REKINDLE EUCHARISTIC AMAZEMENT

Healing and Holiness through the Mass and Holy Hour

Testimony, Teaching and Prayers according to
John Paul II's *Ecclesia de Eucharistia*

Kathleen Beckman

Contributing Authors:
Elizabeth Kim, Ph.D. and Inga Pak, M.D.

Queenship

PUBLISHING COMPANY
P.O. Box 220 • Goleta, CA 93116
(800) 647-9882 • (805) 692-0043 • Fax: (805) 967-5133
www.queenship.org

The Nihil Obstat is hereby granted to your work entitled *Rekindle Eucharistic Amazement.*

Rev. Joseph Son T. Nguyen,
STD Censer Librorum,
Diocese of Orange.

Library of Congress Number # 2008924685
Published by:
　　Queenship Publishing
　　P.O. Box 220
　　Goleta, CA 93116
　　(800) 647-9882 • (805) 692-0043 • Fax: (805) 967-5133
　　www.queenship.org

Printed in the United States of America

ISBN: 987-1-57918-359-X

MARYWOOD PASTORAL CENTER
P.O. Box 14195
ORANGE, CALIFORNIA 92863-1595
(714) 282-3102 PHONE
(714) 282-3029 FAX

Most Reverend Bishop Dominic M. Luong, D.D., M.S.
Auxiliary Bishop of Orange

April, 2008

Dear Kathleen,

This book, *Rekindle Eucharistic Amazement*, is truly an Easter gift to me! The Eucharist is the sacramental enduring Risen Lord to His Church! I used some materials for my Divine Mercy homily, especially chapter six on "Jesus, the Divine Physician."

I enjoyed the book very much and here are some highlights that will help readers.

1   It is a well-researched book in which the author presents a lot of living models from the Church tradition. This indeed makes the Eucharist alive!

2. Some prayers at the end of several chapters are patterned according to the soliloquy style animated by the conversations between friends. These interior dialogues will surely draw many searching souls who are aspiring to join in the journey of interior prayer.

3. Good materials for Lectio Divina for individual or group use.

I highly recommend this work!

Happy Easter in the Eucharistic Jesus,

+Bishop Dominic Luong, D.D., M.S.

What Others Are Saying About
Rekindle Eucharistic Amazement

This book, *Rekindle Eucharistic Amazement*, is truly an Easter gift to me! The Eucharist is the sacramental enduring Risen Lord to His Church! I used some materials for my Divine Mercy homily, especially chapter six on "Jesus, the Divine Physician." I enjoyed the book very much and here are some highlights that will help readers. 1. It is a well-researched book in which the author presents a lot of living models from the Church tradition. This indeed makes the Eucharist alive! 2. Some prayers at the end of several chapters are patterned according to the soliloquy style animated by the conversations between friends. These interior dialogues will surely draw many searching souls who are aspiring to join in the journey of interior prayer. 3. The book is good material for Lectio Divina for individual or group use. I highly recommend this work!

> **Bishop Dominic Luong, D.D., M.S.,**
> **Bishop of Orange, CA,**
> **(author's bishop)**

I love this book. It is such a rich blend of teaching, reflection and sharing. It is like the dewdrop that reflects to us every facet of the Eucharistic Christ: surely an amazing and timely contribution to the rekindling of Eucharistic devotion.

> **Fr. Kevin Scallon, C.M,**
> **Intercession & Retreats for Priests**
> **International, Spiritual Director to**
> **Magnificat, A Ministry to Catholic**
> **Women, Author**

All my life I have tried to promote a love for the Holy Eucharist. In this beautiful book "Rekindling Eucharistic Amazement" I have found the perfect vehicle to help in this work of the Holy Spirit in our time.

> **Sr. Briege McKenna, O.S.C.**
> **International Ministry to Priests,**
> **Healing Ministry. Advisory Team,**
> **Magnificat, Author:**
> *Miracles Do Happen*

Kathleen Beckman is able to incorporate Sacred Scripture, teachings from the *Catechism of the Catholic Church* and various Papal documents, personal experiences, quotes from powerhouse saints, and reflections of mystics with her own personal experience to provide her readers with a dynamic understanding of the Eucharist and to explain how powerful the Holy Spirit can be in the lives of those who are open to it. It is well-researched indeed, but even more, it is evident that she lives what she writes. Her personal story is proof that the power of God prevails in her life. She shares this not to bring attention to herself but to encourage all of us to be devoted to Jesus in the Blessed Sacrament. She relates how devotion to our Lord in the Blessed Sacrament has had a profound role in her life and in the lives of countless others, getting them through many difficulties and helping them to grow deeper in faith. That it is real to her gives credence to how the Lord can work in the lives of each one of us.

The contributions of Doctors Inga Pak and Elizabeth Kim are quite valuable. The connections they make between the spiritual and scientific realm would cause a skeptic to take notice. The book is written in such a way that it is understandable to the reader who has had little exposure to the topics at hand, while at the same time spiritually enriching to the seasoned Catholic to whom the Eucharist is familiar. It is much more than a mere collection of truths and testimonies; it is presented in such a way as to encourage readers to think about their spiritual lives and to consider the great benefits of surrendering oneself to God. It is a jewel for bishops, priests and laity alike. May it be read and referred to regularly by all people of good will who desire to grow in holiness.

> **A Canon Lawyer's Review of**
> *Rekindle Eucharistic Amazement*
> **Fr. Stephen Doktorczyk, J.C.L.**
> **Graduate, Gregorian Pontifical**
> **University, Rome**
> **St. Joachim Church, Costa Mesa, CA**

In this age of spiritual confusion and indifference, Kathleen Beckman, a knowledgeable and inspiring spiritual writer of our time, takes the readers right to the heart of Jesus through sharing of her own experimental knowledge of Him who has captured her heart. Anyone who reads this book will experience a renewed love for the Eucharist and a greater desire to spend more time before the Blessed Sacrament—"the source and summit of the Christian life." Also, her co-authors, Elizabeth Kim, Ph.D. and Inga Pak, M.D., not only contribute their own field of expertise but share powerful personal testimonies of Jesus' merciful love.

Fr. Alex K. Kim, Director, St. Thomas Korean Catholic Center, Anaheim, CA, Chairperson, FIAT Foundation, Inc.

When I read this splendid tome, I immediately recalled the words of Sirach (32:16): "Those who reverence the Lord will form true judgments, and they will kindle righteous deeds like a light." The "true judgments of those who reverence the Lord" are the grace-spawned insights, warmed by basking in his awesome Eucharistic presence. These profound contemplative intuitions will inevitably be "kindled" into righteous deeds - incandescent works that enlighten and inspire others by way of example and inspiration. That is one of the sacrosanct functions assigned to both priests and "priestly people" (1 Pet. 2:5).

This mysterious fomenting of interior grace into exterior deeds was what St. Thomas Aquinas succinctly referred to as "contemplata tradere" - the "handing-down" of heaven-graced insights to others so as to mysteriously inspire ("kindle") virtuous deeds. All grace-responsive readers of this book will find themselves with re-kindled fervor when lofted into contemplative prayer before Jesus in the Blessed Sacrament and in their post-Communion trysts of love. Even their most prosaic "deeds" can then become inflamed with that love. And by those love-burnished deeds they help fulfill the ardent wish of the Divine Master (Luke 12:49): "I came to bring fire to the earth, and how I wish it were already kindled!"

Father John Hampsch, C.M.F. Claretian Teaching Ministry, LA, CA, Who's Who in Religion, Prolific Author

What an honor for me to recommend this book! This book is a treasure that will both inspire and *Rekindle Eucharistic Amazement* in the gift of the Living Presence of Jesus in our midst. As I read the pages in this book "my heart was burning within" with a deeper love and longing for Jesus in the Eucharist.

In speaking to the Curia in 2007, Pope Benedict identified a crucial theme: "To evangelize", he also said, "The Gospel cannot be implemented without a personal encounter with Christ." In the power of the Holy Spirit we can meet Jesus each day in the Eucharist and be transformed and empowered to carry out His mission. Like Mary Magdalene, may we run with haste with the good news, "I have seen the Lord!"

**Marilyn Quirk, Foundress
Magnificat, A Ministry to Catholic
Women**

Contained in this book is an in-depth look at how one is to be drawn into the contemplative gaze of Jesus in the Eucharist and be transformed in the Divine Union of Love. It is my prayer that those who read this book will do so prayerfully; slowly pondering all that is contained herein together with the Holy Spirit and our Lady. Then your hunger and thirst will lead you to "Behold the Lamb of God," through the amazing contemplative encounters with Jesus' Eucharistic Heart. This book will help you to become the very reflection of the Bride who is madly in love with Her Eucharistic Bridegroom! May you allow yourselves to become the gift of love that is blessed, broken and given away to others so that they may inherit eternal life with God!

**Mother Nadine Brown, Foundress
Intercessors of the Lamb,
Bellwether, and author of several
books on Spirituality**

This book is a must-read for all desiring to fall in love in a deeper way with our Eucharistic Lord. Kathleen Beckman, her contributing authors, and Eucharistic Apostles of The Divine Mercy share a common goal and hope – to help an aching mankind understand the great gift of the Eucharist. Using Sacred Scripture, the Catechism of the Catholic Church, the encyclical on the Eucharist, lives of the saints, and personal witness, Kathleen weaves the combination to compile a masterpiece on the pinnacle of our Catholic faith. As a physician, I found the witness and healing stories of Dr. Pak, as well as the section on contemplation and the brain by Dr. Kim, most fascinating.

While reading this manuscript, I recalled a quote in Saint Faustina's Diary where she had a mystical experience that occurred during Eucharistic Adoration. She wrote:

During this hour of prayer, Jesus allowed me to enter the Cenacle [the "Upper Room" where the Last Supper took place], and I was a witness to what happened there. However, I was most deeply moved when, before the Consecration, Jesus raised His eyes to heaven and entered into a mysterious conversation with His Father. It is only in eternity that we shall really understand that moment. His eyes were like two flames; His face was radiant, white as snow; His whole personage full of majesty; His soul full of longing. At the moment of Consecration love rested satiated – the sacrifice fully consummated. Now only the external ceremony of death will be carried out – the external destruction; the essence [of the sacrifice] is in the Cenacle. Never in my whole life had I understood this mystery so profoundly as during that hour of adoration. Oh, how ardently I desire that the whole world would come to know this unfathomable mystery! (*Diary*, 684)

May all who read this book have their hearts set ablaze with the fire of His love, and rekindled with Eucharistic amazement! May the whole world come to better understand the reality of this unfathomable mystery!

> **Bryan Thatcher, M.D., Founder,**
> **Eucharistic Apostles of Divine**
> **Mercy, Lay Outreach of**
> **The Marians of the Immaculate**
> **Conception, Stockbridge, MA**

Kathleen has brought forth in this book a much needed revisiting of the holy gift of the Eucharist. The stepping stone of John Paul II's encyclical *Ecclesia de Eucharistia* exhorts us to "be amazed once again" and this is a solid foundation which is used to help the reader connect to the many facets of the Eucharist. Key words from the chapters speak to us of the wonder that occurs through Eucharistic life. This book addresses the spiritual hunger present in each of us and includes such important topics as healing, joy, protection from evil, hearing God's voice, progressing in prayer, renewal of the Priesthood, Mary as the Woman of the Eucharist, personal Pentecost and so much more!

> **Aggie Neck, Chairman, National**
> **Service Committee USA Catholic**
> **Charismatic Renewal**

In her new book, *Rekindle Eucharistic Amazement*, Kathleen Beckman offers us rich fare indeed! Through insights gleaned from papal documents, the wisdom of the saints, the teachings of the Church, Sacred Scripture, scientific research, and her own personal prayer life, she offers us entry into a deeper appreciation and experience of the Eucharistic Presence of Jesus Christ. In addition, by providing her readers with amazing testimonies and stories of people who have personally witnessed the power and transformative effects of the Blessed Sacrament, Kathleen lights a fire of desire in our hearts to receive through the Eucharist every grace God has in mind for us. Truly this book can help ignite a holy conflagration in the hearts of many.

Johnnette S. Benkovic
Founder and President of
Living His Life Abundantly®
International, Inc. and Women
of Grace®. Seen and heard on
EWTN.

Contents

Dedication

This work is humbly dedicated to the Immaculate Heart of Mary, Mother of the Eucharist; first adorer of the Blessed Sacrament and model of the Church's Eucharistic vocation.

Also this work is gratefully dedicated to our respective mothers, Gloria, Maria Cassy and Angela for sharing their gift of faith and forming us in Catholic piety.

This work is respectfully dedicated to our spiritual mothers including, Marilyn Quirk, Mother Foundress of Magnificat, Mother Nadine Brown, Mother Foundress of Intercessors of the Lamb, and Mother Regina Marie, OCD, Mother Superior of the Carmelite Sisters of the Most Sacred Heart, Alhambra. With gratitude we also include Sister Marie Therese Solomon, ODN, Foundress of the Lestonnac Free Medical Clinic, Sister Catherine Marie of the Intercessors of the Lamb, and the Carmelite Sisters of the Most Sacred Heart, Alhambra.

In this work, we give our personal testimonies of the amazing power of the Eucharist. We are encouraged by these words of John Paul II:

> The world needs to see your love for Christ: it needs public testimony of the religious life as Paul VI once said, "Modern man listens more willingly to witnesses than to teachers, and if he listens to teachers, he does so because they are witnesses." If the nonbelievers of this world are to believe in Christ, they need your faithful testimony—testimony that springs from your complete trust in the generous mercy of the Father and in your enduring faith in the power of the cross and the resurrection. Thus the ideals, the values, the convictions that are the basis of your dedication to Christ must be translated into the language of daily life. Among the people of God, in the local ecclesial community, your public testimony is part of your contribution to the mission of the Church. As St. Paul says: *"You are a letter from Christ…written not with ink but with the Spirit of the living God, not on tablets of stone but on tablets of human hearts."*

Acknowledgments

We humbly acknowledge the prayerful support of our intercessory prayer community: Orange County Intercessors of the Lamb cenacle and Orange County Magnificat Chapter.

We acknowledge particularly, the prayerful theological support of our spiritual advisor, Fr. Raymond Skonezny, STL, SSL whose wise guidance and availability is a priceless gift to us.

Thank you to our priest intercessors and friends including: Fr. Michael Philen, C.M.F., Fr. Joseph Droessler, Fr. Paul O'Donnell, Fr. Steve Doktorczyk, J.C.L., Fr. Alex Kim, (brother of co-author Elizabeth Kim, Ph.D.), Fr. John Hampsch, C.M.F., Fr. Abbot Eugene Hayes, O. Praem., Fr. Pascal, Fr. John Paul, Fr. John Mark, Fr. Kevin Scallon, and Auxiliary Bishop Dominic M. Loung, D.D., M.S.

We also acknowledge the prayers and sacrifices of two seminarian friends at the Pontifical North American College, Rome, Italy: Jeff Droessler and Charlie Cortinovis.

We are grateful to Christopher Gonzales, Esq., Sean and Trudy Buckner for their assistance in proof reading the manuscript.

We give special thanks to John LaBriola for his expert assistance with the manuscript.

Preface

John Paul II's Encyclical, *Ecclesia de Eucharistia* has been a source of many books and articles over the past few years. The title of this book *Rekindle Eucharistic Amazement* is taken from the very beginning of the Encyclical and is the theme around which the author, Mrs. Kathleen Beckman, and her two co-authors, Elizabeth Kim Ph.D. and Inga Pak, M.D., have presented their material.

The book follows the apostolic teaching and tradition of the Church that has been taught from the beginning, that the Lord is truly present Body, Blood, Soul and Divinity in our midst. It is not a purely dogmatic presentation of the Eucharist, but is interwoven with testimony about the authors' personal experiences, on the beauty and power of the Eucharist.

Through judicious choices by the writers, from the Encyclical, Church documents and various authors, mostly Saints, who have written on this subject, it is both very readable and insightful in its presentation about the power of the Eucharist as the "source and summit" of our Catholic Christian life. It is a deeply practical spiritual work that is meant to rekindle within the reader a deeper appreciation of the wonder of this gift given to us in the great act of worship that is the Mass. The book makes a strong argument for the relevancy of Adoration or Holy Hour.

With great spiritual depth Kathleen Beckman brings us to the Upper Room, the place where the history of God with His people reaches its climax. From the Upper Room is born, the Eucharist, its Priesthood and Pentecost. These three Divine initiatives, by the power of the Holy Spirit, form Christ's presence in the world until the end of time.

It is the hope of the author and the two contributing authors that their amazement and wonder of the Eucharist will enkindle a flame in the hearts of the readers. How will this be done? Kathleen quotes The Servant of God, Fulton Sheen, that it isn't by theological knowledge alone nor social action alone that we will come to the love of Christ in the Eucharist. It is rather by "two bent knees before the altar."

The book is truly enriched by the inclusion of prayers that gives the book its remarkable capacity to move the reader into a spirit of meditative prayer. I personally am amazed by the quality of the segments chosen to illustrate the thought of the author(s).

As a priest, the chapter on the priesthood is personally challenging. As an antidote for the vagaries of priestly formation present in different areas of the church it brings back life into the Amazing Mystery the priest holds in his hands at Mass. Telling above all is the realization that Servant of God Fulton Sheen never missed a day without spending an hour before the Blessed Sacrament. This was for him the source of his power and unflagging generous love for God's people.

How often do we see people at Mass who seemingly are there and yet not there? To enter a Church out of the fast moving pace of our modern world with its noise, confusion and sensual delights is a great challenge for the modern Catholic. **I can only stress that this book is both an intellectual feast as well as a spiritual fire for the heart.**

Surely it was not by chance that Pope John Paul II lived long enough to give us this beautiful Encyclical. Who can be so blind and obtuse to not recognize the crisis of the Church in our modern world? The world of today intrudes into our every thought by its sounds, pictures and technology. Where is Jesus? Where can He be found? How can I reach Him? Do I see my life dependent upon Christ, the Eucharist and the Holy Spirit? How can I love my neighbor? How can I find myself? Upon what or whom can I stand and not be swept away? What is love? What is truth? Where is the way? These questions and countless others confuse our hearts.

It is in the meditative reading of this book that we can have a rekindling of our hearts. This is the aim of the book and it finds its source in the encyclical of Pope John Paul II. He, above all, the Vicar of Christ for 25 years had his pulse on the world, secular and religious. What was his answer for all the suffering under the "glamour" of our modern world? It was the Eucharist, the hour of Adoration in heart to heart communion with Jesus.

To rekindle Eucharistic amazement is the reason for this book. The hours spent in its formation by three women filled with the love of Christ bear witness to their personal union with Him who is the way, the truth and the life.

It is my prayer that this book finds its way into a multitude of hearts. It will be for many, a resource to enkindle their faith, hope and love.

Fr. Raymond F. Skonezny, STL, SSL
Spiritual Advisor to the Three Authors

Chapter 1

To Rekindle Eucharistic Amazement, Our Destiny

John Paul II Encyclical, *Ecclesia de Eucharistia*

The late, Pope John Paul II, wrote a program detailing his visionary hope for the Church at the dawn of the Third Millennium. The encyclical letter, *Ecclesia de Eucharistia* details his program that points to the Eucharist for the realization of the new evangelization.

I would like to rekindle this Eucharistic "amazement" by the present Encyclical Letter, in continuity with the Jubilee heritage which I have left to the Church in the Apostolic Letter *Novo Millennio Ineunte* and its Marian crowning, *Rosarium Virginis Mariae*. To contemplate the face of Christ, and to contemplate it with Mary, is the "program" which I have set before the Church at the dawn of the third millennium, summoning her to put out into the deep on the sea of history with the enthusiasm of the new evangelization. To contemplate Christ involves being able to recognize him where he manifests himself, in his many forms of presence, but above all in the living sacrament of his body and blood. The Church draws her life from Christ in the Eucharist: by him she is fed and by him she is enlightened. The Eucharist is both a mystery of faith and a mystery of light. Whenever the Church celebrates the Eucharist, the faithful can in some way relive the experience of the two disciples on the road to Emmaus: "Their eyes were opened and they recognized him" (Lk. 24:31).

It is my hope that the present Encyclical Letter will effectively help banish the dark clouds of unacceptable doctrine and practice, so that the Eucharist will continue to shine forth in all its radiant mystery.

John Paul II, *Ecclesia de Eucharistia*

The prophetic mission of the late, John Paul II, continues to imbue the rich tapestry of the Catholic Church with beauty, wisdom and grace. John Paul II's encyclical letter reveals our glorious destiny to "put out into the deep on the sea of history with the enthusiasm of the new evangelization." His Eucharistic program beckons the Church to contemplate Christ, truly present in the Eucharist, and to do so with Mary. The phrase, *"rekindle Eucharistic amazement"* speaks of rediscovering the beauty and transforming power of the Eucharist. An intensely Eucharistic life refers to frequent reception of the Eucharist and frequent practice of adoration of the Blessed Sacrament.

John Paul II invites the whole Church to contemplate Christ, recognizing him where he manifests Himself, in his many forms of presence, but above all in the living sacrament of his Body and Blood. Every word of his encyclical is filled with insight for the Church toward re-animating Eucharistic devotion. Some may ask what is being done to further the program he has proposed toward rekindling Eucharistic amazement. The answer lies within the heart of each disciple of Christ. When was the last time you were amazed by Christ's True Presence? Consider the meaning of the words chosen by John Paul II in the encyclical, *Ecclesia de Eucharista:*

- **Rekindle**: renew, revive, reawaken, regenerate, and relight.

- **Amazement**: to fill with great surprise, wonder, astonish.

- **Eucharist**: The Eucharist is the "source and summit of the Christian life" (Lumen Gentium 111). The other sacraments, and indeed all ecclesiastical ministries and works of the apostolate, are bound up with the Eucharist and are oriented toward it. For in the blessed Eucharist is contained the whole spiritual good of the Church, namely Christ himself, our Pasch. CCC#1324

John Paul II's program points back to the basics of Christocentric worship, prayer. Rekindling new appreciation for Christ's sacrifice and presence will draw much needed grace for the Church, collectively and individually. John Paul II saw the rekindling of Eucharistic amazement at the heart of "the new evangelization" to bring about "a civilization of love." The many facets of John Paul II's incredible Pontificate point toward a new Pentecost that would enliven the Church and animate the civilization of love. Has the concept of a civilization of love become obscure amidst a culture of increasing violence?

What about the new evangelization? Is it hard to relate to these prophetic proposals when many of our family members, especially our children, have walked away from the Catholic Church? Have you ever been frustrated that you could not effectively evangelize your own family members who are not practicing the faith anymore? Rekindling Eucharistic amazement awakens one soul at a time. In the Bible, the Lord spared a nation for the sake of a few holy people. Holiness is attractive to God and others. Be holy and others will be attracted and want what you have, which is peace and joy. Let Eucharistic amazement begin in your life first. See what happens as one soul ignites another with a living flame of love!

John Paul II's Eucharistic program is a work of the Spirit of the Living God. Our part in the program is to cooperate with God's grace which is always available and sufficient. Like Mary, your receptivity is not a passive reality. It is cooperative, a reciprocal gift of yourself to God. Like Mary, can you assume a posture of receptivity and become a living tabernacle so the Eucharistic Lord can manifest through you? Some questions to ponder:

- What is the level of your expectant faith?
- To what degree is the virtue of hope animating your life?
- Is the fruit of the Spirit, joy, permeating your life?
- Is the Eucharist a priority in your life?

Eucharistic Amazement Leads to Joy

Peter Kreeft, Catholic philosopher, maintains that human beings simply cannot live without truth, goodness and joy. Why is this so? Jesus is the Way, the Truth and the Life. If our lives are not firmly rooted in the

Lord, we can lose our spiritual compass. Since we are created by God to love and be loved, we search after love. We may settle for a weak imitation of God's love. Life can become a burden, not joy.

The goodness of God begets hope in our heart. This enables us to choose rightly to walk and reject the waywardness of the world. The virtue of hope is a powerful catalyst to propel us toward the goal of our heavenly reward. Without hope, there is discouragement and deception. Joy can be quickly extinguished. The goodness of God is a fountain of grace freely given. God always tends toward joy, purity and freedom of heart. Peter Kreeft observes that Catholics are sorely lacking in joy. While truth and goodness has grown in the Church, joy has ceased to grow as steadily.

John Paul II's program to rekindle Eucharistic amazement aims to draw people back into the Church. At Mass today, the priest homilist shared that twenty-million Catholics have "fallen away" from the Church. He said that priests are observing Catholic people coming to Church as few as three times in their lifetime: Baptism, marriage, and their funeral.

As we renew ourselves in Eucharistic piety, conversion will occur; our sadness, discouragement and doubt will assuredly turn into authentic joy. The Mass and Adoration of the Blessed Sacrament contain the amazing power to transform our lives, individually and collectively. If we persist in being Catholics without the joy of the Lord, people will not be drawn to Christ. John Paul II's program for renewing devotion to the Eucharist is a program that will attract people back to Christ-centered living.

When the believer prays and assumes the posture of Mary's receptivity, the Holy Spirit brings forth spiritual union; Creator and creature unite in joyful love. In order to be a Church alive, in order to experience a new Pentecost, we need experiential knowledge of the love of God. The Mass (communal worship) and Adoration (personal prayer) facilitate our encounter with God. His love, which the Spirit has poured into our hearts must be stirred up and fanned into flame! Then zeal for the house of God will be rekindled. When we experience the Eucharist as a penetrating gift of God, the Holy Spirit enkindles love's ardor within our heart. Stony hearts become hearts of flesh. We become responsive to God who loves us first. We come to new life through his Eucharistic species at Mass and Adoration. Whatever the measure of your love of God may be now, there is always more to receive from God.

To Bring the Church to the "Enthusiasm of the New Evangelization"

In his encyclical letter, *Ecclesia de Eucharistia*, John Paul II presents necessary spiritual elements (deeper realization of the transforming power of the Eucharistic Presence) to bring the Church to the "enthusiasm of the new evangelization." Have you noticed the world needs to be re-evangelized? It appears that a whole generation and a half have need of catecheses on the Catholic faith. Can we recognize a wake-up call? Pope John Paul II and his successor, Pope Benedict XVI, are sounding a clarion call to rise up, soldiers of Christ! Rise up to proclaim the good news of Jesus Christ. The world could use some good news, correct? This is why many false religions, cults, and spiritualities are rising up. People are in need of good news, searching to fill a spiritual void. Let us lead people back to the beauty of the true gospel of Jesus Christ. The Eucharist is the means of renewing our faith in Jesus and our love of his Bride. This can happen only as we are filled to overflowing with the dynamism of the Spirit's love.

Do we feel a tug of our conscience telling us that we have ceased to be amazed by the gifts of God? Perhaps we are lethargic about the sacraments? The people of God are busy about many things in our respective vocations. We have only to read a weekly Parish Bulletin to see the numerous "programs" already present in the Church. Presently, we suffer under a yoke of "busyness" in the Church. There are plenty of "Marthas" (people busy about many things) and not enough "Marys" (people choosing to sit at the feet of the Master). Have we lost our vocation of prayer? John Paul II's program for renewing the Eucharistic life of the Church is not a new program to be followed. It is a return to the heart of the Church: Love Personified.

John Paul II's Eucharistic program is an invitation to experience God as Mary who chose the better part: to sit at the feet of the Master. The word "contemplation" is used several times throughout the encyclical. Rekindling Eucharistic amazement can only be realized through a mystical evolution: in contemplation of Christ we will find the way to forge forward to rebuild the City of God in an increasingly atheistic world.

Christ's Bride is to become a "house of prayer for all peoples." Each disciple is invited to become an individual house of prayer. The whole Mystical Body will become revitalized through Eucharistic prayer. The early Church was "devoted" to the "Breaking of the Bread." Life was centered on prayer and the Mass which was celebrated in their homes in the Church's early days. Not only were they devoted to prayer and breaking of the bread, they had expectant faith that they would experience the risen Lord.

One of the fruits of contemplating the face of Christ is to draw so close to him that you begin to see yourself in the reflection of Christ's eyes. When you perceive yourself in the light of Jesus' eyes, you know your dignity as a precious child of God. You can only know this by a close encounter with Christ. This is a healing experience because it corrects any distorted perception of your true identity in Christ.

We are invited to hope in Christ instead of discouragement. The fruit of an intensely Eucharistic vocation is joy and peace, health for your soul. By rediscovering our sacramental gifts, true inner healing can be realized. The fruit of a life centered on the Mass and Adoration is health of body, mind and spirit.

Is It Necessary to Renew
Our Love for the Eucharist?

To answer the above question, consider what St. Faustina wrote in her Diary. Consider it in the light of what Pope John Paul II is saying in the encyclical on the Eucharist.

> *Oh, how painful it is to me that souls so seldom unite themselves to me in Holy Communion. I wait for souls, and they are indifferent toward me. I love them tenderly and sincerely, and they distrust me. I want to lavish my graces on them, and they do not want to accept them. They treat me as a dead object, whereas my Heart is full of love and mercy. In order that you may know at least some of my pain, imagine the*

most tender of mothers who has great love for her children, while those children spurn her love. Consider her pain. No one is in a position to console her. This is but a feeble image and likeness of my love.

Diary of St. Faustina, #1447

This message recorded in her diary indicates that we are indifferent toward him, that we treat him like a dead object. We need to experience further the Risen Lord who is alive. We need to experience the dynamism of the Holy Spirit in our lives every day. Otherwise we can languish in mediocrity. The crisis of faith seems to have developed into a crisis of love. We are starving for authentic Agape Love because our modern experience of love has become disordered. We need to experience falling in love with Christ all over again, to avoid boredom, weariness, dullness and lack of joy. Fr. Raniero Cantalamessa refers to this in the quote below.

Why are faith and religious practices in decline, and why do they not constitute, at least not for most people, the point of reference in life? Why the boredom, the weariness, the struggle for believers in performing their duties? Why do young people not feel attracted to the faith? In sum, why this dullness and this lack of joy among the believers in Christ? The event of Christ's transfiguration helps us to answer these questions.

What did the transfiguration mean for the three disciples who were present? Up until now they knew Jesus only in his external appearance: he was not a man different from others; they knew where he came from, his habits, the timber of his voice. Now they know another Jesus, the true Jesus, the one who cannot be seen with the eyes of the ordinary life, in the normal light of the sun; what they now know of him is the fruit of sudden revelations, of a change, of a gift.

Because things change for us too, as they changed for the three disciples on Tabor; something needs to happen in our lives similar to what happens when a young man and a woman fall in love. In falling in love with someone, the beloved, who before was one of many suddenly becomes the only one, the sole person in the world who interests us. Everything else is left behind and becomes a kind of neutral background.

Something of the kind must happen once in our lives for us to be true, convinced Christians, and overjoyed to be so. Some say, "But the young man or young woman is seen and touched!" I answer: We see and touch Jesus too, but with different eyes and different hands - those of the heart, of faith. He is risen and is alive. He is a concrete being, not an abstraction, for those who know him. Indeed, with Jesus things go even better.

Fr. Raniero Cantalamessa, O.F.M., Cap., *Zenit*

The thought of a renewed love and appreciation for Christ is consistent with the thought of John Paul II toward rekindling Eucharistic amazement. Both John Paul II and Fr. Cantalamessa acknowledge our need to experience the dynamism of Christ's love consistent with what took place in the Upper Room. The Cenacle in Jerusalem, the Upper Room, is a place of origin for the Church. Sometimes when things become obscured, we need to look again at God's original initiative when instituting the Eucharist and Priesthood, and then receive the fullness of the coming of the Spirit at Pentecost (birthday of the Church). Let us return to the Upper Room where three "births" occurred: Eucharist, Priesthood, and Pentecost.

Eucharistic Amazement:
To Gaze at Christ and Be Transfigured

Let us acknowledge our need to experience transfiguration. We need to see Christ, our Savior and King, in a magnified light in order to persevere through the difficult challenges of daily life. Christ is the same yesterday, today and always. But our vision of Jesus, like that of Peter, James and John on Mount Tabor, can be elevated to see the Lord in His glorified reality; to fall in love again with His radiant beauty. Deeper transformation into Christ will strengthen us to pick up our cross daily and follow Him without counting the cost. Daily, discipleship is becoming more costly.

We feel the pressure of a non-Christian world pressing against the Catholic Church. Areas that were once permeated with Catholic thought and devotion are now devoid of the faith. Often in travels to Europe, I observe majestic Catholic Cathedrals used as museums to host a myriad of things other than the Mass and pious prayer. In America, according to a EWTN program hosted by Dr. Scott Hahn, young Catholic people are reporting for college at Steubenville in need of basic catechesis. John Paul II's program for rekindling Eucharistic amazement is pertinent to rebuilding the Church. The time is now to return to lives of prayer and sacrifice.

Jesus promised the Apostles that the Holy Spirit would instruct the Church about His teachings. This is part of the promise of Pentecost. Pentecost was not a single event relegated to a particular time and place. Pentecost is a perpetual event for the Church. The Holy Spirit has not ceased to descend in power! It seems we have simply left the Upper Room: the place of the Eucharist, Priesthood and Pentecost. The Spirit descends to find no one praying around Mother Mary!

The encyclical, *Ecclesia de Eucharistia* points to this:

- Contemplate Christ. (Adoration, prayer)
- Contemplate Christ with Mother Mary. (Marian devotion, rosary)
- Frequently gather around the Eucharistic Banquet. (Mass)
- Be empowered by the Body and Blood of Christ. (Eucharistic transformation)
- Receive the power of the Holy Spirit: be witnesses to Christ to the ends of the earth. (Pentecost)
- Return to the Upper Room: place of Priesthood, Eucharist and Pentecost. (vocations)
- Be vigilant, there are increasing enemies of the Eucharist. (Spiritual warfare)
- Correct the liturgical abuses and disrespect for the Eucharist (Spiritual warfare and intercession)
- Gratitude for the Eucharist (Praise God for the Gift of his Son)

• Amazement (Allow yourself to be a child, one who finds God amazing!)

What is Eucharistic Life?

Christ's Eucharistic teachings are at the heart of the Gospel, which is our compass for life. In John's Gospel, the Lord's catechesis on the Eucharist repeatedly mentions the word "life" because the Eucharist (Christ) affects the life of a person and the world.

> Truly, truly, I say to you, he who believes has eternal life. I am the bread of life. Your fathers ate the manna in the wilderness, and they died. This is the bread which comes down from Heaven that a man may eat of it and not die. I am the living bread which came down from Heaven: if any one eats of this bread, he will live forever; and the bread which I shall give for the life of the world is my flesh. (Jn. 6:47-51)

What is the life that the Gospel promises the people of God? The life of Christ who is one with the Father and the Holy Spirit: Trinitarian life: Love!

> Jesus is the **life**. Christ, the eternal Word, possessed **life** from all eternity (Jn. 1: 4). As Man he is the Word of **life**" (1 Jn. 1:1). He is rightfully the complete master of all **life** (Jn. 5:26), and gives it in abundance (Jn. 10:10) to all those His Father has given Him" (Jn. 17:2). He is the way, the truth and the **life**" (Jn. 14:6), the resurrection, and the **life**." He is the light of **life** (Jn. 8:12); He gives **living** water which in the recipient becomes a "spring of water which bursts forth to eternal **life**" (Jn. 4:14). Christ is "the bread of **life**;" to those who eat his body he gives the power to **live** by Him as He **lives** by the Father.

Xavier Leon Dufour, *Dictionary of Biblical Theology*

The question we might ask is, "Are we living a life in abundance with Christ or have we settled for something less?" Ideally, we would never take the Blessed Sacrament for granted. In reality, we can grow cold in our appreciation of the Eucharist. We may think that we appreciate the Eucharist enough. Perhaps we are very active in ministry, active in the parish, and do charitable good works. Perhaps we are well advanced in the way of prayer and have been living the spiritual life for decades. Do we sometimes think, "I have enough God in my life."

Do you know what St. Augustine said about the word "enough?" Saint Augustine said, *The interior life, like love, is destined to grow. If you say "enough," you are already dead.* Are there any areas of life, spiritual or otherwise that are already dead? Eucharistic amazement may be the catalyst to awaken those areas. Come to the abundant life! Christ said, "Why look for me among the dead? I am the God of the living!" Jesus manifests His loving Presence in fulfillment of His promise, "Lo, I am with you always, to the close of the age" (Mt. 28:20).

John Paul II's encyclical encompasses all aspects of the Eucharist: The Holy Sacrifice of the Mass, Eucharistic Adoration, and the Eucharistic vocation of the people of God. In section 25 he addresses the grace of Eucharistic Adoration outside of Mass stating:

> The worship of the Eucharist outside of the Mass is of inestimable value for the life of the Church. This worship is strictly linked to the celebration of the Eucharistic Sacrifice. It is the responsibility of pastors to encourage, also by their personal witness, the practice of Eucharistic adoration, and exposition of the Blessed Sacrament in particular, as well as prayer of adoration before Christ present under the Eucharistic species.
>
> It is pleasant to spend time with Him, to lie close to His breast like the Beloved Disciple (cf. Jn. 13:25) and to feel the infinite love present in His heart. If in our time Christians must be distinguished above all by the "art of prayer," how can we not feel a renewed need to spend time in spiritual converse, in silent adoration, in heartfelt love before Christ present in the Most Holy Sacrament? How often, dear brothers and sisters, have I experienced this, and drawn from it strength, consolation and support.

This practice, repeatedly praised and recommended by the Magisterium is supported by the example of many saints. Particularly outstanding in this regard is Saint Alphonsus Ligouri, who wrote: "Of all devotions, that of adoring Jesus in the Blessed Sacrament is the greatest after the sacraments, the one dearest to God and the one most helpful to us." The Eucharist is a priceless treasure: by not only celebrating it but also by praying before it outside of Mass we are enabled to make contact with the very wellspring of grace. A Christian community desirous of contemplating the face of Christ in the spirit which I proposed in the Apostolic Letters *Novo Millennio Ineunte* and *Rosarium Virginis Mariae*, cannot fail also to develop this aspect of Eucharistic worship, which prolongs and increases the fruits of our communion in the body and blood of the Lord.

John Paul II, *Ecclesia de Eucharistia*

In the above, section 25 of the encyclical, we are reminded that Eucharistic adoration prolongs and increases the fruit of our communion with the body and blood of Christ. John Paul II states that the Eucharist is a priceless treasure not only celebrated at Mass but also by praying before it outside of Mass. Doing so connects us to the wellspring of grace. We need to draw from Jesus every day. How else shall our thirst for Love be satisfied? Are we not dying of this thirst? Run with haste to the Divine wellspring and drink of living water! Then we will be like the Samaritan woman at the well, a credible witness of Christ! In the Encyclical, John Paul II relays that he experienced renewal, strength, consolation, and support in his time spent in silent adoration and spiritual conversation with Christ. There is no substitute for Eucharistic devotion; no other remedy that will affect our life as thoroughly for the good.

There are excellent books written by theologians on the Holy Sacrifice of the Mass including: *The Lamb's Supper* by Scott Hahn, *The Eucharist* by Fr. Lawrence Lovasik, *In the Presence of the Lord* by Fr. Benedict Groeschel and James Monti, *The Healing Power of the Eucharist* by Fr. John Hampsch, *The Eucharist* by Fr. Bill McCarthy, *The Eucharist, Our*

Sanctification by Fr. Raniero Cantalamessa. These are a few inspirational works that can enrich our receptivity of the sublime grace of the Mass. The more we learn of the exquisite beauty of the Church's liturgy, the more we are able to appreciate the Gift of God that we receive in the Eucharist. Imagine if someone gave us a priceless pearl as a gift, but we did not know how priceless a pearl it was? How could we value it as we should? Jesus offers us a treasury of priceless gifts to enrich our walk with him.

Reparation for Eucharistic Abuses

10. The Magisterium's commitment to proclaiming the Eucharistic mystery has been matched by interior growth within the Christian community. Certainly the liturgical reform inaugurated by the Council has greatly contributed to a more conscious, active and fruitful participation in the Holy Sacrifice of the Altar on the part of the faithful. In many places, adoration of the Blessed Sacrament is also an important daily practice and becomes an inexhaustible source of holiness.

Other positive signs of Eucharistic faith and love might also be mentioned.

Unfortunately, alongside these lights, there are also shadows. In some places the practice of Eucharistic adoration has been almost completely abandoned. In various parts of the Church abuses have occurred, leading to confusion with regard to sound faith and Catholic doctrine concerning this wonderful sacrament. At times one encounters an extremely reductive understanding of the Eucharistic mystery. Stripped of its sacrificial meaning, it is celebrated as if it were simply a fraternal banquet. Furthermore, the necessity of the ministerial priesthood, grounded in apostolic succession, is at times obscured and the sacramental nature of the Eucharist is reduced to its mere effectiveness as a form of proclamation. This has led here and there to ecumenical initiatives which, albeit well-intentioned, indulge in Eucharistic practices contrary to the discipline by which the Church expresses her faith. How can

we not express profound grief at all this? The Eucharist is too
great a gift to tolerate ambiguity and depreciation.

John Paul II, *Ecclesia de Eucharistia*

Unfortunately, we have all heard of Eucharistic abuses and disrespect
that wound the Body of Christ. We can unite our prayers with John Paul
II who intercedes to banish the dark clouds of unacceptable doctrine and
practice pertaining to the Eucharist. How can the *new evangelization* be
realized without rekindling Eucharistic amazement and correcting the
abuses?

Discipleship Is a Eucharistic Vocation

Discipleship is a Eucharistic vocation. A Eucharistic vocation is a life of
intercession for the salvation of souls. This includes a life of reparation for
offenses against the Most August Sacrament of Divine Love. Often when
I am in prayer before the Blessed Sacrament I sense the Lord saying,

*You are here to pray for all those who refuse to pray. You are
here to adore for those who refuse to adore. You are here to keep
company with me, to keep a prayer vigil for those who are not
attracted to me. Bring souls to me.*

When a disciple is imbued with Christ's Presence, a wound to the Heart
of Christ is deeply felt as a wound to the disciple. The daily Communicant
may not be a liturgist, but united to Christ by the Eucharistic bond of love,
there is keen sensitivity to disrespect regarding the Blessed Sacrament.
Presently we observe an increased disrespect for all things sacred and
blatant persecution against all things Catholic. In the midst of a very
tenuous world stands the pillar of the Eucharist to which we should bind
our little ship to weather the present storm of unbelief and lies.

Our Father in Heaven has made a provision for a time such as this, and
the pillar of the Eucharist is the strong tower in which we find refuge and
strength to engage in the spiritual battle of this present age.

There is no new plan in the encyclical letter. John Paul II points to the
apostolic teachings and tradition of the Catholic Church at a time when
faith in the True Presence is waning. How is faith in the True Presence
growing? The Risen Lord lives, reigns and waits for us on the altars

and the tabernacles of the world. He is always present to us. **We need to encourage one another to become more present to Christ, more expectant in faith, more empowered by love. That is the only aim of this book.** There is no extraordinary drama in John Paul II's program per se, simply a turning back to Christ Jesus to rekindle a loving personal relationship with the Lord in the Eucharist. The drama will come when this is accomplished!

Spiritual, Physical, Psychological Health: Priests, Prayer, Physicians, Psychologists

The Eucharistic program John Paul II outlined at the start of the Third Millennium is a treasury to be discovered. The saintly John Paul II foresaw wondrous things to occur when a person takes up a Eucharistic vocation.

This book will look at three disciplines: spiritual, physical and psychological to bear witness to the healing power of the Eucharist. Holiness is healthy for our body, mind and spirit. The dignity of the Eucharist reveals the dignity of the human person.

Neither theological knowledge nor social action alone is enough to keep us in love with Christ unless both are preceded by a personal encounter with Him. Theological insights are gained not only from between the two covers of a book, but from two bent knees before an altar. The Holy Hour becomes like an oxygen tank to revive the breath of the Holy Spirit in the midst of the foul and fetid atmosphere of the world.

Servant of God Fulton Sheen

I appreciate Archbishops Sheen's analogy since I struggle with asthma and can relate to the need for oxygen. My daily holy hour (often two) has become like a spiritual oxygen tank to increase the breath of the Holy Spirit in my life. More important than daily inhalers that regulate asthma is the daily visit to the Blessed Sacrament. What good is health of body without health of soul? Personhood is penetrating integration of body, mind and soul. We can never comprehend the sublime mystery of the Eucharistic Presence of God. We need not understand, only to believe! Our faith is increased by hearing the testimonies of lives changed by the sacramental graces of the Church. Let our lives be a witness of the healing effects of Eucharistic life. This is the mission of the Christian.

The Church proclaims Jesus, the Healer! People sometimes turn toward something or someone that will not provide the remedy that God provides. God often heals through medical physicians as the bible teaches. My brother and sister-in-law are physicians dedicated to the care of the sick. By their sharing, it is edifying to witness the miracles of modern medicine. Medical conditions are affected by emotional and psychological pathology and/or stress on the human body. Science continues to reveal the connection between the mind, heart and body. The Church has always made that connection addressing the dignity of the human person in totality. The Church has the remedy for spiritual, physical and psychological health! An intensely sacramental life is healing! We need physicians, psychologist, priests and prayer! How good it would be if there was more incorporation of all four together.

The present culture of death and hedonistic lifestyle has become toxic. The Lord of the Universe is able to reach into all of these areas and heal his people. The buzz word these days in the health and wellness field is detoxification. It is our experience that a steady diet of an intensely sacramental life; including frequent reception of Holy Communion, adoration of the Blessed Sacrament and regular visits to the confessional, provides the best detoxification of the human heart and mind. This spiritual fortification produces an integrated wholeness in the person. The Lord is concerned with every part of our lives! Grace is granted for healthy bodies, minds and spirits. May it please God to attract people back to His Eucharistic heart containing the medicine for what ails humanity at many levels! This hope of the late John Paul II is also our prayer.

Closeness to the Eucharistic Christ in silence and contemplation does not distance us from our contemporaries but on the contrary, it makes us open to human joy and distress, broadening our hearts on a global scale. Anyone who prays to the Eucharistic Savior draws the whole world with him and raises it to God.

John Paul II, 1996 on the
400th Anniversary of the Forty Hours Devotion

We Do Not Just Adore!

Spending time in contemplation of the Blessed Sacrament is anything but selfish as some people argue. Time spent in prayer before the Blessed Sacrament, compels us to move out toward the service of others. It is not an empty hand that you offer to someone in need. What do you hold in your hand? It is the Lord's bounty that you offer others. His hand holds everything a person needs. A Eucharistic life connects the two: Christ and others. We become servants of all, like Christ became a servant of all.

A servant of the Eucharist lives Jesus and His cross! If you live a Eucharistic lifestyle, you are a burden bearer like the Lord. You take up your cross daily and follow Him. It means you are a victim, but not a victim of oppression. When all hell broke out against the Lord atop Calvary's hill, He was not a victim of oppression. He was a victim of Divine Love destroying all our oppression. He defeated our enemy! The Eucharist empowers us to be a victim of love also. We do not seek after suffering. We lay down our life for others. There is a cost to discipleship. One needs to pay the price. Eucharistic love is heroic! When is the last time the measure of our love was heroic?

God invites us to draw near. Our free will is ours to surrender. He will not violate it. The measure of his transformation in us is to the degree that we desire, and allow it. Will we let the Lord transform us according to his plan? Will we prefer his way over our way? Death to self is not easy. It requires trust. We grow in trust by spending time with the Lord - a lot of time!

May the disposition of our hearts never be "enough Lord!" May our attitude always be "more, Lord!" If we desire more of God, how do we get it? Know that Jesus is one to effect this new amazement for you. Let us not limit Him by refusing His invitation to spend more time in His Eucharistic Presence. Let us not set boundaries for the Lord that we refuse to cross over. What if we became fools for Christ? The history of the Church is filled with people who became fools for Christ. We call them "Saints." These fools for Christ are still alive as Church Triumphant. Christ asks us, "Will you surrender? Will you allow me to act in all my glorious power?"

Rekindling Eucharistic Amazement
is Healing Remedy

During times of long suffering one searches for some remedy. A disciple of Christ is subject to many temptations to escape for a while, to deaden the pain or to find solace in things that distract. Like many non-believers we can look for things that make us feel better for a while, such as mindless or distracting entertainment, entrapping environments with New Age allurement, consumerism and any number of things contrary to Christ-centered healing. Great numbers of people are taking up New Age practices and Eastern philosophies offering mystical revival. People are searching for answers to the complex reality of our post 9-11 lives. Somehow people sense the sickness of our culture without realizing it is sin-sickness that can only be healed through repentance, communion with the God of miracles!

There are countless people duped into discouragement about finding spiritual remedy in the Catholic Church at this time when she is plagued by scandal and undergoing purification. It takes grace to understand that Divine Mercy is at work in every process of purification. It takes grace to understand that God is bringing to light what has existed in darkness to correct the disordered sin-nature of His people. He will restore the Church! This unfolds over time in an organic manner. Throughout the history of the Church, there have been grave, human errors. The need for repentance and reparation is present in every age.

We find no fault in the Blessed Sacrament. Now, when there is a fascination with magic as evidenced by the Harry Potter global phenomena and various forms of the New Age movement, the Church directs us to the Blessed Sacrament to rekindle Eucharistic amazement! The Church has the remedy for what ails mankind! Jesus, the Divine Physician (CCC#1503) is alive, able to bring about complete restoration of His Mystical Body. The omniscient, omnipotent and omnipresent Lord remains with His people in the tabernacles of the world. In the Blessed Sacrament, He is present in a particularly tangible, intimate manner that begs communion and that fills the God-shaped hole in each of us.

In more recent times, the Church has stressed that Christ

is present to His people in many ways, but that none of these detract from the unique experience of the reception of Holy Communion and, in the aftermath of that reception, the adoration of the Real Presence. The following statement of the new *Catechism of the Catholic Church* summarizes this very well: "Christ Jesus, who died, yes, who was raised from the dead, who is at the right hand of God, who indeed intercedes for us," is present in many ways to His Church: in His word, in His Church's prayer, "where two or three are gathered in my name," in the poor, the sick, and the imprisoned, in the sacraments of which He is the author, in the sacrifice of the Mass, and in the person of the minister. But *"he is present...most especially in the Eucharistic species"* (#1373 CCC).

Fr. Benedict Groeschel, *In the Presence of Our Lord.*

Our own belief is that the renovation of the world will be brought about only by the Holy Eucharist.

Pope Leo XIII

Chapter 2

Testimony and Prayers of Kathleen Beckman

The Transforming Power
of a Eucharistic Life: My Story

The Church and the world have great need for Eucharistic worship. Jesus awaits us in this sacrament of love. Let us not refuse the time to go to meet him in adoration, in contemplation full of faith, and open to making amends for the serious offenses and crimes of the world. Let our adoration never cease. CCC #1380

The priest advised: *"Let the liturgy form your spiritual life. Pray before the Blessed Sacrament one hour a day."*

In August, 1992, I traveled to Lourdes, France with a group of Catholic medical volunteers from the St. Jeanne de Lestonnac Free Medical Clinic. Sr. Marie Therese Solomon founded this facility to provide medical care for indigent patients, the "poorest of the poor," she would call them. Sister asked that I organize a spiritual pilgrimage for the Board and volunteers. She was very interested in our spiritual formation since she knew it would be the basis of our continuing commitment to the service of the poor. Together, Sister Therese and I planned the itinerary for approximately forty people. The priest spiritual advisor who served on the Board of Directors would accompany the pilgrimage group to offer the Sacraments each day.

This would be my first trip to Europe. My husband and sons planned to accompany me on pilgrimage. It turned out that my eldest son and I traveled while my husband and youngest son remained at home to care for our business.

The itinerary included flying into Paris, and then a bus trip to Lourdes, where I had a powerful conversion experience. In Paris, we visited Rue de Bac, the place where Blessed Mother appeared to St. Catherine Laboure and gave the message of the Miraculous Medal. We visited the incorrupt body of St. Vincent de Paul, and Notre Dame Cathedral. Then we traveled by bus to Lourdes, visiting Paray Le Monial, where St. Margaret Mary Alacoque received the revelation of the Sacred Heart. We also visited Ars, where St. John Vianney lived. We visited the home of a little known mystic named Marthe Robin, a victim soul who existed on the Eucharist only. She bore the wounds of Christ in her body, and was bed ridden due to extreme physical infirmities. I fell to my knees in her bedroom; the Spirit of God was so present. Several people did the same.

This pilgrimage was an intense time of grace for all who participated. For me, it was like standing under Niagara Falls and becoming saturated with living water! It had been three years since my first conversion from a Sunday Catholic to a daily Communicant, and member of a rosary prayer cenacle. During the pilgrimage I had an opportunity to speak to Fr. Raymond Skonezny, the Chaplain, about my conversion process and he agreed to become my spiritual director.

During our initial meeting for spiritual direction, Father Raymond confirmed that I was attending daily Mass. Then he urged me to do two things:

Let the liturgy of the Church form and fashion your prayer life. Let the Church be a Mother guiding you by her liturgical worship. In this way the liturgy will animate your interior life and anchor you in Christ. Be mindful of the Church's liturgy and draw from it. It will be a fountain of grace for your soul. God will speak to you through the Church's liturgy. Listen for the Lord's voice.

Pray every day for one hour (at least) before the Tabernacle. I do not care if you squirm in the pew. Do not leave until one hour passes. If your mind wanders and you are thinking a myriad of other things, stay with the Lord, in front of the Blessed Sacrament. If you experience no consolation or perceive nothing, it is still a good prayer. You need not do anything but sit there. He will do everything. The Lord Himself will teach you.

His advice struck a chord in my heart. I did as he said. I perceived this priest to be a man of prayer. But I did not know that he was a Trappist Monk for seventeen years in Our Lady of the Most Holy Trinity Monastery in Utah until our initial meeting. He studied in Rome where he received a Licentiate in Sacred Scripture from the Pontifical Biblicum as well as a Licentiate in Theology from the Angelicum Pontifical University. After returning from Rome, the Lord called him out of the Monastery to become a Diocesan priest in the Diocese of Orange.

He was assigned as parochial vicar of a parish, priest spiritual advisor of Cursillo and Magnificat, A Ministry to Catholic Women. Sixteen years later, he is still my spiritual director, praying with me once a week. In the first meeting, Father Raymond advised that the Holy Spirit is the true director of a soul and the Church would be my spiritual mother. At daily Mass I was attentive to the liturgy. The flow and ebb of Eucharistic grace streamed in a synchronized rhythm with the liturgy of the Mass.

The priest's advice to pray before the Blessed Sacrament sounded familiar. I recalled that my childhood family practiced visits to the Blessed Sacrament. My mother was a full-time homemaker raising five children, eighteen months apart. Often during the week, especially on Fridays, we walked 1.5 miles to St. Pancratius Church to "make a visit." I observed my mother gaze at the Tabernacle and the Crucifix above. I sensed she was talking to God. I imitated her and imagined that He heard my every silent prayer. As a child this seemed natural. Our family was formed by this practice; we knew we had a friend in the Lord.

I ceased making visits to the Blessed Sacrament for fifteen years while I was busy with college, career, marriage and children. It seems my life with Christ has been "all or nothing." If I pushed God aside, I did so completely. For fifteen years I led a life of selfish ambition. Worldly enticements made me forgetful of a relationship with God. Our lumber business became successful through consistent hard work. The more money was available, the more self-reliant we became. I became forgetful of pious practices I grew up with. The world's enticing allurements eclipsed God for me.

In 1990, when I accepted an invitation to join a rosary prayer group, spiritual conversion began. The prayer group consisted of some mothers from St. Jeanne de Lestonnac School and parishioners of the Cathedral parish. Their dedication to prayer quickened my faith.

Here is an example of what I experienced in prayer group. At the beginning of the fifteen decade rosary (no Luminous Mysteries back then!) everyone stated prayer intentions. A lady named Cassie, closed her eyes and peacefully began, "I offer my rosary tonight for the woman my husband is involved with. Lord, please send someone else to help her and her son. Bless them and keep my husband safe." I was stunned to hear such a prayer. I wondered, "How does a person become so big-hearted?" Shortly afterward Cassie was diagnosed with cancer. She suffered and died. In the process of her battle with cancer, her husband converted and remained faithful to her. At the funeral he told me, "She was a saint. She helped save me from myself."

Another member of the group, a lady named Lorraine, hoped to start Magnificat, A Ministry to Catholic Women. She was going to pray for this intention at Lourdes with the group from the Free Medical Clinic. Prior to leaving, she had a stroke that left her paralyzed, unable to speak clearly anymore. I visited her in the hospital before leaving for Lourdes. She kept trying to say the word "Magnificat." At that time, I did not know what she meant. She suffered as a victim soul for Christ and then passed to the Lord. From a worldly life, I found myself in the midst of victim souls who kissed the Cross for love of God. This small faith community became a school of prayer for us. Eighteen years later, the prayer group continues to meet each Friday night. From this prayer group the Lord called forth Magnificat, A Ministry to Catholic Women, Orange Diocese Chapter. A few years later, the Lord called forth the Intercessors of the Lamb Orange Chapter. We are blessed to have a seminarian studying in Rome, a Religious vocation, Sr. Catherine Marie and three priest members.

Since 1992, I have made a daily holy hour as Fr. Raymond advised. The practice of this spiritual discipline led to a personal relationship with

Christ that proved to be healing for all areas of my life. In the radiance of the Monstrance, I discovered my true identity as a child of God. The graces received during holy hour, prepared me for a remarkable journey, first to Mount Tabor, then to Mount Calvary. In the past twelve years, terrible trials shattered the easy existence of our family.

The Blessed Sacrament Exposes Sin Areas

One of the first signs of authentic conversion is repentance. At the beginning of my conversion, the Holy Spirit revealed my faults and sins. I returned to the sacrament of reconciliation on a weekly basis. This is where my liberation came. Conversion requires the purification of the capital sins: pride, anger, envy, lust, gluttony, sloth, and avarice. The quote below reflects what was happening in my interior life.

> The Christian way is different, harder and easier. Christ says: Give me all. I do not want so much of your time, and so much of your money, and so much of your work: I want you. I have not come to torment your natural self, but to kill it. No half measures are any good. I do not want to cut off a branch here and a branch there, I want to have the whole tree cut down. I do not want to drill a tooth, or crown it, or stop it, but to have it out. Hand over the whole natural self, all the desires which you think innocent as well as the ones you think wicked - the whole outfit, and I will give you a new self instead. In fact, I will give you my self: my own will shall become yours.
>
> C.S. Lewis, *Mere Christianity*

At the start of my conversion, I had a dream in which I saw a white sphere covered by many cancerous growths. My first instinct was to turn away from such ugliness. The Lord indicated this was a representation of my soul, sickened by the spirit of the world. I had a strong urge to hide myself from the Lord; not wanting him to behold such a wretched thing. I turned away from his gaze and ran in the opposite direction. Then I seemingly bumped into the Blessed Mother who whispered, "Ask for Divine Mercy." I turned back to God and prayed, "Lord, have mercy on me, a sinner." The sphere, image of my soul, began to be cleansed of its ugliness. During the first year of spiritual conversion, Jesus provided the grace of true repentance for sin. I no longer wanted to offend the Lord.

The Eucharist Strengthens for Co-Redemptive Suffering

On the Feast of Our Lady of Lourdes, 2008, Cardinal Javier Lozano Barragan celebrated Mass for the sick and for pilgrims at the 16th World Day of the Sick. During his homily, the cardinal recalled that it was the 150th anniversary of the apparition of the Virgin Mary to Bernadette Soubirous in the grotto of Massabielle in Lourdes.

He posed the question, "Is it possible to experience the suffering of Christ in our own suffering, to find therein happiness and joy?" He said, "The answer can only come from the Holy Spirit, fusing our suffering with that of Christ through his infinite love. The Eucharist is the memorial of Christ's suffering. The reality of the mystery of suffering, which in Christ becomes positive, creative, redeeming, happiness and joy, while not ceasing to be extremely painful, is the Eucharist. Participation in the Eucharist is the authentic way to make our own suffering part of Christ's suffering. This is the Eucharistic communion. The Eucharist is thus our cross and our resurrection. It is the only true remedy to pain. It is the medicine of immortality."

The Cardinal added, "Responding to the love of the cross implies pronouncing an unreserved 'yes' to the mysterious plan of the Redeemer. This complete 'yes' of love is the Immaculate Conception of our dear Mother, Mary, who participated 'on Calvary as the co-redeemer of the Savior....Christ on the cross suffered all the pains that his most holy mother suffered. And she in Christ suffers all our pains; she assumes them and knows how to commiserate with us. Our suffering is also her suffering. Suffering has value inasmuch as the death of Christ inherently comprehends his resurrection.'" (Zenit.org news agency, February 12, 2008)

Daily Mass and Holy Hours proved to be times of intense grace to prepare me for traumatic events that would touch our family. God's grace is extremely practical and His timing perfect to prepare us for what is coming. The intensity of my conversion corresponded to the intensity of the crosses to come. My prayer life was progressing so I could recognize the voice of the Good Shepherd when he spoke through the liturgy or during times of prayer. Time spent in his Eucharistic Presence caused my heart to simply sink into his. I was experiencing much spiritual consolation.

Praying before the Blessed Sacrament, Jesus gave me an attraction to his Passion. Daily I meditated on the sorrowful mysteries of the rosary imagining every scene of the Passion as if I were the only person for whom he was dying. This must have been the prompting of the Holy Spirit since my nature tends to comfort. The contemplation of Christ's passion was penetrating; becoming incredibly personal. Most of my life, I appreciated that Christ suffered and died to save the world but it was not personal for me yet. I began to understand the principle of St. Paul's teaching on co-redemptive suffering. This made the difference between embracing and rejecting the Cross.

The Eucharist Upholds Us through Trauma

Quite suddenly our comfortable family life was shattered. It was a beautiful spring day, a Saturday morning when the boys had their sport games which we enjoyed as a family. A phone call came advising us to go immediately to St. Mary's Hospital. My father-in-law had arrived via paramedics. Two women driving by the front of our family lumber business found dad lying in a pool of blood on the sidewalk. They covered him with a blanket and called the paramedics. At the hospital we discovered that dad had been brutally beaten about the head with a piece of timber. When we saw him in the emergency room there was no semblance of his former countenance; he was unrecognizable. It was shocking to behold the violence done unto him. He needed brain surgery to save his life. He underwent a surgical procedure called a frontal lobectomy wherein the front lobe of the brain is removed to allow for the swelling from blunt force trauma. Surgery did not save him. He died that day at the hands of two thieves. The case aired on the television program *America's Most Wanted*. To this day, it is an unsolved mystery.

To be at the bedside of a dying loved one is a special blessing and sorrow. To observe a person you love breathe his last and the body rendered lifeless is incredibly painful. One moment there is life and the next it is rendered back unto God. Gloriously our faith enters to help make sense of the whole dying process; bringing much needed consolation. I kept reminding myself, "He is alive in God."

There are no words to describe this kind of trauma to a family. I struggled to reconcile the reality of such a violent murder with the permissive will of God who is love! How cheap life has become in a culture where a person kills an innocent man to steal a few things like a microwave and office equipment!

I felt the horror of disrespect for life to the core of my being. There was a loss of innocence in my heart, in the family. I experienced the culture of death that day and felt vulnerable to it for the first time in my sheltered life. I associated the culture of death with contraception, abortion, and euthanasia. This cold blooded murder seemed the result of a culture turned away from protecting human life. This dark reality entered my family and was terribly personal.

On the day of the funeral the Church overflowed its capacity since my father-in -law was a well known, beloved pillar in the business community. Every person's face seemed to radiate a mystified sorrow. In a way, every person had been violated. For me, I could only reconcile such pain by contemplating the Man of Sorrows.

As it turns out, the family has never recovered fully from this violent loss. There has never been cohesive unity in the extended family since that time. Our grief was too quickly pushed aside in an effort to return to normalcy. The copious tears shed in the hospital room and at the funeral were the last of them. We could not talk about the situation; it was too hard to articulate the grief and loss. The family dug in to keep the business going. Our pain was repressed in an effort to cope with the traumatic loss of the father who was the glue that kept the family united.

I could not manage to repress this. After my husband left for work, I would cry each day for months following the murder. I ran to the Blessed Sacrament, bringing my pain, expressing my bewilderment. Not only was I grieving the loss of a father whom I loved as my own, but also the loss of innocence, the reality that horrible things happen in the world. Only Jesus could bring solace to my wounded heart. In the silence and solitude of those holy hours I felt Jesus healing me from the trauma.

The Eucharist Empowers Us to Draw Divine Mercy for Sinners

Providentially, I was reading the diary of St. Faustina, secretary of Divine Mercy, when the murder occurred. A grace came through the message of Divine Mercy. I felt the Lord ask me to pray for the eternal salvation of the murderer. At first, I was taken aback and put aside the inspiration. Daily before the Blessed Sacrament I sensed this call to intercession from Jesus inviting me to ask for mercy so the murderer would not be eternally lost.

During holy hours following the murder, the Lord taught me that He alone knows the disposition of a person's heart. He gave me to understand that no one gets away with murder. I could count on Divine Justice. Would I intercede for Divine Mercy? I began to realize the magnanimity of Divine Mercy. God so loves the sinner He does not want anyone to be lost eternally!

I was able to pray for the soul of the murderer. Grace made my heart docile and I did not refuse the Lord. In this sacrifice of intercession, I could fully appreciate the words of Jesus from the Cross, "Father, forgive them for they know not what they do." I simply desired to echo His forgiving plea. Grace led daily intercession for the murder and my heart grew in its capacity to forgive. This would be the first of many lessons on becoming a vessel of mercy for others. God grants me awareness that I have been the recipient of Divine Mercy; therefore I must extend mercy to others.

This trial deepened my reliance on God and confirmed the efficacious power of praying before the Blessed Sacrament. Words cannot express the solace I found in the Eucharist. I could run to him, talk to him, listen to him, hear him and simply rest in him. Never did I leave the tabernacle without having been enriched for being there. The more suffering bore down on me and the family, the more I relied on those hours in communion with God. The Lord never disappointed. He gave me precisely what I needed, when I needed it; bringing good out of every trial and temptation.

The Sacrifical Nature of the Sacrament of Matrimony

As a medical assistant I saw patients in terrible pain due to sickness of body. All medical resources were utilized to alleviate suffering and restore wellness. Medical science teaches that the human body is in a perennial process of purification and regeneration. There is also a consistent process of degeneration called the aging process that ultimately leads to physical death. This is one type of human suffering.

There is another type of suffering that is invisible, occurring in the soul of the person. My suffering has been hidden in the depths of my heart. No one can see the insult and injury that caused my wounds yet I know the reality of an interior torment that is as all consuming as any physical pain in the body. These interior wounds are real, painful and beg the attentive mercy of Jesus the Healer.

In my opinion, the science of the Cross very much parallels the science of medicine. The body's process of purification and regeneration is at once, life and death. It is the same for the soul who yields to the Divine Physician. In the sacrament of Baptism, you enter mystically into the death and resurrection of the Lord and are born into the Mystical Body of Christ. So begins an interior life of grace that suffers a process of death and life toward transformation into Christ.

I have struggled to discern the truth from the lie about the meaning and value of human suffering. Discernment of spirits was vital to my experience that I now share with you. It is for the purpose of thanking the Lord and reinforcing the practical value of a Eucharistic vocation.

I was asked to share my testimony throughout many chapters in Magnificat. What surprised me afterward were the long lines of women (and sometimes men) that approached me to share their own similar stories. It is for the sake of encouraging people to trust in the sacramental grace of matrimony that I continue to tell what Christ has done for me.

Scripture tells us: "The Enemy is defeated by the Blood of the Lamb and the word of your testimony" (Rev. 12:11). This is the reason I share such an intimate reality with you: to defeat the Enemy who is coming against Catholic marriages and families. Sacramental grace is more than sufficient to carry marriages through stages of discord.

I met the man I married at thirteen years of age. We went through grade school, high school and college together. We were best friends through those years and our families also socialized together. I was twenty years old when we married in the Church with the blessing of our parents. I had no doubt this was a match made in heaven. It was the fulfillment of a dream to marry a prince of man and begin a family. I knew my husband to be a good, Catholic man and a righteous person. We desired to create the same loving Catholic family environment in which we had been nurtured.

Our married life was blessed, though we were not always faithful to the practice our faith. Through hard work and good financial investments in real estate, by the age of thirty we were living in a neighborhood of million dollar homes. We were blessed with two sons and I was able to stay at home to raise the children. My husband proved to be a good father to his sons, and devoted to me. Our lumber business prospered and we lived a comfortable, if not extravagant lifestyle. We were living the American dream.

My husband suffered from chronic serious medical conditions as early as his thirties. I was concerned about his health since he lost forty pounds in two months time. One day, he was sick and resting in our bedroom. When I entered the room to see if he needed anything, his words would pierce my heart like a thousand swords. Nothing prepared me to hear these words: "I do not love you. We should never have gotten married. It was a mistake." After twenty-two years of what I perceived to be a good marriage, suddenly this rejection came forth.

Utterly shocked, tremendous grace came upon me. My husband was emotionally distraught after sharing his feelings so I moved to comfort him. I became forgetful of myself and concentrated on consoling him. Though I could not process what I just heard, I was filled with love (from the Lord) and began to thank my husband for allowing me to feel that I was loved for the past twenty-two years. He seemed in agony. I thought there must be some mistake.

In the dark days and nights that followed this revelation, I was thrust from a position of security into an uncertain future. He wanted to separate. We agreed that it might be good to get away to ponder things. We planned that he would take an apartment by our business for one month and then return. Of course, I prayed this would be a time for him to come to his senses. Then everything would return to normal. The months passed into years.

My husband transformed into a person I scarcely recognized because of sudden indifference to me and the family, so unlike his former self. St. Maximilian Kolbe said the most deadly poison of our time is indifference. These are matters of the heart that cut to the core of a person. Suffice to say that I struggled daily for the sake of holding our family together. The rupture of this sacramental union felt like the cutting in two of my person. Scripture states: "Two shall be become one" in the covenant of marriage. Little did I realize how much my identity was interwoven with my husband! The Lord would teach me now the true power of sacramental grace of Catholic marriage. Daily Mass and Holy Hour enabled me to carry on for our eleven year old son.

In the area of my personal dignity, the evil one toyed with me, presenting an image of myself as one spurned because of my own faults and imperfections. I began to perceive myself as one worthy of rejection shouldering all the blame. The battleground of my mind became a place of spiritual warfare. The spiritual battle was intense; required constant discernment of spirits to distinguish the lie from and truth. In the discernment of spirits I relied on the help of my priest spiritual advisor.

For years I resisted the reality of the separation and bore the weight of the cross with clenched fists just trying to hold it together until all would be normal again. There were normal stages of denial, grief, anger, and then surrender. Each stage brought a corresponding grace. The Holy Spirit guarded my tongue from speaking negativity. Grace moved me to desire only to forgive the one who caused the hurt, though there were terrible temptations to retaliate. Intercession for my husband had to be Spirit led because I did not know how to pray for him; what to make of this situation. Even while separated we remained friends, business partners and he supported the family in the same manner as always. Though we went to our sons' football games together, spent holidays together and went to some family counseling, there was a painful divide in our marriage.

The Eucharist and holy hour became my strength. I would drive our son to school, then attend Mass and remain in prayer for one or more hours desperately seeking God's will and some relief from the bleeding wounds of my heart. In the light of the Tabernacle, I began to understand that God is so preoccupied with my salvation that He allowed my husband to become the instrument of my personal crucifixion. He allowed me to be broken open, to be brought low, to re-establish the proper hierarchy in my life. God would now move to the foremost place in my heart. The pride I took in my husband and family was a reflection of self-love. Our financial success gave me license to do whatever I wanted. I felt myself to be the master of my life. God would teach me the truth of my spiritual poverty now.

The perfect family that we once presented had become sick. Now the light of truth was going to draw out the poison. As wife and mother, there was unspeakable pain observing our close knit family go into separate worlds of grief. Seemingly a thread held us together. The course seemed obscured as we lived moment to moment in uncertainty. I had never experienced such instability in my life.

By uniting my suffering to Christ Crucified, I felt myself to be an intercessor for my family. I felt the Lord's invitation to lay down my life for the sake of the salvation of our family. I understood though physically separated, we are still spiritually bound by the sacramental grace of matrimony. The highest purpose of this union is each other's eternal salvation. I recall a priest once preached that God does not give us the spouse that we desire rather, the spouse that we need to get to Heaven.

It has been eleven years since we separated and yet our marriage is in transition. The course was rockiest in the first seven years. The past four years have been a process of much healing. Each person seems to have reconciled, at some level, with what happened in our family. It is a testament to God's merciful fidelity that we are together still. My husband is returning to his true self and works long hours to support the family. The children have passed through phases. Because of the respect they see between me and their father, because of the love I still profess for my husband, they feel secure and are moving forward in their own lives. They understand how fragile is the gift of family and I believe they will take great care in their own families. What we have gone through has taught the importance of fidelity to one another and reliance upon God.

On pilgrimage to the Shrine of Divine Mercy in Poland, I placed my head on the first class relic of St. Faustina; a large fragment of bone, encased on the altar rail that is positioned in front of the miraculous image of the Divine Mercy. There I prayed, "O, Lord, I bring you my husband and children." Immediately, I heard in my heart these words of Jesus, "Would you bring me only your husband and children? Rather bring all husbands and children!" Such is the role of an intercessor. The Lord widened my scope of love to include prayer for all marriages and families.

The Eucharist Enables Me to Love Those Who Do Not Love in Return

This trial in our marriage helped me to discover that it is altogether possible to love without being loved in return. Is this not how God first loved me? Love is a decision of the will. I desired only the Lord's will for our marriage.

A Marian priest volunteered to lead me through a process of discernment through the St. Ignatius Exercises to seek God's will in this situation. After one year of weekly spiritual exercises, reading Pope John Paul II writings on marriage and Theology of the Body, it was discerned that God was calling me to remain true to my marriage covenant. The Lord filled me with enough love to bless my husband. Eucharistic grace empowered me be as Christ for my family during these tumultuous years.

By looking at the lives of women saints who suffered marital discord, I found examples to live by during these years. There are many women saints, St. Monica and St. Rita for example, who suffered in their marriages and were able to transcend the situation. I drew strength from the examples of the lives of women saints. In our modern culture, God's proven way of sanctity still exists for those of us who persevere to believe in the saving power of the Cross.

Whenever I speak this testimony I mention also that there are women saints who divorced because of marital oppression, such as St. Fabiola and

Cornelia Connolly, whose cause for beatification is underway. As Rhonda Chervin states in her book, *A Kiss from the Cross*, the issue of whether to choose a path of outward resistance or inward self-offering will depend on the character of the husband, the circumstances, the needs of the children and one's own emotional survival.

In my case, when all illusion was stripped from me, by God's grace, I entered into the abode of the Sacred Heart. The love of God captured me so thoroughly, it eclipsed the self-negation. My pain was intense and it was not taken away. The Lord provided a place for me to put it - namely in his heart. He gave me to understand that I could win grace for my husband's conversion and for the lives of the children if I would embrace the Cross. We know that in everything God works good for those who love him, who are called according to his purpose (Rom. 8:28).

The Lord more than supplied for our family's needs. Divine mercy flooded each member like a protective blanket so we would not self destruct. Somehow in the midst of this trial, we entered into our true identity as dependent children of the Eternal Father, as redeemed souls, not helpless victims. There were years of confusion and sadness as we hung together by a golden thread of grace. We each were being transfigured according to God's grace. The Cross was the means of transformation for each of us. He heals the broken hearted, and binds up their wounds (Ps. 147:3).

One evening, in adoration of the Blessed Sacrament at St. Michael's Norbertine Abbey, I looked up at the large, detailed Crucifix above the altar and prayed, "O Lord, there is such disorder in my family. How can you be in this?" In the depths of my heart, I heard the Lord, "Look closely at the Crucifix. Is there anything more disordered? I am here in the midst of disorder to restore creation." I stood corrected. My Savior is compelled by His nature that is all Love, to enter into human disorder to bring forth the tranquility of order. His Divine order does not necessarily look like our concept of order. I will restore you to health, and your wounds I will heal, says the Lord (Jer. 30:17).

The tragedy of this world is that so much pain is wasted. There is a bright jewel of merit for suffering united to Christ's passion, death and resurrection. St. Paul teaches the truth of the disciples' mission to co-redeem with Christ. The call to co-redemption resounded in my heart and I persevered. If my suffering was co-redemptive, it had meaning and value. This truth kept me grounded and balanced, in the midst of the tornado ripping through my household.

Be sober and vigilant. For your adversary, the devil is like a roaring lion, traveling around and seeking those whom he might devour. Resist him by being strong in faith, being aware that the same passions afflict those who are your brothers in the world. But the God of all grace, who has called us to his eternal glory in Christ Jesus, will himself perfect, confirm and establish us, after brief time of suffering. (1 Pt. 5:8-10)

My vocation is wife and mother. But within this vocation I find a Trinitarian call. As daughter of the Father, I am called to spiritual childhood. As a spiritual bride of Christ, I am called to transforming union with the Beloved. As a temple of the Holy Spirit, I am called to sanctification. If I focused only on my vocation as wife and mother and ignored the spiritual Trinitarian call, I would falter. God gave me the bigger vision. A sacrifice now would procure a great reward eventually.

My marriage situation continues to evolve in the hands of the Almighty One. The disordered years of torment have given way to a new heart surrendered to God's will. I did not close off my heart or cease to love because of pain or fear. My Eucharistic vocation proved to be a source of courage and hope. The Lord ministered to my broken heartedness daily. Padre Pio said, "Love is the first ingredient in relief of suffering."

Joy eventually returned! Worn out from trying to fix things my way, I let go and let God. The Cross proved to be the means by which God could increase and I would decrease. Only an experiential knowledge of God's ineffable charity heals the human heart. There is no other method of healing that will last. All who suffer are in need of the delicate, yet strong hand of Jesus, the Healer. He remains in our midst, accessible to each person in all the Tabernacles of the world. Not only is he waiting there but he longs for us to come to him. Did he not say, "Come to me, all you who are weary and I will give you rest." Resting in the Eucharistic Heart of Jesus brings about revival and hope.

Testimony at the National Assembly of the Council of Major Superiors of Women Religious

In October, 2005, I had the privilege of sharing my testimony at the National Assembly of the Council of Major Superiors of Women Religious at the Shrine of Our Lady of the Snows, Belleville, Illinois. The Theme of the National Assembly was *Healing and the Mystery of Suffering*. The Keynote speaker was George Weigel whose presentation was entitled, The Mystery of Suffering in the Teaching and Life of Pope John Paul II. As the biographer of the late Holy Father, he relayed the martyrdom of love that John Paul II lived. The world could witness John Paul II's physical infirmities and his spiritual radiance was easily perceived. His biographer had a more intimate perspective to share.

During the course of the long weekend, I gathered with many Superiors of various Women Religious Communities to worship the Lord at daily Mass. Different bishops, including Bishop Bruskewitz and Archbishop Raymond Burke, celebrated the Mass. The lectures included topics of human suffering, matters of life and death. Among the many Religious Orders represented in the CMSWR, it was edifying to see the multi-faceted services the various orders provide the Church in fields including medical care, healing arts, legal, teaching and prayer and spiritual formation. If before I was discouraged at the declining numbers of Consecrated Women, I was now encouraged to see many vocations and depth of dedication to Christ. God is renewing the Church in this area. These spiritual brides of Christ are a treasury of grace for the Church!

Mother Regina Marie, O.C.D., Carmelite Sister of the Most Sacred Heart of Jesus, suggested my name as a speaker on suffering in the family. Mother assured me the Committee would consider many other speakers as well. I felt it unlikely that my testimony would be selected. Approximately nine months passed when I received a phone call from the CMSWR in Washington, D.C. inviting me to speak at the National Assembly. Then the letter of confirmation came with the list of speakers which included Archbishop Raymond Burke among other bishops, George Weigel and various other doctors and lawyers. Then there was my name. I immediately found myself before the Blessed Sacrament asking, "Lord, how can this be?" I prayed fervently to comprehend how I fit into such an assembly of consecrated people. Then, in the depths of my heart, the Lord seemed to say, *Ordinary! I chose an ordinary soul so I can manifest my Eucharistic Heart to the assembly by the example of your ordinary life. A life of prayer is a gift for the whole Church. I will be with you.* God was faithful to uphold an ordinary soul called to bear witness to his abundant grace! The CMSWR National Assembly was edifying to all who were present.

The Eucharist Enables Us
to Say Yes to the Divine Will

Yielding to the Divine Will is captured in one word: Fiat! By taking the posture of Mary Immaculate; echoing her Fiat, we allow God to reign in our lives. The highest form of wisdom is surrender to God: Fiat! If the Virgin Mary did not say "Fiat" to the angel Gabriel she would never have become the Living Tabernacle of God, and her womb would not have borne fruit: the Word Incarnate (Lk. 1:38). If Jesus did not say yes to the Father's will in Gethsemane, we would not be redeemed, eternal life would not be our hope (Mt. 26:42). If the great cloud of witnesses had not given their personal fiat, the communion of saints would not be our helpers. If I did not give my fiat to God's will I would be caught in the snare of the carnal world, perhaps losing my inheritance as a child of God. God saved us once and for all, but a personal fiat is given one soul at a time.

By echoing the fiat of the Savior and the fiat of the Mother of the Savior, I discovered an empowerment of the Holy Spirit that brought forth a new dynamism of faith, hope and love. As a disciple of Christ, I am mindful of the condition for discipleship given by the Lord in Mark's Gospel, "Whoever wishes to come after me must deny himself, take up his cross, and follow me" (Mk. 8:34).

No one is without suffering in this earthly exile. There is every kind of cross and particular suffering unique to each person. But there is one, the Word Incarnate, who suffered all in His body, mind, heart and soul so as to heal me. "Upon him was the chastisement that makes us whole, by his stripes we are healed" (Is. 53:5). This truth became my anchor and consolation when I needed healing in all areas of my life.

I am free to choose His will or mine, a decision between life and death. The Lord respects my dignity so perfectly that He can only invite me to choose His will as He never violates my freedom. My fiat was the key to a world of Divine Revelation that led to spiritual intimacy. This spiritual intimacy brought healing to my broken heart. The touch of Jesus renders a person healed in the precise area of the wound. For me, it was a wound of rejection that required the salve of Divine Love. My daily Eucharist was the source of this love.

Sometimes in the midst of the most painful years, there were days when my feet, seemingly did not touch the ground because I felt my heart inebriated with Divine Love. There were seasons when my joy was so complete I would remind myself, "I should be in pain but I am not!" There were seasons when He took away sadness and preoccupied me with things of Heaven. The cross, at times so terrible, became at times, sweet. How? It was terrible when I fought against it. It was sweet when I yielded my will in totality.

I experience the heartache of separation to this present day. The deprivation of human intimacy in a sacramental marriage is a sacrifice I offer God in reparation for the sins of my family. It is not ideal by any means but it is the way it is for now. Joy is quite possible amidst sufferings on earth when united to Christ's passion. The Lord taught me to never look at the Cross without seeing it in the light of Resurrection. Resurrection is what Jesus is about! The family continues to grow in the grace of God.

This past summer our eldest son married a beautiful lady from Berlin, Germany. As they stood at the altar of the Mission Basilica where, as a family, we attended Sunday Mass for ten years, I gazed at the beautiful young couple with so much love and hope for a future of marital joy. I was not afraid for them. My husband and I stood together praying for our son and new daughter. I harbored no more anger or anxiety over what transpired in our marriage. As I listened to the scripture reading of the Mass, I realized they had chosen the same scripture that my husband and I chose for our wedding thirty-three years ago. I still cling to the truth and beauty of that scripture.

> Love is patient, love is kind. It is not jealous, love is not pompous, it is not inflated, it is not rude, it does not seek its

own interests, it is not quick-tempered, it does not brood over injury, it does not rejoice over wrongdoing but rejoices with the truth. It bears all things, believes all things, hopes all things, and endures all things. Love never fails. So faith, hope and love remain, these three, but the greatest of these is love. (1 Cor. 13: 4-8, 13)

Meditation on Carrying the Family to His Eucharistic Heart

Imagine this dialogue between the Lord and a servant of the Eucharist:

Lord, I adore you in the Most Blessed Sacrament. The Holy Spirit prompts me to remain in a vigil of prayer. After Holy Communion my soul is inebriated with your Presence and I find it difficult to go immediately back to the "busyness" of my day. I remain to thank you, to love you for those who cannot because their duties beckon them elsewhere. I remain to pray for those who do not pray. I desire to intercede for the salvation of all souls because you love the human family. I gaze upon the Tabernacle and I perceive you as entirely present. I see the infinite Lord of the universe right here, right now. I see the glory of the God-Man shrouded in a Humble Host. Lord, look with mercy upon my family. Forgive us our sins.

I am here with my heart opened wide to impart blessing. I draw you to myself to carry you to the core of the Trinitarian family. You are changed each day as my love transforms and perfects you. You love me imperfectly but the perfection of my love purifies and increases your love of me. Our union is of the heart, of the spirit, and strengthens the Mystical Body because one person of prayer draws grace upon the Church.

I form you into a co-redeemer and intercessor, expanding your heart to include all souls because I do not wish to lose one of them whom the Father has given me. It is man who separates himself from me. I do not separate myself from man. Mercy flows like a torrent of grace for the Church. I defend and rescue my people. One soul who offers reparation becomes a vessel of Divine Mercy for all souls.

As for your family, by carrying them in your heart to the Altar of

Sacrifice, you do them the highest good. Your faith shall bear fruit for their souls. I accept your reparation on their behalf and pursue them patiently. Receive my peace.

Jesus, faith allows me to peer through that golden tabernacle into your heart. Your ineffable beauty draws me daily. May it be so all the days of my life! Lord, thank you for humbling yourself that I might approach you, My King! Help me to be a good wife, mother and servant in the Church, please. I love you imperfectly yet with all of my heart.

Disciple, intercede for more people to attend the Holy Mass. In this way, I can heal more people. Many have left who once worshipped at my altar. The enemy has targeted the Mass; led countless people away from the summit of Divine worship and source of Divine life. Intercessor, pray for a great increase in attendance at the Mass! Here is where I am in the greatest miracle of Divine Love! I am like a beggar, with my heart in my hand offering myself to a multitude of sin-sick people. Come back to me! Do not run from me! Do you not realize that you are sick and in need of healing?

Lord, I pray for my family members who are not attending Mass. Lord, I surrender them unto you. I pray also for all those people who have left the Church.

Keep bringing them to the Mass in your heart. Keep placing them in the Chalice of the Precious Blood during the Mass. Persevere to intercede for them, to stand in the gap. Be patient and loving as I am patient and loving. Never cease to hope, for great is my mercy. No one is beyond my reach. Your intercession builds a reservoir of grace for their conversion of heart. Surrender your loved ones each day at the Mass. When you remain with me afterward, you cause my light to shine upon their souls. Love excludes no one. Blessings and peace be yours.

In Gratitude for My Conversion: Mary Magdalene Hymn of Praise

Of all the women in the Bible, I most relate to Mary Magdalene. In gratitude to God for the grace of my conversion, I wrote a hymn of praise in honor of Mary Magdalene.

Rabbi, Teacher, Jesus, Savior, Messiah and Lamb,
When I was lost in sin and did not recognize myself,
You did not condemn me in punishment or death.
Full of perfect charity, your heart ablaze with love,
Moved to pity for sinners, of whom I was the greatest,
You chose to forgive my transgressions freely.
Bending from the heights of your holiness,
You stooped to the ground to find me there,
Wallowing in my sinful choices, seeking love,
Without knowing what I was seeking after.
Driven by human passions, I walked with spirits of darkness,
And shunned the light of truth.
I saw myself fit for the darkness; tried to hide myself
In the din of lustful and greedy desires.
My sinful heart became a whirlpool of contamination.
Driven by a lifestyle of disordered affection, I lost my way.
Shunned by the righteous and lawful people,
I became shame to those who beheld me and talked.
Then came that moment of truth when our eyes met
For the first time and you knew everything about me.
You saw my blindness and sickness of soul.
You desired to heal and restore my soul to wellness,
My shame and scars were taken away.
You conquered your sinful servant
In the revelation of your Divine Heart
Full of Mercy, you lavished your healing
Upon a heart mired in sin and darkness.
Your extravagant love thoroughly cleansed,
And I was born again of Water and Spirit.
To be in your service and the company of Miriam,
To care for the needs of apostles and holy women,
Was the honor given to me; the fruit of contrition.
The fire of Divine charity set ablaze my heart,
When you took my hand in your own and revealed,
I am the Way, the Truth and the Life.

I witnessed your passion, death and resurrection;
I saw the terrible price that you paid for my sins,
The river of tears that flooded the face of our Mother
At the foot of the Cross of Salvation on Calvary's Hill
Through the countless days of ages and then some
I sing my hymn of gratitude and praise to your mercy.
The choirs of angels proclaim your Majesty,
The Apostles, Prophets and Saints above and below
Give endless thanksgiving and honor to you, Lord.
Your wounds forever heal the sins of creation.
Sinners are saved covered in your Precious Blood.
Hosanna to the King and Glory to you forever,
My Savior, I am all yours.

Chapter 3

Adoration: I Look at Him and He Looks at Me

What is the precise meaning of Eucharistic contemplation? In itself, it is really the ability or better, the gift, of es-
tablishing a heart to heart contact with Jesus really present in
the Host, and through him, of raising oneself to the Father in
the Holy Spirit.

Fr. Raniero Cantalamessa, *This is My Body*

As I come before the Blessed Sacrament, a heart-to-heart contact is
made, an interior conversation ensues that eventually gives way to silent
contemplation wherein I look at him and He looks at me. How do I know
that I have prayed at all? Contemplation of the Blessed Sacrament produces
the very practical fruit of the Spirit lived out in daily life; the theological
virtues of faith hope and love flower. One becomes Christ-centered, other-
centered, generous with one's time and talent, placing oneself at the service
of others for the sole purpose of pleasing God. Life becomes ordered to
Divine Love's initiative. Intimacy of love occurs, and this is a powerful
healing balm since we are created to love and be loved.

Definition of contemplation:

A loving look at God.

St. Bonaventure

In the parish of Ars there once was a peasant who used to
pass hours in church immobile, looking at the tabernacle, and
when the Saint Curate of Ars asked him what he was doing

there every day like that, he replied: "Nothing. I look at him and he looks at me!" This tells us that Christian contemplation is never a one-way gaze and neither is it directed at "Nothing" (as in certain Oriental religions, in particular Buddhism). It is always the meeting of two looks, our look at God and God's look at us. If, at times, our gaze weakens, God's never does. Sometime Eucharistic contemplation just means keeping Jesus company; being there under his gaze, giving him the joy of contemplating us, too. Although we are but useless creatures and sinners, we are still the fruit of his passion for whom he gave his life.

Eucharistic contemplation is not, therefore, hindered by any arid empty state that can be experienced, whether this is due to our own dissipation or permitted by God. Jesus can dispose of eternity to make us happy - we have only this short space of time to make him happy. How could we resign ourselves to missing a change that will never occur again for all eternity? At times Eucharistic adoration may simply seem to be a pure waste of time - we gaze and see nothing. Instead, what strength and proof of our faith it holds! Jesus knows we could leave and busy ourselves with a thousand other more gratifying things, but we stay, simply giving him our time. When we cannot pray with our minds we can always do so with our bodies and that is prayer of the body.

Fr. Raniero Cantalamessa, *This is My Body*

During a recent Holy Hour I considered the many hours over sixteen years spent before the Blessed Sacrament in the light of the Monstrance or Tabernacle. I had a fleeting temptation. What if this was a waste of time? What if I should have been volunteering at the Medical Free Clinic to help indigent patients instead? The enemy of my soul did not waste time to tempt me further: "God will judge against you for this waste of time! The Master seeks to make a big return for His investment and here you sit doing nothing!" Such is the battleground of the human mind. Suddenly, the Lord seemed to break through saying, *Do you not spend time with those you love: family and friends, simply enjoying their company? How often do friends become forgetful of time when they are together? This is how it is with you and me. What is time that passes between two friends? It is mutually life giving. I give you my life and you give me your life. It is a gift exchange. It is love given and received. Then you are prepared to serve those in need. I am the Lord of time and time spent in the Light of this Tabernacle will bare eternal fruit. This is the truth. Banish the lie.*

I recall the years when our children were small, when my husband and I would stand at their crib, or hold them in our arms, and gaze at them adoringly. As mother I never tired of looking at my children even as they slept. Being in the company of those we love is the truest joy in life. How often do lovers waste time together!

Once when our oldest son was in seventh grade, twelve years old, he contracted bacterial spinal meningitis. He ended up in Mission Hospital for one week. After the spinal tap confirming his diagnosis, he slipped into an unconscious state for five days. I could not bear to leave him alone and arranged to have a hospital bed brought into the room so that I could remain with him. Days and nights passed and time was no object for me. I could not take my eyes off of him lying there with an intravenous drip of medicine that would bring him recovery. I watched and waited that week for some sign that he was getting better, praying unceasingly. That focus is the fruit of love. When he finally opened his eyes and smiled, I was right there to comfort him. Love does not count the cost of time or energy. Love makes us capable of heroic self-giving.

Jesus in the Blessed Sacrament is my Lord and King. While it is my duty to adore Him, adoration is more a small gesture of the love I have for him; a sign that he comes first; before him there are no others. What amazes me is that I sense his gratitude for my being there. I perceive that he simply wants to act as God and give me many graces. He is grateful that I come to receive them. Consider that many graces fall to the ground unused at every moment. I often perceive the Lord with his heart in his hand extended outward, willing to give his heart away to anyone who will receive him. St. Therese, the Little Flower perceived that Jesus was like a beggar for the sake of love. I understand what she means. Christ thirsts for his people. What is the measure of our thirst for him?

They Shall Look Upon Him Whom They Have Pierced

In contemplating Jesus in the Sacrament of the altar, we actualize the prophecy made at the moment of Jesus' death on the Cross: "They shall look on him whom they have pierced" (Jn. 19:37). This contemplation is itself a prophecy for it anticipates what we shall do forever in the heavenly Jerusalem. It is the most eschatological and prophetic act that can be done in the Church. In the end the Lamb will no longer be slain and his flesh will no longer be eaten. Consecration and Communion will cease, that is, but contemplation of the Lamb slain for us will not cease. This is precisely what the saints in Heaven are doing (cf. Rev. 5:1ff.). In front of the tabernacle we form one choir with the Church in Heaven, they, as it were, facing the altar and with us behind it; they, face-to-face in the beatific vision, and we in faith.

When Moses came down from Mount Sinai, he did not know that the skin of his face shone because he had been talking with God" (Ex. 34:29). Moses did not know and neither shall we. But maybe it will happen even to us after one of those moments, that some will see our face shining because we have contemplated the Lord. It would indeed be the most wonderful gift we could give them.

Fr. Raniero Cantalamessa, O.F.M., Cap., *This is My Body*

The above quote is true, beautiful and pertinent to defining the efficacy of a daily Holy Hour. Love communicates; its nature is outward: for love is not love until it is given away. Of the many needs of the human person, knowing that we are loved by the Creator God is the greatest gift. God is the necessary Gift to becoming fully human, realizing our full potential as Christ-bearers.

The world is in desperate need of the Good News that is borne by an authentic witness radiantly alive in the love of God! May our faces shine with His light like Moses when he descended from the mountain after communing face to face with the Great I Am! In His Presence, one's countenance is truly transfigured and made radiant. I perceive this on peoples' faces whose lives are one continuous prayer and act of love.

Like the disciples on the road to Emmaus, we recognize him in the breaking of the Bread. Our reaction is praise and gratitude. Peace permeates our hearts in the light of his presence. A cloud of credible witnesses continue to live this reality. A person of prayer draws untold grace upon the world. God so appreciates the smallest offering of prayer from the heart, of sacrifice and time spent with Him.

Recently, I was privileged to hear Fr. Raniero Cantalamessa preach a retreat in Los Angeles for the Catholic Charismatic Renewal. Like his spiritual father, St. Francis, not only were his words anointed by God's Spirit, but his entire being radiated Jesus. The large assembly perceived a tangible presence of the Lord in our midst whether he was praising, sitting, or preaching. I have since forgotten many of his words that day. However, I will never forget the experience of feeling I was in the presence of a priest in persona Christi, a holy man of prayer. We received the fruit of his union with Christ. We were spiritually richer. Such a living witness inspires a disciple onward.

To Distinguish Between Adoration and Contemplation

Eucharistic adoration may be personal or communal; in fact, it expresses the full force of what it signifies when an assembly is before the Blessed Sacrament, singing, praising, or simply kneeling. This invitatory psalm, with which the Liturgy of the Hours opens every day, aptly expresses the shared character of adoration: "O come, let us worship and bow down, let us kneel before the Lord, our Maker!" (Ps. 95:6)

Contemplation, instead, is an eminently personal activity; it calls for silence and requires that one be isolated from everything and everyone to concentrate on the object contemplated and to be lost in it.

Fr. Raniero Cantalamessa, *This is My Body*

Contemplative prayer is a gift of God freely given and no human formula can bring it about; it is His prerogative to grant it to a person. However, it behooves us to desire and dispose ourselves to receive the gift. Contemplation is simply having an experience of God so we perceive his presence, love and Word within us. The awareness of His presence within us is a revelation that consecrates us in the Truth.

St. Paul speaks of Christ's presence: "...the mystery hidden from ages and from generations past. But now it has been manifested to his holy ones, to whom God chose to make known the riches of the glory of this mystery among the Gentiles; it is Christ in you, the hope for glory" (Col. 1:26, 27).

How can we dispose ourselves for the gift of contemplative prayer? We can cultivate a desire deep within to draw closer to God. But we should realize that it is God who is actually initiating such a desire within us. The Lord has said, "Come to Me all you who are thirsty" (Jn. 6:35). He said, "Blessed are they who hunger and thirst...for they will be satisfied" (Mt. 5:6). He said, "Come to me, all you who labor and are burdened, for I will give you rest" (Mt. 11:28).

In contemplation, we enter into that interior castle that exists in each person and there we connect with the Lord of the castle. In that communion there is refreshment like no other refreshment. To dispose ourselves for the gift of contemplation, we must enter into silence and assume the posture of listening. In this type of prayer, we are in a mode of receiving, of being acted upon by God. We are still so he can act. We cease to be the doer. God said, "Be still and know that I am God" (Ps. 46:10).

How often in the Gospel did Jesus set himself apart and enter into silence and solitude to commune with His Father. He was receiving from His Father. If Christ did this; go apart and receive from his Father, all the more do we, his struggling disciples need to receive from our Father. There are four means of disposing ourselves to receive the grace of contemplation, and these are: prayer, penance, silence and solitude. Scripture tells us, "Every morning he opens my ears to hear" (Is. 50:4). Every day brings with it the grace of His presence which is ever ancient, ever new.

The Eucharistic Empowerment of Love

What is this empowerment? Christ Himself! His power is at work in you as you bask in his Creative Presence. His nature is agape Love, more dynamic than anything of this world. Having chosen the better part, you receive empowerment to become like him! To become like him is the fulfillment of your purpose. It is why you are created: to perpetuate his life on earth and to be with him eternally in paradise. He gives you the grace to love as he asks. The empowerment to love as God loves releases in us a new dynamic life: the ability to put on the mind of Christ, the ability to rise above every circumstance, to spiritualize pain or suffering without fear or shame. It is written that perfect love casts out fear. If I am no longer afraid of failure, afraid of what others think, afraid of becoming vulnerable, afraid of risk, afraid of suffering, afraid of rejection, or death, then am I liberated. This type of freedom comes from being reconciled with God, others and my self. Spiritual empowerment is freedom to choose love in every circumstance. When the question arises, "What would Jesus do?" I am free to act as Jesus does, lovingly, mercifully, peacefully, patiently, kindly, gently, prudently and wisely.

The Blessed Sacrament is the supreme lesson of love since we find no greater charitable condescension: the Lord of the Universe hidden in the humble species of the Sacred Host so we fear not to approach him. He desires to draw us close to him.

The Blessed Sacrament reveals the truth about him and about you. His Spirit overshadows your sin sickness, purifies intentions and actions to sanctify you. Realize that you are his beloved! If you receive him, contemplate him and allow yourself to become formed by him, he will create a most beautiful image of himself within you. He chose you before the foundations of the world to be like him in love, to be holy as our Father in Heaven is holy. He meets you right where you are. The Blessed Sacrament effects the greatest change in you because the dynamism of Divine Love beautifies and begets new life.

Every self-image is disordered until we see ourselves through His eyes. To do so, you must draw close and be not afraid. There, in the mirror of his merciful gaze, you see yourself as he sees you: beloved of his Father;

temple of the Spirit! In his loving gaze is reflected your true self image, free from illusion and disorder. This occurs organically by grace. You cannot make it happen. You are acted upon by God. He is the architect of your true identity and freedom. Your part is to yield to his touch.

In ministry for sixteen years I have known many good people whose lives became more peaceful and opened to God's will, because they began the practice of Eucharistic contemplation. Often people say that allowing themselves to be acted upon, to simply receive, is difficult. Recall the Virgin Mary's fiat: "Let it be done unto me according to your word." This is key to receiving the fullness of grace offered. Pray to assume the posture of receptivity. Yielding to God's grace and timing is necessary for a servant of the Eucharist.

In our modern culture, there is a yoke of "busyness" that deprives us of choosing the better part: sitting at the feet of the Master. I, too, am a busy person with many duties. My prayer before the Blessed Sacrament empowers me to be faithful to all of my duties. It enables me to live every hour of the day in the service of Love.

Once at a Bellwether conference on intercessory prayer, a person asked one of the leaders, a mother with nine children, how she could possibly make a daily holy hour with the demands made on her time? The mother of nine children shared that she gets up very early, before the children, to give God the first hour of her day. What an ideal example she is giving her children. Hers is an example of a life ordered to God's will.

At the time of my initial conversion, when I resumed prayer, I was a full time mother with two sons and a nephew who lived with us. Two children were in high school and one in grade school. Our business was thriving, requiring my husband to travel. Our household was very busy. My hunger for God and thirst for prayer compelled me to either get up early or stay up late to spend time in silence and solitude to pray. When the children were in school, I would go the Tabernacle and spend an hour with the Lord. This was simply a priority in my life and I saw that I was a better spouse and mother because of this time in prayer.

In an article Leo Sands, C.S.B., makes the following statement backing it up with the teaching of Pope Paul VI: "But as we have probably observed, those Catholics who pray before the Blessed Sacrament are often the same ones who are active participants at the Eucharist, particularly on week-days. The two actions reinforce one another." This explains the repeated advocacy shortly after Vatican II of Eucharistic devotion, exposition and Corpus Christi processions. Pope Paul VI spoke of "the indescribable gift of the Eucharist of the Church received from Christ as a pledge of his love....not only while the sacrifice is being offered...but as long as the Eucharist is kept in our churches and oratories, Christ is truly the Emmanuel, the God with us...Day and night he is in our midst...Anyone who approaches this August sacrament with special devotion...experiences how great is the value of com-muning with Christ...for there is nothing more effective for advancing on the road to holiness."

Fr. Benedict Groeschel, *In the Presence of Our Lord*

How great then is the value of communing with Christ in the Eucharist since there is nothing more effective for advancing in holiness! Do you desire to advance on the road to holiness? Your attitude in reception of Holy Communion, in adoration of the Blessed Sacrament, makes a difference in the effect in your soul. The fruitfulness of the grace corresponds to your openness to enter into the fullness of the life of the Most Holy Trinity. St. Thomas Aquinas teaches that if a "false person" (we are a "false self" when we are in a state of sin) receives the Lord there can be no good effect. One must desire to receive the fullness of the Lord and enter into His life of holiness.

Christ wills that you become holy. Did he not say, "Be holy as your Father in Heaven is holy?" He said this because He made a provision for us to become holy, giving His Body and Blood as the transforming reality that sanctifies. Christ wills your sanctification because this is your purpose; to abide with the Holy One; to be transfigured into Him, to enjoy Him in His kingdom. The question I often hear the Lord ask of me is simply, "Am I enough for you?" He knows well the duplicity of our human nature. His word teaches that our yes must mean yes and our no mean no. Are you saying yes or no to His invitation to enter fully into His Eucharistic life? He will not violate your free will.

Nature and Qualities of Eucharistic Service: Love

The Eucharistic service of Jesus Christ should be a service of love. How could it be otherwise? The Eucharist is the Sacrament of Love, and the grace which flows from it in torrents is a grace of love. Divine Love is responsible for its institution; love should then also quicken the entire life of the adorer. The all too generous love that made this marvel a reality is a challenge to the love of man.

The love of the servant of the Eucharist must therefore be great; never will it attain the height and the depth, the breadth and the length of the blessing that is the Eucharist. It must be tender, as tender as the Heart of Jesus who gives Himself to him. It must be pure; the adorer must serve his good Master for His sake, for His glory, for His good pleasure, like the child who serves very dear parents, like the devoted knight who serves his beloved king, like the saints who serve the God of Heaven.

Our Lord is the only one to be left alone and abandoned in His home, in the palace of His glory, on the throne of His love in the Most Blessed Sacrament of the altar. He is left alone there day and night, while the waiting rooms of the great of this world are crowded. Or if Jesus has a few adorers, they are the poor and simple folk. The mighty of the earth hardly ever enter His temple any more. The learned no longer pay Him the homage of their intellect. The rich no longer honor Him with their gifts. He is the unknown God, often deserted even by His own.

And yet He remains in the Eucharist only for man. It is His infinite love that keeps Him night and day close to man's home with all the gifts and graces of Heaven: Oh! Why are men so indifferent?

Let the faithful souls bestir themselves and get together; let them become adorers in spirit and truth of Jesus Christ in the Most Blessed Sacrament; let them organize a guard of honor for the King of kings, a devoted court for the God of love!

St. Peter Eymard, *Eucharistic Handbook*

The above quote from St. Peter Eymard, Founder of the Blessed Sacrament Fathers, written almost 200 years ago, is prophetic in content. It speaks to the modern world of the Third Millennium. It challenges the Church. Perhaps some of the questions raised by St. Peter Eymard were in the mind of John Paul II as he explained his hope to rekindle Eucharistic amazement. We pray for the Church to become a devoted court of adorers for the God of love.

The challenge of St. Eymard's teaching is also a personal one. It speaks of a return to the basics and the relevancy of Eucharistic piety. The Eucharistic service of Jesus Christ should be a service of love. Consider that the present crisis of faith is also a crisis of love. This is a mutual crisis: the thirst of Jesus and the thirst of humanity. The crisis of faith became a crisis of love that developed into a crisis of hope. There is a great deal of discouragement and despair in the world presently. That is why our present Holy Father, Pope Benedict XVI, has written an encyclical on the need for hope. His introduction, first paragraph, states:

Redemption is offered to us in the sense that we have been given hope, trust-worthy hope, by virtue of which we can face our present; the present, even if it is arduous, can be lived and accepted if it leads towards a goal, if we can be sure of this goal, and if this goal is great enough to justify the effort of the journey."

In paragraph 2, he states:

"...the Gospel is not merely a communication of things that can be known - it is one that makes things happen and is life-changing. The dark door of time, of the future, has been thrown open. The one who has hope lives differently; the one who hopes has been granted the gift of a new life."

Pope Benedict XVI, *Spe Salvi Encyclical*

In all simplicity, I came to the Blessed Sacrament knowing full well that I did not know how to adore or contemplate him rightfully. I began this practice as a matter of obedience to my spiritual director because I perceived it to be the will of God. The Lord helped me to understand that Eucharistic contemplation is not a formula, a multiplication of words, or an opportunity to impress him with profound sentiments or fluency of prayer.

He made me understand that it was an opportunity to come to him as I am: poor, weak, broken and sinful. It was an invitation to silence, to spiritual transparency. It was a time when I should simply bask in his Presence and receive his loving light to pierce my darkness, weakness, and brokenness. After years of adoration, it remains a daily new adventure of spiritual communion. I am not satisfied to remember what he said or did for me yesterday, rather let me hear his voice today, let me receive his portion anew, let me experience his Divine embrace of love, the intimacy I require to be well and whole! The Lord infuses knowledge into the heart of a person of prayer.

Since my initial conversion, each year I embarked on spiritual pilgrimages to grow in knowledge of the Church's rich treasury that captured my heart. On pilgrim journeys to Paris, Rue de Bac, Lourdes, Lisieux, Ars, Fatima, Avila, Toledo, Loyola, Rome, Assisi, San Giovanni, Sienna, Cascia, the Holy Land, Medjugorje and Betania, profound graces were received which still animate my spiritual life. Walking in the footsteps of the Lord in the Holy Land, and the footsteps of the Saints in their respective cities, definitely built up my faith in the God of Miracles! It was the exhortation of John Paul II that provided encouragement to embark on spiritual pilgrimages. He exhorted us to step away from our routines on occasion to go apart to enjoy nature and God! During these travels, I witnessed supernatural realities like the incorrupt bodies of Saints, Eucharistic miracles in Lanciano, Cascia and Venezuela.

Several times I had the privilege of being in the presence of Pope John Paul II in St. Peter's Square or Paul V1 Hall for liturgies or special celebrations including Pentecost Events with Ecclesial Movements from around the world in 1998 and 2006. In the presence of John Paul II, my response was always the same; I burst into tears! Why? Christ was passing me by! One glance from his radiant face was like Christ peering into my heart, reading it like a book. At the Presentation in the Temple, Simeon said to Joseph and Mary, "Behold, this child is destined for the fall and rising of many in Israel, and to be a sign that will be contradicted (and you, yourself a sword will pierce) so that the thoughts of many hearts may be revealed" (Lk. 2:34, 35). In the presence of John Paul II, I sensed his priestly heart being pierced by a sword, so the thoughts of many in the Church would be revealed. This redounds to the glory of God and good of the Church. We have yet to fathom the measure of his sacrificial papacy and the fruit that is to come for generations! His life was a dynamic manifestation of Eucharistic Presence!

While these "Mt. Tabor" experiences blessed me, they could not sustain me daily, amidst the many demands as wife, mother and servant in the Church. Above every other experience of the Lord is the need for consistent union with Jesus in the Eucharist! This has been the greatest cause of joy, consolation, empowerment, liberation and teaching in my life. It is like receiving an intravenous infusion of Divine life every day.

The Eucharist Leads to Intimate Conversation with the Risen Christ

In the book entitled, *In the Presence of the Lord: the History, Theology, and Psychology of Eucharistic Devotion,* the authors state,

...there is another dimension to the mystery of the abiding Eucharistic Presence, a dimension that revealed itself to whose willing to venture into the restful quiet of a darkened church, where under the flicker of the sanctuary lamp the only voice to be heard was that which spoke within the deep recesses of the human heart. The realization that steadily deepened that prayer before the Blessed Sacrament was nothing less than an intimate conversation with a living Person-the Risen Christ-about as close as we can come in this life to talking with God face to face.

As this realization permeated the collective consciousness of the Church, it served to foster a spirituality that in a certain sense re-created so many of the beautiful scenes from the Gospels of troubled souls in need going to Christ to beg the healing of soul or body. Among the first to give voice to this

new awareness was Saint Alphonsus Ligouri (1696-1787),
who discovered his calling to the priesthood on his knees before the monstrance, as had the first Apostles summoned by
their Master along the Sea of Galilee. Thus in his classic Visits
to the Blessed Sacrament and the Blessed Virgin Mary, first
published in 1745, he observes,

Oh, what a delight it is to be in front of an altar and speak
familiarly with Jesus in the Blessed Sacrament: asking him to
forgive out offenses; to reveal our needs to him, as a friend to
a friend; and to ask for his love and the fullness of grace.

Fr. Benedict Groeschel & Monti, *In the Presence of the
Lord*

The same book tells the story of the convert, Venerable John Henry
Newman (1801-1890), who like Saint Paul became an ardent apostle of
the religion he had originally sought to refute. The discovery of the continuing presence of Christ in the reserved Blessed Sacrament came after
his entrance into Catholicism and served as an unanticipated consolation
of such magnitude that to him the thought of Christian worship devoid of
it seemed in retrospect insipid by comparison.

Once Newman wrote to a new convert in 1846, "I could
not have fancied the extreme ineffable comfort of being in
the same house with Him who cured the sick and taught his
disciples....When I have been in Churches abroad (before
becoming Catholic) I have religiously abstained from acts of
worship, though it was a most soothing comfort to go into
them - nor did I know what was going on; I neither understood
nor tried to understand the Mass service - but now after tasting
of the awful delight of worshipping God in His Temple; how
unspeakably cold is the idea of a Temple without that Divine
Presence! One is tempted to say what is the meaning? What
is the use of it?

I am writing in the next room to the Chapel - it is such an
incomprehensible blessing to have Christ in bodily presence
in one's house, within one's walls, as swallows up all other
privileges and destroys, or should destroy, every pain. To

know that He is close by - to be able again and again through the day to go in to Him...."

Fr. Benedict Groeschel & Monti, *In the Presence of the Lord*

The Cure of Ars, Saint John Vianney (1786-1859), who would rise from his sleep to spend long hours before the sunrise prostrate in the presence of the Blessed Sacrament, pleading for the salvation of his people:

"My God, grant me the conversion of my parish: I am willing to suffer all my life whatsoever it may please Thee to lay upon me...only let my people be converted."

Gradually the shepherd had the consolation of seeing his flock following his example- by 1825, according to the schoolmaster of Ars, "even before the great rush of pilgrims, besides M. le Cure, who spent all his time before the Blessed Sacrament, there were always people engaged in prayer in the church....I cannot recollect a single occasion when, on entering the church, I did not find someone or other in adoration.

Fr. Benedict Groeschel & Monti, *In the Presence of the Lord*

For Saint Peter Julian Eymard (1811-1868) the mission of the Eucharistic adorer did not merely begin and end at the door of the church; the adorer was to go forth to live a life consonant with what he had experienced on his knees before the tabernacle. This concept of the adorer as an ambassador of the Eucharistic Christ is made implicit in Peter Eymard's writings on the Blessed Sacrament which are extensive. He composed reflections upon the Eucharist that in the nearly one and a half centuries since they were first set to paper have lost nothing of their beauty. Here is an example:

Jesus wishes to reign in me; that is His whole ambition. That is the kingliness of His love; that is the end of His Incarnations, of His Passion, of His Eucharist.

To reign in me, to reign over me, to reign in my soul, in my heart, over my whole life, over my love, that is the second Heaven of His glory. Oh! Yes, Lord Jesus, come and reign! Let my body be your temple, my heart your throne, my will your devoted servant; let me be yours forever, living only of you and for you.

> Fr. Benedict Groeschel & Monti, *In the Presence of the Lord*

When we come into the presence of the Lord in the Blessed Sacrament, we dispose our hearts to listen, hear and converse with Jesus. Each day, there must be a silent time and place to which we bring a listening heart to encounter our Friend, Jesus who says, "Be still and know that I am God" (Ps. 46:10).

Dialogue: When you look at Him and He looks at you

Beloved, the rays of Divine Love are piercing your heart as you adore me in the Blessed Sacrament.

Lord, I am at peace before the Tabernacle; simply happy to be here near you.

Do you want to know more about what happens when you come to me in the Blessed Sacrament?

Lord, I am here to listen as you will.

When you come to me in the Blessed Sacrament;
I am the Christ Child inviting you to be a child;
I am the Son of Mary sharing My Mother;
I am the Obedient Son imparting obedience;
I am the Word Incarnate speaking unutterable mysteries;
I am the Light of the World dispelling your darkness;
I am the Savior ransoming you;
I am the Divine Physician healing you;
I am Wisdom Incarnate imparting wisdom;
I am the Divine Teacher instructing you;
I am Humility making you humble;
I am the Good Shepherd reaching for His lamb,
I am the Eternal High Priest interceding for you;
I am the Perfect Sacrifice covering you;
I am the Resurrection bringing new life;

I am the Cornerstone upon which I set you;
I am Truth consecrating you;
I am Living Water satisfying your thirst;
I am The Divine Mercy forgiving you;
I am Love imbuing you;
I am the King conferring a kingdom upon you;
I am the Door you enter;
I am the Gate you pass through;
I am the Vine you are attached to;
I am the Tree of Life sheltering you;
I am the Living God communing;
I am the Pierced Heart opening;
I am the Strong Arm enfolding;
I am the Lover searching;
I am Paradise opened for you.
I am Who Am.

My Lord, what do you see when you look at me?

Beloved, I see before me a sinner who is forgiven;
A creature chosen from the beginning;
The work of My Hands;
Clay that I am molding;
Vessel that I am purifying;
Child that I carry;
Someone more precious than gold;
The gem I refine;
A temple of the Holy Spirit;
A ship in the river of grace;
The apple of My eye;
Imitator of My mother;
Messenger of the Word;
Prophet of reconciliation;
Servant of the King;
Apostle of Mercy;
Shepherdess of souls;
Intercessor!

I see a maternal heart;
A generous soul;
Daughter of the Father;
A city being constructed;
A garden blooming;
A lover striving;
You did not spare extravagant oil to anoint My Body;
You are like an alabaster jar broken open;
You have anointed my feet; My head with the balm of
  your love;
You are listener;
A pupil who sees with the eyes of your soul;
You are sick with love;
Vigilant and engaging in battle;
Impatient for consummation;
Lover of Truth;
You are devoted and single-hearted;
Faithful and true;
Weakness and strength;
This is what I behold in you,
Servant of the Blessed Sacrament!

Thank you Good Jesus for drawing me to the Blessed Sacrament and for condescending to remain on earth in the humble species of the Sacred Host. Be adored! My God! My All! Amen.

Chapter 4

The Priest Makes
the Eucharist Present

Rekindling Eucharistic amazement
and renewal of the priesthood

We cannot separate the dignity of the Eucharist from the dignity of the priest. Understand that rekindling Eucharistic amazement is intertwined with renewal of the priesthood. The priest has the singular dignity of making the Eucharist present. The priest is a sacrificial victim to perpetuate the life of Jesus for his Mystical Body. The absence of the priest could mean the difference between the loss and gain of eternal life for souls. All priests have their sacramental being in Jesus, the Eternal High Priest. We are mindful that God humbly obeys their priestly prayer to cause the transubstantiation at every Mass. Through the consecrated hands of the priest we receive the Bread of Life.

As the Church more fully embraces its intensely Eucharistic vocation, our amazement in the Eucharistic Heart of Jesus will undoubtedly increase appreciation of the Priesthood. This is the genius of John Paul II at work. His prophetic vision already foresaw the good fruit of rekindling Eucharistic amazement soon to be realized in many different facets. The renewal of the priesthood and increase of vocations to the priesthood will be a first fruit of his pastoral plan.

Basking in the light of the monstrance, we acknowledge the dignity of the priest since we are sitting in the presence of the Eternal High Priest whose risen heart contains the whole brotherhood. Through daily hour, our hearts are conformed to the Eternal High Priest. Therefore our hearts perpetuate his love and gratitude for the men he has chosen to be vessels of election.

Servant of God Fulton Sheen: The Eucharist and the Priest - Victim

The following quotation from Archbishop Fulton Sheen eloquently presents a biblical picture of the relevancy of the Priesthood to the Eucharist.

The Canon of the Mass (in the first Eucharistic Prayer) enumerates three kinds of victims who, by prefiguring the sacrifice of Christ, become models for all priests. They were, in order, the offerings of the just son Abel; the sacrifice of our Patriarch, Abraham; and that which the high priest Melchizedek offered, a sacramental sacrifice. A priest may be victim to each of these ways.

Abel offered to God the choicest lamb of his flock, while his brother, Cain offered only the fruits of the earth (Gen 4:3-4). God looked with favor on Abel and on his blood sacrifice, but he rejected the sacrifice of the Cain, as though it implied that sin could be forgiven without the shedding of blood. The blood sacrifice of Abel is the model of the missionaries who are martyred for their faith, for the priests who are victims of anti-God persecution and for all the faithful who suffer death rather than deny faith.

The sacrifice of Abraham serves as a model for the sacrifice of those who endure all the stages of martyrdom under tyranny yet are denied the formal crown of the shedding of their blood. One brings to mind those who suffered under Communism in the twentieth century. It is for such especially that the figure of Abraham's sacrifice was intended. For them it was emphasized that the sacrifice received its full reward even though the blood of the victim was not poured out (Heb. 11:19). This is the assurance for all who undergo a thousand martyrdoms by not being permitted to die by their persecutors, for those who are brainwashed and who spend their lives in prison or labor camps. They share in the promise and in the reward bestowed on Abraham because he was willing to sacrifice his own flesh and blood, his son, Isaac.

The third kind of priest-victimhood is that of Melchizedek. It is offered by all priests who live the mystery they enact sacramentally in the Mass. But how? By understanding the secondary meaning of the words of consecration. The primary reason is clear and needs no elaboration. The mystery of transubstantiation takes place as we pronounce the words of the consecration. There is, however, a secondary meaning, because we are priest victims. When we say, "This is My Body," I must also, mean, "This is *my* body;" when I say, "This is My Blood," I must also means, "This is *my* blood." "Thou, O Jesus, are not alone in the Mass," the consecrating priest must pray in his soul, "On the Cross, Thou were alone; in the Mass, I am with Thee. On the Cross, Thou did offer Thyself to the Heavenly Father; in the Mass, Thou still offers Thyself, but now I offer myself with Thee."

The Consecration is, then, no bare, sterile repetition of the words of the Last Supper; it is an action, a reenactment, another Passion in me. "Here, dear Jesus, is my body, take it. Here is my blood, take it. I care not if the species of my life remain - my particular duties in school, parish or office; these are only "appearances." But what I am in my intellect, my will - take, possess, divinize, so that I may die with Thee on the altar. Then the heavenly Father, looking down, will say to Thee and to me in Thee; "Thou are my beloved son; in thee I am well pleased (Mk. 1:11).

"When I come down from the altar I will then, more than ever, be in Mary's hands as when she took Thee down from the Cross. She was not a priest, but she could say the words of consecration in a way no priest ever said them of that Body and Blood. As she held Thee she could say, as at Bethlehem, "This is *my* Body; this is *my* Blood. No one in all the world gave Him body and blood but me."

Servant of God Fulton Sheen, *The Priest is Not His Own*

The above quotation illumines the union of the priest and Christ in their sacramental bond of charity. The priest bears the indelible seal of the sacrament of Holy Orders upon his heart. This makes him "another Christ" for the Church. The priest lays down his life for the sheep. Let us be mindful that the priest is paying the price of his life for the sake of our soul. The title of Archbishop Fulton Sheen's book, *The Priest is Not His Own*, reflects the reality of the sacrifice the priest makes to perpetuate the life of Christ on earth. It has pleased God to work through these men. It has pleased God to make the sacramental fountain of grace flow through their consecrated hands.

The above quotation also illumines the Eucharistic vocation of the Church as the Body of Christ. What does it imply? It implies that our hearts shall be pierced as Christ's was on Calvary! It implies that our union with Christ will be through sacrifice. It is the Lord's Risen Heart that we receive at Mass; and his Risen Heart that we adore in adoration. But we are mindful that resurrection follows Good Friday. If we are not mindful of this simple truth, we could get discouraged by the suffering that touches every life on earth.

Our hearts will beat with peace amidst the storms of life if our heart is also set on reaching the place of resurrection. In a manner of speaking, we die a thousand deaths on earth and we rise a thousand times to begin again. This is the life of a Eucharistic people. The life of Christ is perpetual on earth through the Eucharist. Think of St. Paul saying to us, "I live not now, Christ lives in me." That is the Eucharistic life! It sounds so beautiful. But we know that transformation into Christ requires death to self. This is more difficult.

As often as we surrender our will in favor of God's will, we are choosing the better part. The fruit of such surrender is healing. God's way is perfect healing. I am convinced that when we insist on doing things our way, tension of body, mind and spirit results. Each time we let go and let God, we receive healing. The grace that enables us to live complete abandonment to God comes to us through the Eucharist. Our fiat to God's plan and God's timing is necessary to enjoy the beautiful fruit of complete surrender. Surrender to God is simply allowing God to be God. The beauty of surrender to God is in acknowledgement that I am a child in need of a Savior from myself and I am in need of a Father in Heaven to watch over me. When we humble ourselves by surrender to God, Divine Love rushes into our hearts and lives to put everything in order. This is healing and wholeness. God's will is to put order in the hierarchy of our values so we may fulfill our mission on earth. The priest's mission is to be as Christ wedded to the Mystical Bride, the Church. The priests are not bachelors. They are wedded to Christ's Bride, the Church. The priest vocation bears fruit in the generation of spiritual children, carried to Christ through the sacrificial gift of himself to God and the children of God. Is there any higher calling?

A Bishop's Holy Hour

Recently, praying before the Blessed Sacrament, I observed an auxiliary bishop enter to pray before the Tabernacle. When he sat down in the pew, he exhaled loudly and seemed to sink into the presence of the Lord. After sitting for some time with his eyes closed, he proceeded to take up his breviary and read the Liturgy of the Hours. I closed my eyes and continued contemplating the Blessed Sacrament. When I opened my eyes to gaze at the Tabernacle, I somehow saw two rays of light, one red, one white, coming from the Tabernacle, radiating toward the Bishop praying his breviary. This reminded me of the Divine Mercy Image of the Lord as given to St. Faustina. The Bishop's breviary was bathed in light. It appeared as if angels were supporting the breviary for him. I have seen this Bishop pray before the Tabernacle on other occasions. He remains for a long time, and often prays with deep groaning. It is edifying to observe his devotion to the Blessed Sacrament. Let us pray for all bishops. Please pray that priests pray!

Blessed Mother's Priest Sons

A servant of the Eucharist will be led to intercede for priests and pray for vocations. I once said to a bishop that I, too, take responsibility for the priest scandal, because I did not pray enough on behalf of priests who are the foremost target of the Enemy.

At one Orange County Magnificat Prayer Breakfast, the historian took a photograph of Father Skonezny, spiritual advisor, seated at the head table as usual. Later, when she developed the photograph she was surprised to see that over his heart appeared a clear image of the Blessed Mother as our Lady of Grace!

She took the photo to her workplace, a hospice facility, and showed it to a fellow worker who is Jewish. Her co-worker desired to take the photo home to give it a closer examination with special equipment. With this equipment, she saw the image became even more defined; clearly it looked like our Lady of Grace. This extraordinary photograph sits on the nightstand in Father's room; for his eyes only. No one was more surprised by the appearance of the image of Blessed Mother over his heart than he was. A life long devotion to Mary has animated the life of this priest. The Lord allowed the Blessed Mother to show herself as Queen of his priestly heart.

Mary's maternal protection is over the hearts of all priests if they permit. Magnificat has statutes which call forth a lively faith in God, growth in holiness, and intercession for priests. Our local chapter of Magnificat, A Ministry to Catholic Women, intercedes with the intention of offering reparation for offenses against the priesthood.

Reparation *and* Repentance
for offenses against the Priesthood

- For the times we have not recognized or appreciated the gift of the ministerial Priesthood: **R. Lord, forgive us and have mercy.**

- For the times we compete with priests rather than complement them. **R. Lord...**

- For the times we thought our worth in the Church was compromised because of the chosen men of the Priesthood. **R.**

- For the ways we have not agreed with the teachings of the Church about priests but rather rebelled through words or actions, showing disrespect. **R.**

- For the times we gossiped or slandered a priest using our speech to tear down rather than build up. **R**

- For anger we harbored for the priest scandal, becoming suspicious of all priests. **R**

- For the times we have been inappropriate toward priests. **R.**

- For the times we neglected to pray and sacrifice for priests. **R.**

- For the times we neglected to express gratitude to priests. **R.**

- For the times we allowed our hearts to grow cold, uncompassionate and failed to love the priests with your love. **R.**

- For the times we have not forgiven priests and withheld mercy from them. **R.**

- For selfish demands we make on priests while failing to sacrifice for them. **R.**

- For the times we failed to pray for vocations or did not nurture them in children. **R.**

- For the times we have not spent time in prayer so that we appreciate fully the incomprehensible gift of the Priesthood. **R. Lord, forgive us and have mercy. Amen.**

St. Francis of Assisi, Eucharist and Priesthood

The lives of the saints are examples of Eucharistic piety that fosters deepest appreciation and intercession for the Priesthood. St. Francis of Assisi's devotion to the Eucharist intertwined with his devotion to the priesthood.

God inspired me, too, and still inspires me with such great faith in priests who live according to the laws of the holy Church of Rome, because of their dignity, that if they persecuted me, I should still be ready to turn to them for aid. And if I were as wise as Solomon and met the poorest priests of the world, I would still refuse to preach against their will in the parishes in which they live. I am determined to reverence, love and honor priests and all others as my superiors. I refuse to consider their sins, because I can see the Son of God in them and they are better than I."

Fr. Cantalamessa and Carlo Maria Martini, *St. Francis and the Cross*

In a retreat preached in Assisi for priests, Fr. Cantalamessa teaches in the tradition of St. Francis:

But Francis' love and zeal for the Eucharist has some even deeper motives. For the Eucharist is Christ present in his "most holy Body." St. Leo the Great said that "everything that was visible to you of our Lord Jesus Christ after his Ascension was incorporated into sacramental signs."

Francis' tender love for the Child Jesus and for Jesus crucified - the humility of the incarnation and the charity of the passion - were all contained in the Eucharist. For Francis, the Eucharist is not simply a ritual, a mystery, a truth, a dogma or a sacrament, even if it is the most sublime of all. The Eucharist is a humble, defenseless, living person. It is, as one of the Eucharistic prayers say, God, who places his body in our hands.

Let us consider some of Francis' own words on how to rekindle Eucharistic piety in our lives that we too, arrive at a place of renewed appreciation for the Priesthood of the Lord.

Listen to this, my brothers: If it is right to honor the Blessed Virgin Mary because she bore him in her most holy womb; if St. John the Baptist trembled and was afraid even to touch Christ's sacred head (see Mt. 3:13-14); if the tomb where he lay for only a short time is so venerated how holy, and virtuous, and worthy should not a priest be; he touches Christ with his own hands, Christ who is to die now no more but enjoy eternal life and glory; *upon whom the angels desire to look* (1 Pt 1:12). A priest received him into his heart and mouth and offers him to others to be received.

Remember your dignity, then, my friar-priests. *You shall make and keep yourselves holy, because God is holy* (Lv. 11:44). In this mystery God has honored you above all other human beings, and so you must love, revere and honor him more than all others. Surely this is a great pity, a pitiable weakness, to have him present with you like this and be distracted by anything else in the whole world. Our whole being should be seized with fear, the whole world should tremble and Heaven rejoice, when Christ the Son of the living God is present on the altar in the hands of the priest.

What wonderful majesty! What stupendous condescension! O sublime humility! O humble sublimity! That the Lord of the whole universe, God and the Son of God, should humble himself like this and hide under the form of a little bread for our salvation. Look at God's condescension, my brothers, and *pour out your hearts before him* (Ps. 62:8). Keep nothing for yourselves, so that he who has given himself wholly to you may receive you wholly.

Fr. Cantalemessa and Carlo Martini, *St. Francis and the Cross*

At the foot of the Cross Jesus said to his mother, "Woman, behold your son" (Jn. 19:26). Obediently, Mary adopts John, the beloved disciple and priest. In so doing, she spiritually adopted every priest in the apostolic line to love, protect and guide them. She alone can truly comprehend the singular dignity bestowed upon the priest. We would do well to imitate Mary's solicitude for priests.

St. John Vianney, Cure of Ars, the Eucharist and the Priesthood

St. John Vianney is named the patron saint of diocesan priests. On a spiritual pilgrimage we visited the little town of Ars, France in 1992. We toured the Saint's parish and living quarters. His bedroom is preserved for all to observe the humble abode where he prayed and lived. In his bedroom there are burn marks still visible from Satan's attacks against him. It is easy to imagine the spiritual battles that took place in his room. How did it happen that one, humble priest in a remote village like Ars, France would draw such intense fire from the powers of darkness? St. John Vianney was a threat to Satan's camp; he was destined to save thousands of souls through his priestly vocation. He is just one example of the power of the priesthood conformed to Christ's passion, death and resurrection. St. John Vianney's devotion to the Mass and Adoration of the Blessed Sacrament is exemplary.

St. Augustine exclaimed, "Marvelous dignity of priests! In their hands, as in the womb of the blessed Virgin Mary, the Son of God becomes incarnate." St. Paul said, "They are ministers of Christ and dispensers of the mysteries of God." Commenting on these words, the Cure of Ars said, "Without the priest the death and passion of our Lord would be no use; the priest has the key of the heavenly treasures; he is God's steward and the administrator of His goods." Let us ask the Holy Spirit to give us knowledge of these truths. It will inspire us with a religious veneration for the character of the priest, and a lively gratitude towards our Lord who has invested him with it. What is this priest? A man who holds the place of God, a man clothed with all the powers of God. Go, our Lord, said to the priests, "As my Father has sent me, I also send you." Behold the power of the priest! The tongue of the priest makes God from a morsel of bread! It is more than creating the world. How great is the priest! He will only rightly under-stand himself in Heaven... To understand it on earth would make one die, not of fear, but of love. The priest is everything, after God! Leave a parish for twenty years without a priest, and the beasts will be worshipped there. ...If I were to go away, you would say, "What is there to do in that Church? There is no more Mass. Our Lord is no longer there; we may just as well pray at home." When men want to destroy religion they begin by attacking the priest, because where the priest is no more, there is no more sacrifice, there is no more religion. The priesthood is the love of the heart of Jesus. When you see the priest, think of our Lord Jesus Christ.

St. John Vianney, *Eucharistic Meditations*

O priest, know your dignity! In your singular dignity you remind the laity of our dignity, too. We need you to be a sign of contradiction in the world. We need to hear a clarion call by your priestly example and courage! You are set apart for God alone. So be it!

Servant of God Fulton Sheen to the Priests: Why Make a Holy Hour?

In the last chapter of his book, *The Priest is Not His Own*, Archbishop Sheen exhorts the brotherhood of priests to make a holy hour in a teaching quoted below. Though Fulton Sheen is speaking specifically to priests, his reasoning is applicable to the lives of lay people as you will see.

What concrete recommendations may be given to the priest to make him worthy of the supernatural vocation to which he is called? One immediate and essential answer is the Holy Hour. But why make a Holy Hour?

1. Because it is time spent in the Presence of Our Lord Himself. If faith is alive, no further reason is needed.

2. Because in our busy life it takes considerable time to shake off the "noonday devils," the worldly cares that cling to our souls like dust. An hour with Our Lord follows the experience of the disciples on the road to Emmaus (Lk 24:13-35). We begin by walking with Our Lord but our eyes are "held fast," so that we do not recognize Him. Next, He converses with our soul as we read the Scriptures. The third stage is one of sweet intimacy, as when "He sat down at the table with them." The fourth stage is the full dawning of the mystery of the Eucharist. Our eyes are "opened"; and we recognize Him. Finally, we reach the point where we do not want to leave. The hour seemed so short. As we arise we ask, "Were not our hearts burning within us when He spoke to us on

the road, and when He made the Scriptures plain to us?" (Luke 24:32).

3. Because our Lord asked for it. "Had you no strength, then, to watch with me even for an hour? (Matthew 26:40)" The word was addressed to Peter, but he is referred to as Simon. It is our Simon-nature that needs the hour. If the hour seems hard, it is because "the spirit is willing enough, but the flesh is weak" (Mk 14:39).

4. Because, as Saint Thomas Aquinas tells us, the priest's power over the *corpus mysticum* follows from his power over the *corpus physicum* of Christ. Practically, this means that he walks into the confessional from the foot of the altar, that he mounts the pulpit after having enacted the mystery of Redemption. Every sick call, every word of counsel in the parlor, every catechism lesson taught to children, every official act in the chancery flows from the altar. All power resides there, and the more shortcuts we take from the tabernacle to our other priestly duties, the less spiritual strength we have for those duties. If all the sacraments, if all our preaching, confessing, administrating and saving start with the Flame of Love, then how can we refuse to be sparked by it an hour a day?

5. Because the Holy Hour keeps a balance between the spiritual and the practical. Western philosophies tend to an activism to which God does nothing and man everything, the Eastern philosophies tend to a quietism in which God does everything and man nothing. The golden mean is action following rest; Martha walking with Mary, *contemplata aliis tradere*, in the words of Saint Thomas. The Holy Hour unites the contemplative to the active life of the priest. Thanks to the hour with Our Lord, our meditations and resolutions pass from the conscious to the subconscious and then become motives of action. A new spirit begins to pervade our sick calls, our sermons, and our confession. The change is effected by Our Lord, Who fills our hearts and works through our hands. A priest can only give what he possesses. To give Christ to others, one must possess Him.

6. Because revelations made by the Sacred Heart to saintly souls

indicate that still unexplored depths of that Heart are reserved for priests. There are veils of love behind which only the priest may penetrate and from which he will emerge with an unction and power over souls far beyond his own strength.

7. Because the Holy Hour will make us practice what we preach. It grieves the Sacred Heart to see a scandalous disparity between the high ideal of the priesthood and its poor realization.

8. Because the Holy Hour makes us obedient instruments of the Divinity. In the Eucharist there is this double movement: first, of the priest to the Eucharistic heart, and secondly, of the priest to the people. The priest who has given himself the Heart of Our Beloved Lord is known by Our Lord as "expendable" for His purposes. The priest becomes endowed with an extra power because of his suppleness in the hands of the Master. God gives some graces directly to souls, as a man gives alms to the poor man he happens to meet. But the Sacred Heart wished great graces to be distributed to souls through the hands of His priests.

9. Because the Holy Hour helps us make reparation both for the sins of the world and for our own. When the Sacred Heart appeared to Saint Margaret Mary, it was His Heart, and not His head, that was crowned with thorns. It was Love that was hurt. Black Masses, sacrilegious communions, scandals, militant atheism - who will make up for them? Who will be as Abraham for Sodom, a Mary for those who have no wine? The sins of the world are our sins, as if we had committed them.

10. Because it will restore our lost spiritual vitality. Our hearts will be where our joys are. One reason why many fail to progress after many years in the priesthood is that they shrink from casting the whole burden of their lives upon Our Lord. They fail to seek their joy in the union of their priesthood with the victim-hood of Christ. They will sometimes remain stubborn, clinging to the things of sense, forgetful that the Eucharistic door is really not a door at all; it is not even a wall, for there we have the "breaking down the wall that was a barrier between us" (Eph. 2:14).

11. Because the Holy Hour is the hour of truth. Alone with Jesus, we there see ourselves not as the people see us - always judging us to be better than we are - but as the Judge sees us. If we take praise seriously, nothing so deflates our pomposity as the recognition of the helplessness to which the Lord of Heaven has reduced Himself under the species of bread.

12. Because it reduces our liability to temptation and weakness. Presenting ourselves before Our Lord in the Blessed Sacrament is like putting a tubercular patient in good air and sunlight. The virus of our sins cannot long exist in the face of the Light of the world. Our sinful impulses are prevented from arising through the barrier erected each day by the Holy Hour. Our will becomes disposed to goodness with little conscious effort on our part. Satan, the roaring lion, was not permitted to put his hand to touch righteous Job until he received permission. Certainly then will the Lord withhold serious fall from him who watches (1 Cor. 10:13).

13. Because the Holy Hour is a personal prayer. The Mass and the breviary are official prayers. They belong to the Mystical Body of Christ. They do not belong to us personally.

14. Because meditation keeps us from seeking an external escape from our worries and miseries. When difficulties arise in the rectory, when nerves are made taut by false accusations, there is always a danger that we may look outward, as the Israelites did, for release.

15. Finally, because the Holy Hour is necessary for the Church. No one can read the Old Testament without becoming conscious of the presence of God in history. How often did God use the nations to punish Israel for her sins! The history of the world since the Incarnation is the way of the Cross. The rise of nations and their fall remain related to the Kingdom of God. We cannot understand the mystery of God's government, for it is the "sealed book" of Revelation. John wept when he saw it (Rev. 5:4). He could not understand why, at this moment prosperity, and at that hour, adversity.

What we often forget is that all the judgments of God begin with the Church, as they began with Israel. Not politics but theology is the key to the world. We bemoan the wickedness of men, but is not the Lord all the while looking at our failures? Judgment begins with us. The hand of God will strike first the Church, then the world. We who are the watchmen set on the walls are the first to be judged. Jerusalem was destroyed only after Our Lord purged the temple. Jacob's house felt the famine before the Egyptians did. The Jews were carried into captivity before the Assyrians fell to the Medes and Persians. If judgment thus starts with the sanctuary, then so shall mercy. Thus can the world be saved!

The alleged superiority of being "in the chancery" or the alleged inferiority of being "only an assistant" dissolves before the Tabernacle. What ultimate difference does it make if one is passed over for a "good" (rich) parish or if the "second best" man in the diocese is made an *officialis*? Self-assertiveness gives way to Christ-assertiveness in the presence of the tabernacle. The priest who makes the Lord everything for an hour each morning is not seriously wounded by an Episcopal "Passover" when the promotion was logically his. The *littleness* of the Lord in the Eucharist makes *bigness* in the priest an absurdity.

Servant of God Fulton Sheen, *The Priest Is Not His Own*

Fulton Sheen's writings are conducive also for meditation before the Blessed Sacrament. All fifteen reasons for making a holy hour are included because their teaching is rich and relevant. The laity will better understand our own Eucharistic vocation by reflecting on Fulton Sheen's teaching on the efficacy of the holy hour.

From the Heart of the Eternal High Priest: Message to Priests

I present a poignant message received from the Lord to an anonymous priest who receives mystical favors. It is taken from a book entitled, *From the Heart of the Eternal High Priest*. In this prophetic message the Lord speaks first person to his beloved priests.

My priest sons, who I gather to my side, listen to me and observe the treatment of your King. I suffered unimaginable ignominy, pain, ridicule, mockery, defilement, blasphemy, every terrible thing at the hands of the enemy whose hatred for me knew no limits! Every insult, every wound inflicted came as the sting of malice, treachery, and wickedness. Satan hates your King! This you know, but do not forget my elected vessels, his hatred for you is of the same measure, the same degree. For in your soul you bear the eternal seal of the Most High Eternal Priest. Satan spies into your souls and sees me! Know that he seeks too your destruction, your end! He unleashed his legions against you so that you might not make your way to the Summit. How many of my priest sons have been lost to his treachery, his deception, his wickedness. These priest sons of mine suffer eternal defilement as chained dogs who suffer every humiliation by such a cruel master!

My sons be vigilant! I cannot bear to lose another son to the enemy! The enemy is always spying, calculating and measuring his snares for your capture. Only in the company of My Priestly Heart, only walking in the Spirit of the Father can you see what snares lay upon you. My sons you suffer treachery, ugliness, rejection, malice, mockery, every evil thing and you wonder wrongly, "Why such things would happen to me?" I tell you this again, if they hate me, they will hate you. The enemy and all of his legions, his servants hate you. You are targeted for destruction, to rip your flesh apart, to grind your bones into fine powder. Woe to you priests who do not recognize the snare laid for you. Woe to you priests who have crossed into the enemy's camp. You "Judases" will come to the same end!

My faithful sons do not fear! In the company of your King, crowned with thorns, you will receive an eternal crown of victory from the hands of your Priestly King. Will you wear My Robe of Passion? Will you suffer your pride for me and know my glory through humble docility? My priests I love you. You are my own; my own image in your eternal soul. Victory to My priest sons!

Fr. Evan, *From the Heart of the Eternal High Priest*

Prayer for Vocations to the Priesthood

Adore the living Christ in the Eucharist, falling ever more in love with Him, Who is our brother and true friend, the Bridegroom of the Church, the faithful and merciful God Who loved us first. Thus, you young people will be ready and willing to welcome His call, if He wants you totally for Him in the priesthood or in the consecrated life.

O Father, raise up among Christians abundant and holy vocations to the priesthood, who keep the faith alive and guard the blessed memory of your Son Jesus through the preaching of his word and the administration of the Sacraments, with which you continually renew your faithful. Grant us holy ministers of your altar, who are careful and fervent guardians of the Eucharist, the sacrament of the supreme gift of Christ for the redemption of the world. Call ministers of your mercy, who, through the sacrament of Reconciliation, spread the joy of your forgiveness. Grant, O Father, that the Church may welcome with joy the numerous inspirations of the Spirit of your Son and, docile to His teachings, may she care for vocations to the ministerial priesthood and to the consecrated life. Sustain the Bishops, priests and deacons, consecrated men and woman, and all the baptized in Christ, so that they may faithfully fulfill their mission at the service of the Gospel. This we pray through Christ our Lord. Amen. Mary, Queen of Apostles, pray for us.

Pope Benedict XVI

Prayer to the Mother of Priests

O Mary, Mother of Jesus Christ and Mother of priests, accept this title which we bestow on you to celebrate your motherhood and to contemplate with you the priesthood of your Son and of your sons, O Holy Mother of God. O Mother of Christ, to the Messiah-priest you gave a body of flesh through the anointing of the Holy Spirit for the salvation of the poor and the contrite of heart; guard priests in your heart and in the Church, O Mother of the Savior. O Mother of Faith, you accompanied to the Temple the Son of Man, the fulfillment of the promises given to the fathers; give to the Father for his glory the priests of your Son, O Ark of the Covenant. O Mother of the Church, in the midst of the Disciples in the upper room you prayed to the Spirit for the new people and their shepherds; obtain for the Order of Presbyters a full measure of gifts, O Queen of the Apostles. O Mother of Jesus Christ, you were with him at the beginning of his life and mission, you sought the Master among the crowd, you stood beside him when he has lifted up from the earth consumed as the one Eternal Sacrifice, and you had John, your son near at hand; accept from the beginning those who have been called, protect their growth, in their life ministry accompany you sons, O Mother of Priests. Amen

John Paul II, Pastores Dabo Vobis,
Apostolic Exhortation, March 25, 1992

Chapter 5

Progressing in Prayer in the Presence of the Blessed Sacrament

Eucharistic Piety according to John Paul II, *Ecclesia de Eucharistia*

Let us take our place, dear brothers and sisters, at the school of the saints, who are the great interpreters of true Eucharistic piety. In them the theology of the Eucharist takes on all the splendor of a lived reality; it becomes "contagious" and, in a manner of speaking, it "warms our hearts." Above all, let us listen to Mary Most Holy, in whom the mystery of the Eucharist appears, more than in anyone else, as a mystery of light. Gazing upon Mary, we come to know the transforming power present in the Eucharist. In her see the world renewed in love. Contemplating her, assumed body and soul into Heaven, we see opening up before us those "new Heavens" and that "new earth" which will appear at the second coming of Christ.

In the humble signs of bread and wine, changed into his body and blood, Christ walks beside us as our strength and our food for the journey, and he enables us to become, for everyone, witnesses of hope. If, in the presence of this mystery, reason experiences its limits, the heart, enlightened by the grace of the Holy Spirit, clearly sees the response that is demanded, and bows low in adoration and unbounded love.

John Paul II, *Ecclesia de Eucharistia*

John Paul II exhorts us to take our place at the school of the saints, who are the great interpreters of true Eucharistic piety. The theology of the Eucharist takes on all the splendor of a lived reality, it becomes contagious and in a manner of speaking, it warms our hearts. This is absolutely true, as I know by experience. We stand on the shoulders of the saints!

The school of the saints is the school of prayer. John Paul II speaks of the theology of the Eucharist becoming a lived reality. How does this happen? By the continuity of grace that penetrates our heart in the worthy reception of Holy Communion and also, in the sacrifice of praise before the Tabernacle! We are made for dialogue with God. The simplest person can converse with God. When we present ourselves to the Blessed Sacrament, we are disposed for an interior dialogue with God.

There is no need to make an effort to hear this voice. The difficulty is to shut your eyes to it (Is. 33:15). The voice speaks up; it makes itself heard; it does not cease to knock on everyone's door (Rev. 3:20). "Forty years long," he says, "I was with this generation, and I said, "They err constantly in their hearts" (Ps 94:10). He is still with us. He still speaks, even if no one listens.

St. Bernard of Clairvaux

The Everyday Mystic
before the Blessed Sacrament

The Jesuit Father Karl Rahner repeatedly said, "The Christian of the future will either be a mystic, one who has experienced "something," or he will cease to be anything at all." The term, "mysticism" in our time can be associated with strange, singular or psychic phenomena. These have nothing to do with normal Christian life. Rahner identifies mysticism as the elemental experience of God in every human life. In his view the human person is a mystical man. A mystical person simply means a "spiritual" person. The bible tells us, "Become spiritual men." Of course, we are referring to authentic Christ-centered mysticism, not the counterfeit New Age mysticism. Rahner said, "Thus, each and every human being's experience of immense longing for complete happiness contains within itself the seeds of mysticism. Strictly speaking, therefore, everyone is at least a sleeping, distracted, or repressed mystic. To deny this experience is to deny one's deepest self. It is damnation."

This is worth mentioning in this chapter on prayer, because if the Lord Jesus desires to grant us a mystical grace in prayer: an experience of his loving presence, or insights into the scriptures with images or words expressed in the depths of our heart, or a prophetic image, we should be gracious to receive the grace that is offered. St. John of the Cross cautions souls about seeking after such grace. This would not be Spirit led prayer. But if we come before the Blessed Sacrament in a humble posture of receptivity, like Mary, and God initiates some close interior spiritual movement or close encounter of the supernatural kind, we should not be afraid. Judge the fruit of the prayer experience.

If the mystical experience draws us closer to the Truth (enkindles love) then it is of God. If the encounter feeds our ego or pride, it is from self or the enemy. I know many daily Communicants and daily Adorers who experience authentic mystical graces, not to mention priests and religious. Thank the Lord! When we read the lives of the saints, we are being fed by their mystical experiences, are we not? Thank God they were open to receive them! St. John of the Cross cautions that we do not seek after them, and this is true. He, himself, received countless mystical graces! His writings are mystical experiences!

What Karl Rahner said, "The Christian of the future will either be a mystic, one who has experienced "something," or he will cease to be anything at all," is a prophecy for the times we are living. Why do we doubt that God, who is love, does not want to give his needy children spiritual experiences of Divine Love? The bible is filled with mystical experiences of God to every people and nation: dreams, prophecies, visions, locutions, messages, healings and miracles! If this ceased to happen in the Church, it would be inconsistent with God's behavior throughout the history of creation! Oh, how generous is God in his desire to bring his children into transforming union! What transformation can occur in our hearts, and in our Church, if every person became "a spiritual person," or mystic! Before the Blessed Sacrament this can and should unfold according to God's timing.

Fr. Garrigou-Lagrange, O.P., On the Interior Life and Conversation with God

Fr. Reginald Garrigou-Lagrange, O.P. teaches on the interior life and intimate conversation with God in the following excerpt.

To give a clear idea of what the interior life should be, we shall do well to compare it with the intimate conversation that each of us has with himself. If one is faithful, this intimate conversation tends, under the influence of grace, to become elevated, to be transformed, and to become a conversation with God. This remark is elementary; but the most vital and profound truths are elementary truths about which we have thought for a long time, by which we have lived, and which finally become the object of continual contemplation. As soon as man ceases to be outwardly occupied, to talk with his fellow man, as soon as he is alone, even in the noisy streets of a great city, he begins to carry on a conversation with himself.

In a man's hours of solitude, this intimate conversation begins in spite of everything, as if to prove to him that it cannot stop. He would like to interrupt it, yet he cannot do so. The center of the soul has an irrestrainable need which demands satisfaction. In reality, God alone can answer this need, and the only solution is straight away to take the road leading to Him. The soul must converse with someone other than itself. Why? Because it is not its own end; because its end is the living God and it cannot rest entirely except in Him. Saint Augustine puts it, "Our heart is restless, until it rests in Thee."

The interior life is precisely an elevation and a transformation of the intimate conversation that everyone has with himself as soon as it tends to become a conversation with God."

St. Paul says, "For what man knows the things of a man but the spirit of a man that is in him? So the things also that are of God no man knows but the spirit of God" (1 Cor. 2:11). "The Spirit of God progressively manifests to souls of good will what God desires of them and what He wishes to give them. May we receive with docility all that God wishes to give us! Our Lord says to those who seek Him, "You would not seek Me if you had not already found Me."

This progressive manifestation of God to the soul that seeks Him is not unaccompanied by struggle; the soul must free itself from the bonds which are the results of sin, and gradually there disappears what St. Paul calls "the old man" and there takes shape "the new man."

The interior life thus becomes more and more a conversation with God, in which man gradually frees himself from egoism, self-love, sensuality, and pride, in which, by frequent prayer, he asks the Lord for the ever new graces that he needs.

As a result, man begins to know experimentally no longer only the interior part of his being, but also the highest part. Above all, he begins to know God in a vital manner; he begins to have an experience of the things of God. Little by little the thought of his own ego, toward which he made everything converge, gives place to the habitual thought of God; and egotistical love of self and of what is less good in him also gives place progressively to the love of God and of souls in God. His interior conversation changes so much that St. Paul can say, "Our conversation is in Heaven." St. Thomas often insisted on this point.

Therefore the interior life is in a soul that is in the state of grace, especially in a life of humility, abnegation, faith, hope, and charity, with the peace given by the progressive subordination of our feelings and wishes to love God, who will be the object of our beatitude.

Hence, to have an interior life, an exceedingly active exterior apostolate does not suffice, nor does great theological knowledge; nor is the latter necessary. A generous beginner, who already has a genuine spirit of abnegation and prayer, already possesses a true interior life which ought to continue developing.

In this interior conversation with God, which tends to become continual, the soul speaks by prayer, *oratio*, which is speech in its most excellent form. Such speech would exist if God had created only a single soul or one angel; for this creature, endowed with intellect and love, would speak with its Creator. Prayer takes the form now of petition, now of adoration and thanksgiving; it is always an elevation of the soul toward God. And God answers by recalling to our minds what has been said to us in the Gospel, and what is useful for the sanctification of the present moment. Did not Christ say: "But the Paraclete, the Holy Spirit, whom the Father will send in my name, He will teach you all things and bring all things to our mind, whatsoever I shall have said to you" (Jn. 14: 26).

Man thus becomes more and more the child of God; he recognizes more profoundly that God is his Father, and he even becomes more and more a little child in his relations with God. He understands what Christ meant when He told Nicodemus that a man must return to the bosom of God that he may be spiritually reborn, and each day more intimately so, by that spiritual birth which is a remote similitude of the eternal birth of the Word. The saints truly follow this way, and then between their souls and God is established that conversation which does not, so to speak, cease. Thus it was said that St. Dominic knew how to speak to only of God or with God; this is what made it possible for him to be always charitable toward men and at the same time prudent, strong, and just. Let us strive to be of the number of those who seek Him, and to whom it is said, "Thou would not seek me, if Thou had not already found Me.

Fr. Garrigou-Lagrange, O.P., *The Three Stages of the Interior Life.*

Prayer: As a Child before the Blessed Sacrament

During Adoration recently, I felt compelled to pray to the Lord in the following manner which reflects the truth of Fr. Garrigou-Lagrange's teaching, "Man becomes more a little child in his relations with God."

Lord, I adore you without knowing how to adore you.

Lord, I contemplate you without knowing how to contemplate you.

Lord, I praise you without knowing how to praise you.

Lord, I thank you without knowing how to thank you.

Lord, I perceive you without knowing how I perceive you.

Lord, I believe you are present without knowing how you are present.

Lord, I love you without knowing how to love you.

Lord, I draw close to you without knowing how to draw close to you.

Lord, I experience you without knowing how I experience you.

Lord, I feel your gaze without knowing how I feel your gaze.

Lord, I am sure of you without knowing how I am sure of you.

Lord, I know you are near me without knowing how you are near.

Lord, I know you instruct me without knowing how you instruct.

Lord, I know I am healed in your presence without knowing how I am healed.

Lord, I know you extend your heart to me without knowing how you extend your heart.

Lord, I know you take my intentions to the Father without knowing how you take my intentions to the Father.

Lord, I believe you draw the veil aside to show me Heaven without knowing how you draw the veil aside to show me Heaven.

Lord, I know this time with you is the most important time of my day without knowing why this time with you is the most important time of my day.

Lord, I know I am changed in contemplating you without knowing how I am changed.

Lord, I am happy to be with you in this way without knowing how you make me happy.

Lord, I know this is right according to your ordinance of love, that

I stay near you in the Blessed Sacrament without knowing why it is right.

Lord, I know my "keeping watch" with you for an hour per day has infinite meaning and value without knowing why this is so. Nor do I care to understand all these mysteries. It is enough for me to love you, Lord, in all simplicity. It is enough to believe that you love me in simplicity also.

Lord, the whole world is passing away but you will never pass away. So it is right that I hide myself in you since you will it, since you make it happen, and since you make fruitful this encounter.

Lord, it is enough for me to know that I am lost and found in you, that for an eternity you will delight in me and I will delight in you. Such is your humility and condescension for your lowly creature.

Lord, love is all that I need. Let my soul sink into your silent glory.

O pierced heart of Jesus, hide me! Not that I escape this life but that I taste of the abundant life that you promised for those who love you.

Glory to you, My God.

Hush my soul. Silence now! Amen.

After some silence, the Lord seemed to speak in the depths of my heart: *Child, know that your prayer is pleasing to my ear and consoling to my heart. I come to you in the Blessed Sacrament, hidden in a little Host. My littleness is a goal for you. You behold Resurrected Life and infinite fullness of love for you personally. Your prayer echoes the words of Peter, James and John on Mount Tabor when they said, "Lord, it is good to be here! Let us remain here!" Child, see me through the eyes of faith. Faith is not a deceiver. Continue to tell me what is on your mind, unburden your heart and present your body as a living sacrifice of praise to my glory. Know that each time you come to me in the Blessed Sacrament my glory is unveiled for you. I expand your soul to receive more of my Glorified Being. I do this to draw you to myself, to heal you and make you free. Child, of all the things that you could do with your time, your being here with me is highest good, producing fruit beyond measure. Here you have a foretaste of the heavenly banquet. You give yourself to me as gift and I give myself to you as gift. Look around, child, not many people are interested in receiving the gift of God! To those who come, I extend my Sacred Heart and welcome you into the deep recesses of Divine Love. I am the Hidden God waiting to be found. I come to live in you and do not leave unless you take in other things that cause me to flee. If your heart erects an idol within, you then send me away. But if you keep yourself pure and free of sin, I am present within you. Nothing of your poverty can drive me away! Know that I want to do extraordinary things though ordinary people of prayer! Be still now and know that I am God.*

Prayer According to the Catholic Catechism

2559 Prayer is the raising of one's mind and heart to God or the requesting of good things from God. But when we pray, do we speak from the height of our pride and will, or "out of the depths" of a humble and contrite heart? He who humbles himself will be exalted; humility is the foundation of prayer. Only when we humbly acknowledge that "we do not know how to pray as we ought" (Rom. 8:26), are we ready to receive freely the gift of prayer. "Man is a beggar before God" (St. Augustine, Sermon 56, 6, 9: PPL 38, 381).

2560 "If you knew the gift of God!" (Jn. 4:10) The wonder of prayer is revealed beside the well where we come seeking water: there, Christ comes to meet every human being. It is he who first seeks us and asks us for a drink. Jesus thirsts; his asking arises from the depths of God's desire for us. Whether we realize it or not, prayer is the encounter of God's thirst with ours. God thirsts that we may thirst for him.

2561 "You would have asked him, and he would have given you living water" (Jn. 4:10). Paradoxically, our prayer of petition is a response to the pleas of the living God: "They have forsaken me, the fountain of living waters, and hewn out cisterns for the themselves, broken cisterns that can hold no water" (Jer. 2:13). Prayer is the response of faith to the free promise of salvation and also a response of love to the thirst

of the only Son of God.

#2562 Where does prayer come from? Whether prayer is expressed in words or gestures, it is the whole man who prays. But in naming the source of prayer, Scripture speaks sometimes of the soul or the spirit, but most often of the heart (more than a thousand times). According to Scriptures, it is the heart that prays. If our heart is far from God, the words of prayer are in vain.

#2563 The heart is the dwelling-place where I am, where I live; according to the Semitic or Biblical expression, the heart is the place "to which I withdraw." The heart is our hidden center, beyond the grasp of our reason and of others; only the Spirit of God can fathom the human heart and know it fully. The heart is the place of decision, deeper than our psychic drives. It is the place of truth, where we choose life or death. It is the place of encounter, because as image of God we live in relation: it is the place of covenant.

#2564 Christian prayer is a covenant relationship between God and man in Christ. It is the action of God and of man, springing forth from both the Holy Spirit and ourselves, wholly directed to the Father, in union with the human will of the Son of God made man.

#2565: In the New Covenant, prayer is the living relationship of the children of God with their Father who is good beyond measure, with his Son, Jesus Christ, and with the Holy Spirit. The grace of the Kingdom is "the union of the entire holy and royal Trinity"...with the whole human spirit (St. Gregory of Nazianzus, Oratio, 16, 9: PG 35, 945). Thus, the life of prayer is the habit of being the presence of the thrice-holy God and in communion with him. This communion of life is always possible because, through Baptism, we have already been united with Christ (Rom. 6:5). Prayer is Christian insofar as it is communion with Christ and extends throughout the Church, which is his Body. Its dimensions are those of Christ's love (Eph. 3:18-21).

St. Therese of Lisieux describes prayer in this way: "For me, prayer is a surge of the heart; it is a simple look turned toward Heaven, it is a cry of recognition and of love, embracing both trials and joy."

The Catholic Catechism on prayer is sublime, clear, and useful to deepen our understanding of heart to heart prayer, conversational communing with the Lord. Especially in the Presence of the Blessed Sacrament, our hearts are able to turn toward Heaven since the True Presence is Heaven. Somehow, the physical focus of a Tabernacle or Monstrance helps us to elevate our hearts to God. This is because we are looking at sacred objects of beauty containing within, Beauty Himself! We can imagine the Lord as a Prisoner of Love, so little in the Eucharistic Host! This quickens our desire to run to him with haste and to become little like him.

The Holy Spirit leads us to spend time in the presence of Jesus. Let the Holy Spirit lead our prayer when we arrive at the Tabernacle. Recollect, enter into some silence of soul. Breathe out the cares of the day. Breathe in the Presence of Jesus! Let his peace overcome your heart. Quiet your mind. Perhaps pick up the rosary. Let the rhythmic beauty of the rosary aid your recollection. Contemplate the mysteries of Christ's life, death and resurrection and allow the Lord to place you in the prayer of quiet if he pleases! Say to Jesus, "Lord, it is good to be here with you!" Listen and absorb his Light of Love! Let the healing progress.

When it is not possible to receive Holy Communion, or to remain before the Tabernacle or Monstrance, it is very efficacious to make a spiritual communion, praying with true desire to unite with the Eucharistic Heart of Jesus wherever we may be. The Lord honors our desire to unite to him spiritually when it is impossible to do so sacramentally. The grace of a spiritual holy communion provides a powerful outpouring of his Eucharistic Presence. O how merciful God is to grant the desires of our heart, especially when our desire relates our need of the Eucharist.

The God of the Bible is not only the most high: He is the all near God as well (Ps. 119, 151). He is not a supreme being isolated from the world by His perfection, but on the contrary a reality which could be joined with the world. He is God the creator present to His work (Ws. 11:25) and (Rev. 1:20), God the Savior present to His people (Ex. 19:4 ff), God the Father present to His Son (Jn. 8:29) and to all those whom the Spirit of His Son vivifies and who love Him as His sons (Rev. 8:14, 28). He is present at all times for he dominates time, he who is the First and the Last. The Presence of God, in order to be real is not material, however. If this presence manifests itself through sensible signs, it is still the presence of a spiritual being whose love envelops His creature and vivifies it, whose love wishes to communicate itself to make and make of him a luminous witness of His presence. (Jn. 17:21).

Xavier Leon Dufour,
Dictionary of Biblical Theology

The Presence of God is constant and yet how often we are forgetful of Him. How often we struggle through life independent of Christ who is always present to us. It takes a long period of steady discipline to practice the Presence of God. By constancy in prayer, we are mindful that He is our constant companion and friend. A Eucharistic life of prayer becomes as natural as breathing. Before the Blessed Sacrament, simply speak to Jesus from your heart. He is a perfect listener. Often, we just need to get things off our chest. Tell Jesus exactly what you are experiencing. For example, if you are feeling angry at God or his church, tell the Lord! He can handle it. He has heard it before and he understands. Never be afraid to reveal your wounds to Christ. He wants to heal you.

Be in conversation with God throughout the day and night. Train your heart to pick up the rhythm of his heart. Train your ears to hear his voice. Express your love and gratitude for him. His abiding Presence opens the entire spiritual realm of the communion of saints and angels. He is the door to the whole treasury of the Church, militant and triumphant. The Divine Groom and his Mystical Body is for your enjoyment and salvation. Prayer is a lifeline to Christ's heart. Prayer is not only life giving and healing, it is joy!

Chapter 6

Testimony and Prayers of Inga Pak, M.D.

Jesus, the Divine Physician

Then he said to me: Prophesy over these bones, and say to them: Dry bones, hear the word of the Lord! Thus says the Lord God to these bones: See! I will bring spirit into you that you may come to life. I will put sinews upon you, make flesh grow over you, cover you with skin and put spirit in you so that you may come to life and know that I am the Lord. I prophesied as I had been told, and even as I was prophesying I heard a noise; it was a rattling as the bones came together, bone joining bone. I saw the sinews and the flesh come upon them and the skin cover them, but there was no spirit in them. Then he said to me: Prophesy to the spirit, prophesy, son of man, and say to the spirit: Thus says the Lord God: From the four winds come, O spirit, and breathe into these slain that they may come to life. I prophesied as he told me, and the spirit came into them; they came alive and stood upright, a vast army.

Ez. 37:4-10

This verse from Ezekiel is particularly meaningful to me as God's beloved daughter, and to my vocation as a family physician. The Lord allowed me to breathe His spirit of life into seemingly hopeless situations which I will share. I began to understand what Isaiah meant when describing Jesus and his redemptive healing power.

> For the yoke that burdened them, the pole on their shoulder, and the rod of their taskmaster you have smashed, as on the days of Midian. For every boot that tramped in battle, every cloak rolled in blood, will be burned as fuel for flames. For a child is born to us, a son is given us; upon his shoulder dominion rests. They name him Wonder-Counselor, God-Hero, Father-Forever, and Prince of Peace."
> Is. 9:3-5

Jesus Christ, the Divine Physician, great and compassionate high priest, wants to heal us and save us from our sins (Ps. 103:3-4, Rom. 8:1-2, Heb. 2:17-18, Gal. 5:1-2). Where can we find this Jesus you ask? Jesus is ever present and alive right now in the Blessed Sacrament in all the tabernacles of the world where He awaits us to come, rest, and be healed! (Mk. 6:31).

> Come to me, all you who labor and are burdened, and I will give you rest. Take my yoke upon you and learn from me, for I am meek and humble of heart; and you will find rest for yourselves. My yoke is easy, and my burden light.
> Mt. 11:28-30

Jesus more than understands our trials and sufferings (Heb. 2:17-18, Heb. 4:15) and WANTS TO HEAL US NOW!

> Those who are well do not need a physician, but the sick do. I did not come to call the righteous but sinners.
> Mk. 2:17

What does Jesus want to do for us you ask? He wants to "pardon all our sins, heal all our ills, deliver our life from the pit, and surround us with love and compassion" (Ps. 103:3-4). It was this very compassion for the sick that moved Him to lay hands on them and make them well (Mt. 14:14, Mk. 1:29-34, Mk. 1:40-42, Mk. 3:1-5, Mk. 3:7-11, Mk. 5:21). He is waiting for us to come to Him with our sin sick hearts (Ps. 51:17) laden with shame, guilt, anger, hatred, unforgiveness, just to mention a few. There are various other physical and mental infirmities desperately in need of Christ's purifying and healing graces. The catechism says this about Christ the physician.

Jesus has the power not only to heal, but also to forgive sins; he has come to heal the whole man, soul and body; he is the physician the sick have need of. His compassion toward all who suffer goes so far that he identifies himself with them: "I was sick and you visited me" (Mt. 25:36). His preferential love for the sick has not ceased through the centuries to draw the very special attention of Christians toward all those who suffer in body and soul. It is the source of tireless efforts to comfort them.

CCC#1503

He waits for us to come on our knees to seek Him in the midst of overwhelming needs. He knows what we need, beyond our understanding.

Trust in the Lord with all your heart; on your intelligence rely not. In all your ways be mindful of him, and he will make straight your paths. Be not wise in your own eyes, fear the Lord and turn away from evil; this will mean health for your flesh and vigor for your bones.

Pv. 3:6-8

Jesus Christ, the Divine Physician is present and alive today in the Blessed Sacrament, and continues to heal today as He did two thousand years ago when He was walking the face of the earth. Let this no longer be the best kept secret of all times! Remember that "He himself bore our sins in his body upon the cross, so that, free from sin, we might live for righteousness. By his wounds you have been healed" (1 Pt. 2:24).

Do we recognize the Lord himself in the Blessed Sacrament? Are we like the disciples on the road to Emmaus who recognized Jesus only when He broke the bread with them and said afterwards, "Were not our hearts burning within us while he spoke to us on the way and opened the scriptures to us?" (Lk. 24:32). Jesus invites us to spend time with Him so that we too will experience our hearts burning within us and allow the Word made flesh (Jn. 1:14) to breathe His way, His truth, and His life (Jn. 14:6) into our broken and wounded minds, bodies, and spirits.

We need to be restored and healed back to health, wholeness, and holiness NOW more than ever before in this "faithless and perverse generation" (Mt. 17:17) that we are living in today. Satan's blatant attack on marriage, family, the sanctity of life, the priesthood and the church, and the concomitant rise of many false Gods and new age practices are luring us away from the very source and breath of life. What is the effect of all this we ask? It has left us more restless, emptier, alone, and sicker than ever before as individuals, families, and societies; in effect weakening the body of Christ.

St. Paul asks, "Do you not know that your bodies are members of Christ?" (1 Cor. 6:15). God calls us today in urgency to "repent, for the kingdom of Heaven is at hand!" (Mt. 3:2). He calls us to restore our faith in Jesus Christ, our Lord and Savior who invites us to come and spend time with Him in the Blessed Sacrament so that we will know, love, and serve Him as the Lord of our lives. Jesus wants to give us a new heart. Will we receive it?

As the prophet Ezekiel says, "I will sprinkle clean water upon you to cleanse you from all your impurities, and from all your idols, I will cleanse you. I will give you a new heart and place a new spirit within you, taking from your bodies your stony hearts and giving you natural hearts. I will put my spirit within you and make you live by my statutes, careful to observe my decrees" (Ezk. 36:25-27). It is this very transforming process of undergoing 'heart surgery' that allows the floodgates of the rivers of living water (the Holy Spirit) to open up and flow forth within us to bring much needed healing and restoration (Jn. 7:38). The Lord declares, "I will restore you to health and heal your wounds" (Jer. 30:17).

Jesus, the Divine Physician says to us now, "Come away by yourselves to a deserted place and rest a while" (Mk. 6:31) inviting each one of us into His glorious presence in the Blessed Sacrament knowing that this is precisely what the doctor ordered to make us well. It is this transcendental grace poured upon us when receiving the Eucharist that we come into this transforming union with Him and are healed. Before receiving the Eucharist, we say "Lord, I am not worthy to receive you, but only say the word and I shall be healed." St. Paul says: "Whoever is joined to the Lord becomes one spirit with him" (1 Cor. 6:17). Let us be one mind, body, and spirit with him!

The Glorious Victory: My Story

When reflecting upon my life, I am drawn to the story of the sinful woman who washed the feet of Jesus with her tears. Jesus said to her who showed great love, "Your sins are forgiven. Your faith has saved you, go in peace" (Lk. 7:47-50). Jesus said, "I came so that they might have life and have it more abundantly" (Jn. 10:10). After having encountered the living Christ, this woman lived a new life of faith. I can relate to this sinful woman in my own encounter with Jesus in the Blessed Sacrament. Living a Eucharistic lifestyle, with all its ups and downs, brought me a new life of faith as well!

I can never be the same again after having encountered the living Christ who loves me to no end (Is. 43:4, Ps. 136) and who died for me so that I could have new life in him (Is .65:17, 1 Cor. 5:17, Col. 3:10). Believe that Jesus, the Divine Physician hears your cries (Ps. 22:25) and wants to heal you! "So let us confidently approach the throne of grace to receive mercy and to find grace for timely help" (Heb. 4:16). If you have a hard time believing, ask the Lord to help you in your unbelief as did the possessed boy's father when crying out to Jesus to heal his son. Jesus immediately rebuked the unclean spirits and the boy was made well. (Mk. 9:24)

When the initial excitement of collaborating on this book settled down and the reality of it finally sunk in, I began to wonder, "Why me? I have nothing interesting to share about my life." Then the realization hit me like a rocket ship launching full throttle that I do indeed have a story to share about the great things that Christ has done for me through the power of the Blessed Sacrament!

To provide a little background of myself, I was born in Oak Lawn, IL in 1972 to immigrant parents who are from Korea. They gave life to four beautiful daughters of which I am the third. Although born and raised in America, I grew up in a traditional Korean family where my father was the breadwinner, strict and set in his ways; while my mother was the housekeeper who tended to the needs of the family. Although my father had few spoken rules, he was clear in his expectation that we girls focus on our studies. When it came to boys in our lives, they were simply out of the question as far as he was concerned.

Being the obedient daughter, I complied thinking that father must know best. And besides, I sure did not know a thing about boys having grown up alongside three sisters and my mother who was ever present in the good and the bad times. On the other hand, my father, the lone male in the house (and feeling outnumbered I'm sure!), was always working and had little time for us. Despite his absence, my father's words became engrained in my mind as a young girl. We were all craving for Daddy's love and approval, and would take whatever we could get of it without qualms. From that moment onwards, boys became an unknown entity to be avoided lest they dared to take me away from my studies which later became a hiding place to shield myself from the harsh realities of the immigrant life.

My parents married in Korea in haste shortly after meeting each other through an arranged encounter, not having taken the time to get to know one another. They immigrated to the United States shortly thereafter with my oldest sister who was six months old at the time, and struggled to get along with each other and raise a family in a foreign land without the support of family or friends. I did not know much about relationships, but knew early on that I did not want a marriage like my parents.

I continued to focus on my studies. I had finally reached my last year of medical school at which time I met this man, a surgical resident, who showed interest in me. I experienced all these newly stirred up "giddy" emotions, and things progressed quickly from there as he wanted me to be his girlfriend. Being caught up in the excitement of it all, I sighed to myself, "This must be love." In order be closer to this man, I immediately decided to do my family medicine residency north of Boston which meant moving from the West Coast to the East Coast. What a surprise this was to my Mom when I told her (she may still be recovering from the shock!).

I didn't know what love was, but soon discovered the hard way what it was not! To my surprise, this nice man began to pressure me to have sex. As tempting as this was and presented as convincingly in the guise of "love," I knew in my heart of hearts that I could not give into his desires and compromise my integrity as a woman of grace. The following verse has always left a lasting impression on my heart and mind. St. Paul says that women, and in particular wives, should present themselves to their husbands "holy and without blemish" as Christ presented himself to the church (Eph. 5:27). Although naïve and lacking in self-esteem, I knew better. I was being treated as an object and this made me angry! It was a holy anger stirred up in me to shed light and truth into the situation. Certainly, this was not the life-giving love that God intended between man and woman. The relationship fell apart. How perfect the timing was, as my focus shifted towards surviving residency, which required all my attention and energy, and was not without trials.

After finishing my family medicine residency in February of 2006, I moved back to Southern California and this time was introduced to a Catholic man who also showed interest in me. Once again, this was new and exciting for me and things progressed quickly as he wanted me to be his girlfriend. Sound familiar? The plot thickens. Shortly thereafter, caught up in the rapture of the moment, we got engaged; after all, we were in love and wasn't that what happy couples that are in love do?

As quick as all this happened reality set in as quick as we realized just how little we really knew of each other (sound like my parents' story?) and proceeded to backpedal furiously in trying to get to know each other as we now had the added pressure of being engaged. Our relationship got off to a shaky start, but I was not going to worry. I had a handle on things, or so I thought. During the next months, we tried with all our might to make it work and struggled to keep our heads above water. My attempts to mold him into my desired image continued and naturally led to more conflict. A year had gone by and the relationship remained stagnant.

Only later, through prayer, did I come to realize my own human limitations, faults, and weaknesses more clearly. God wanted me to surrender my agenda to Him so that His will, and not mine be done. I prayed daily for the healing of this man and in particular that the stronghold of his addiction to tobacco (sixteen years) would be broken. What was impossible became possible through the power of intercessory prayer (Lk. 1:37). He attended prayer meetings and received prayer ministry which brought healing of mind, body and spirit. He was not alone in the battle. One day, he stopped smoking cold turkey! He never really believed that he could quit, but the grace of God provided healing and deliverance. Praise God for His mighty works!

However, the relationship did not last and one day unexpectedly came to an abrupt end. Despite all the signs pointing to this inevitable outcome, I was left utterly crushed and heartbroken! It was as if someone had sneaked up on me and suddenly pulled the rug from under me and that the world was now crumbling beneath me. I was crumbling.

I pleaded with the Lord, "Oh no! Please no, don't let it end this way! This is not how it is suppose to be! No! Lord, don't you know that I wanted a happy ending? What about all my effort and sacrifices? Where did I go wrong? Lord, why, oh, why, have you abandoned me?" I desperately needed some answers quick as the pain of this rejection tormented me. This dream gone awry was simply insupportable. I was crumbling and had no strength to pick myself up.

Through the depths of my despair came a voice that belonged to my dear friend and principal author of this book, Kathleen Beckman who advised me to sit in front of the Blessed Sacrament and simply receive the Father's healing love. This brings to mind the words of Father Tadeusz Dajczer who says in his book, *The Gift of Faith,* "One of the most fundamental psychological needs in a person is the need for acceptance and love. However, do not look for acceptance and love in people through whom you will often experience disappointment and embitterment. Faith tells you that in reality you need only one acceptance, the acceptance from Christ, who always accepts you. John Paul II said: In Holy Communion, you do not receive Him as much as He receives you. He accepts you as you are. He receives which means He accepts and loves." How timely this invitation was as I was desperately in need of the Father's love due to my own father wound of rejection that I was carrying so deeply in my heart. This wound was hidden for all these years, so how could it have affected me you ask? It affected me profoundly as this wound caused me to seek out men like my father hoping to fill that "love" void that I have come to realize over time, could only be filled by our Abba, Father (Rom. 8:15).

In the past, my ignorance of the real presence of Jesus in the Blessed Sacrament, together with being preoccupied with many things, and the fear of the unknown blocked me from receiving manifold Eucharistic grace. Besides, I thought that only a select few who were especially holy made visits to the Blessed Sacrament. I did not really consider it available to all, especially a sinner like me. These things no longer mattered. I had reached a point of desperation where I had no other place to turn. Even receiving prayers from my faithful prayer companions, however consoling, was not enough.

I needed to experience the Father's restoring love and healing touch as I was broken, heart sick and exhausted as life's travails and "busyness" had taken its toll on me. I, a physician myself, accustomed to taking care of others in need, now desperately needed the Divine Physician to take me into His arms and nurture me back to health. Jesus said to me as He said to Martha: "There is need of only one thing. Mary has chosen the better part and it will not be taken from her" (Lk. 10:42). I then began to sit at the feet of Jesus wanting to experience the better part, having no idea what that better part was.

During one of my first Holy Hours, this is how my dialogue with the Lord went. I cried out to him, "Lord, I am afraid of trusting again and being disappointed again. What is wrong with me? Why do I choose wrong? Why didn't I guard my heart? Where can I find my hope? Help me Lord. I desire to be a woman of grace like our Blessed Mother, but I don't know how. Be my rock and fortress, in whom I trust, and will never be disappointed. I thank you Lord for revealing to me the need to heal my own father wound. Please heal my father wound so I can break free from this pattern of being in unhealthy relationships."

This is what I sensed the Father saying to me,

Inga, you have made the right choice in coming to me this day. Let me be your Abba, Father who nurtures and cares for you. Let me affirm you and fill you with my love. Then, you will regain your true self and will be able to trust in your decisions which will now be spirit-led. Can't you see that I am doing a new thing in you? (Is. 43:19). The fact that you have discovered your true beauty in me and are rejecting the lies that have been told about you in the past is a tremendous victory!

You will begin to know my voice and reject the voice of the Evil one who attempts to rob you of your peace and livelihood, and perpetuates the lies. Refuse to believe his lies that tell you that you are worthless or that you amount to nothing. Counter his lies by proclaiming my words of truth that remain with you and will set you free. You are truly wonderfully made as I formed you in your inmost being and knit you in your mother's womb (Ps. 139:13-14). I have created you in my Divine image (Gen. 1:27). You are valuable and lovable in my eyes. Now is the time to get to know me, your Maker and be nurtured in the gentlest of hands. Know of my awesome plans for you; plans to help you to prosper and not to harm, plans to give you a hope and a future. You will call upon me and I will listen to you. You will seek me and find me when you seek me with all your heart. I will be found by you and will bring you back from captivity (Jer. 29:11-15). You are not alone. Reach out and get help and comfort from others in your time of need. Know that I am here ministering to your wounds at this very moment. You need not appear strong in front of me. Come just as you are. Let me love you just as you are. I will bring good people into your life, friends that will affirm and uplift you. How will you know them you ask? You shall know them by their fruits. Unite your pain and suffering to the cross and there you will find solace and hope in the joys to come in your life. Yes, I said joys! Do not doubt, worry, or fear, you of little faith. Know that I am with you always and go before you. Be patient in all things. I love you, my precious daughter and woman of grace for this is your true identity.

What consolation and joy it was when I discovered my Abba Father's infinite love for me and came to know my true identity in Him. May you experience the fullness of our Abba Father's love for you!

For as long as I can remember, I have always envisioned having a holy family, a family united in faith, hope, and love. That was an unspoken desire buried deep in my heart unbeknownst to anyone. I quickly learned to suppress my desires and needs as a child seeing the overwhelming struggles of my mother trying to raise four children practically on her own.

My father, as the breadwinner, was busy working and not available to help much in raising us. As a family, we found out quickly that trying to achieve the American dream was not without costs. While growing up, my own dream of having a holy family seemed unrealistic and far-fetched, and had to be pushed aside for awhile.

Feelings of guilt welled up inside of me to even desire this for myself; regularly seeing my mother sick from exhaustion and suffering from the emotional neglect and lack of support from her husband. It was only through the grace of God that my mother endured each waking day for the sake of fulfilling her duty to keep the family together at all costs. It was this very suffering that brought her to the Catholic Church where she encountered Jesus on the cross, and there found the much needed solace and hope that only He could bring.

It was all in the Lord's plan for her she says, to leave her comfortable life in Korea and settle down in America in order to discover life's greatest treasure in Him! Her greatest gift to us has been that of faith, which as you can see, makes all things possible! I am eternally grateful to my mother for her fiat and for exemplifying our Blessed Mother in carrying her cross with fidelity and hope that always springs eternally. May you always find hope in Him in all the circumstances of your life.

Therefore, since we have been justified by faith, we have peace with God through our Lord Jesus Christ, through whom we have gained access by faith to this grace in which we stand, and we boast in hope of the glory of God. Not only that, but we even boast of our afflictions, knowing that affliction produces endurance, and endurance, proven character, and proven character, hope, and hope does not disappoint, because the love of God has been poured out into our hearts through the holy Spirit that has been given to us (Rom. 5:1-5).

Adoration of the Blessed Sacrament: Inner Healing of the Child Within

It was in front of the Blessed Sacrament that I was able to return to being a child again and what joy that brought me! When I look at young children, they are so beautiful and precious, full of life, joyful, carefree, innocent, trusting, fearless, honest, open, present in the moment, and needing to be cared for. They don't have fears or worries that bog them down. They don't have pretenses. What you see is who they are. Along the way, I lost that child in me, but now have been found! (Lk. 15:24).

We need to go back to being children again in our relationship with the Lord in the spiritual sense, as Mother Nadine, Intercessors of the Lamb teaches us. How did I experience this during my visits with the Lord in the Blessed Sacrament? I became a child again. I grieved, vented, complained, and cried to Jesus all the while receiving heart surgery and it turns out, a heart transplant, too! He began to piece my heart together again one precious piece at a time.

Jesus was saying to me, "I will give you a new heart and place a new spirit within you, taking from your bodies your stony hearts and giving you natural hearts" (Ez. 36:26). I simply sat and soaked in His love for me (which was not easy at first!) and allowed His words of truth and life to penetrate my broken heart and eventually transform it into a new heart. It was then that I experienced a new found freedom and peace that was unlike any that I had experienced before! It was wonderful to receive and be loved just as I was! Thank you, Jesus!

I had found a true friend in Jesus in the Blessed Sacrament, a priceless treasure available to us all! (Mt. 14:44). And it was only in this prayerful silence and solitude that the Lord began to show me just how consuming and draining this former relationship with this man, had been on me. This also was not the love that God intended between man and woman. Despite my insecurities, I asked the Lord, surprising myself with this new holy boldness, "Please show me the love that God intended between man and woman. Teach me and show me as you alone are the way, the truth, and the life (Jn. 14:6), and sure enough, this is exactly what He did!

One day in front of the Blessed Sacrament, I had the desire to ask the Lord and our Blessed Mother this question, "Do you have a St. Joseph for me?" and this is what I sensed the Lord saying to me.

"Trust me to provide you with a St. Joseph in due time. You are a new creation in me. I have given you a new discerning heart. Your integrity as woman of grace will shine forth as your Blessed Mother and I are preparing you both for the journey ahead."

I then saw two sail boats, one ahead of the other and the Lord saying to me through this image, "You will be free to be who you are. The man who loves and fears the Lord will lead you. He will be like St. Joseph and have his virtues of gentleness, humility, purity, and self-control. He will affirm you, challenge you, and help you to be the woman of grace that you have always desired to be. A solid rock he will be to you, your best friend and companion for life.

I felt encouraged by these words and pondered them in my heart during which time my eyes came to rest on these bible verses that illuminated the message, "Believe!" As Peter said to Jesus, "Master, to whom shall we go? You have the words of eternal life. We have come to believe and are convinced that you are the Holy One of God" (Jn. 6:68-69). I, like Peter, now believed with the eyes of faith, undeniable a fruit of prayer.

Ask and it will be given to you; seek and you will find; knock and the door will be opened to you. For everyone who asks receives; and the one who seeks, finds; and to the one that knocks, the door will be opened. Mt. 7:7-8

May he give you the desire of your heart and make all your plans succeed. We will shout for joy when you are victorious and will lift up our banners in the name of our God. May the Lord grant all your requests. Now I know that the Lord saves his anointed; he answers him from his holy Heaven with the saving power of his right hand. Ps. 20:4

In you they trusted and were not disappointed. Ps. 22:6

Jerusalem, take off your robe of mourning and misery; put on the splendor of glory from God forever. Bar. 5:1

Remember not the events of the past, the things of long ago consider not; See, I am doing something new! Now it springs forth, do you not perceive it? Is. 43:18-19

Christ-centered Courtship

While sailing in this new-found freedom and joy of the spirit, I indeed met my St. Joseph who was everything that I had hoped for and more! This time, we began a Christ-centered courtship, seeing the reflection of Christ in ourselves and in one another which brought such inexplicable freedom and joy!

> The truth that Christ loves another person through you implies that you cannot love a person without loving God. You alone are unable to love. It is Christ who loves in you. You can give Christ to others to the extent that you accept Him and to the extent that you allow Him to encompass you.
>
> Father Tadeusz Dajczer, *The Gift of Faith.*

The courtship glided in serene waters. And, oh, how incredibly sweet it was, the moment he got down on his knees and officially proposed to me in front of the BLESSED SACRAMENT! What a glorious crowning moment it was as I felt our Blessed Mother's radiant presence and my crown of thorns being replaced with a crown of roses! I still savor the moment. The song, "He makes all things beautiful in His time," surfaces. God is truly good and has done great things for me as you can see! (Lk. 1:49). He delivered my life from the pit and surrounded me with love and compassion! (Ps. 103:4). He is waiting for you in the Blessed Sacrament and wants to do the same for you! What are you waiting for?

Jesus' Mission of Healing *and* Faith in Him

If you are praying for healing for a loved one, remember the story of the faithful friends of the paralytic man. Unable to reach Jesus due to the massive crowds (never letting that be an obstacle) they opened up the roof of the home that Jesus was in, and let down the mat that the paralytic man was sitting on. He received healing not only in body, but in mind and spirit! Jesus saw the great faith of the friends, and said to the paralytic, "Child, your sins are forgiven" and then ordered him to "Rise, pick up your mat, and walk" which is indeed what he did. All were astounded and glorified God (Mk. 2:1-12). And take heart in the story of Jairus, a faithful official of the synagogue, who despite almost being crushed by the crowds, came forward and fell at the feet of Jesus. Jairus begged Jesus to heal his only daughter who was about 12 years old and dying. When news came that it was too late that the daughter had died, Jesus said to Jairus, "Do not be afraid; just have faith and she will be saved" (Lk. 8:50), and indeed it happened just as the Lord said.

How come we don't hear about miracles happening everywhere as they did in Jesus' time? Is it that Jesus is no longer healing? Not at all! Jesus is the same, yesterday, today, and forever more. Then we are led to look inwardly and ask ourselves these questions: "In whom or in what are we putting our faith in? Is Jesus truly our personal Lord and savior?

Oh, how we can relate to Thomas, one of the twelve disciples, in looking at our own spiritual journey that calls us to daily conversion and unwavering faith in Jesus alone! Thomas believed only after seeing Jesus in the flesh that He had resurrected. Jesus is saying to us now as he said to Thomas: "Do not be unbelieving, but believe. Have you come to believe because you have seen me? Blessed are those who have not seen and have believed" (Jn. 20:28, 29).

Our lack of faith in the living Christ is a reason that we are not seeing more miracles, as was the case in Jesus' time. When he went back to his hometown, Nazareth, he did not do many miracles there because of their lack of faith (Mt. 13:58). As Isaiah prophesied, "You shall indeed hear but not understand; you shall indeed look but never see. Gross is the heart of this people, they will hardly hear with their ears, they have closed their eyes, lest they see with their eyes and hear with their ears and understand with their heart and be converted, and I HEAL THEM" (Mt. 13:14-15).

Mark tells us about Jesus' commissioning of his disciples, "These signs will accompany those who believe: in my name they will drive out demons, they will speak new languages...They will lay hands on the sick, and they will RECOVER" (Mk. 16:14-18). He is commissioning us to go forth and do as he did! This is what the catechism says in reference to healing the sick:

> The risen Lord renews this mission and confirms it through the signs that the Church performs by invoking his name (cf. Acts 9:34; 14:3). These signs demonstrate in a special way that Jesus is truly "God who saves" (cf. Mt. 1:21; Acts 4:12).
> CCC #1507

The question then arises, "Well, then, why isn't everyone healed? The Catechism says:

> But he did not heal all the sick. His healings were signs of

the coming of the Kingdom of God. They announced a more radical healing: the victory over sin and death through his Passover. On the cross Christ took upon himself the whole weight of evil and took away the "sin of the world" (Jn. 1:29; cf. Isa. 53:4-6), of which illness is only a consequence. By his passion and death on the cross Christ has given a new meaning to suffering: it can henceforth configure us to him and unite us with his redemptive Passion.

CCC #1505

But even the most intense prayers do not always obtain the healing of all illnesses. Thus St. Paul must learn from the Lord that,

My grace is sufficient for you, for my power is made perfect in weakness, and that the sufferings to be endured can mean that, in my flesh I complete what is lacking in Christ's afflictions for the sake of his Body, that is, the Church (2 Cor. 12:9; Col. 1:24).

CCC #1508

Furthermore, this is what the catechism says concerning the sacrament of the sick addressing the above question as well:

The liturgy has never failed to beg the Lord that the sick person may recover his health if it would be conducive to his salvation (cf. Council of Trent 1551).

CCC #1512

Where do we find the living Christ who is as real as the air that we breathe? We can not see the air, but we know that it sustains our existence. It is the same way with our faith in the living Christ. Jesus is present in the many forms of Eucharistic Presence.

Eucharistic advent is above all an attitude of faith. It is faith in the love of Jesus who awaits you as a loved one. It is so important for you to believe that Jesus desires to come into your heart, that he desires the celebration of the Eucharist. He waits for you to receive Holy Communion because He wants to give Himself to you fully through The Most Blessed Sacrament, the main source of graces.

As faith is the reliance on Christ and entrusting yourself to Him, then in the Eucharist you should entrust to Him all your affairs, fears, and anxieties. The Eucharist will then bring you peace born of the faith in the redeeming power of Jesus' sacrifice. This faith means believing that He redeemed you from fear, uncertainty and stress, and from all that destroys your spiritual life, as well as your physical or mental health. Through faith, you will be able to receive the fruits of redemption. The catechism says this about healing the sick.

Father Tadeusz Dajczer. *The Gift of Faith*

The Catechism Says This About Healing the Sick

The Church has received this charge from the Lord and strives to carry it out by taking care of the sick as well as by accompanying them with her prayer of intercession. She believes in the life-giving presence of Christ, the physician of souls and bodies. This presence is particularly active through the sacraments, and in an altogether special way through the Eucharist, the bread that gives eternal life and that St. Paul suggests is connected with bodily health (Jn. 6:54, 58; 1 Cor. 11:30).

CCC #1509

St. Paul says: Therefore whoever eats the bread or drinks the cup of the Lord unworthily will have to answer for the body and blood of the Lord. A person should examine himself, and so eat the bread and drink the cup. For anyone who ears and drinks without discerning the body, eats and drinks judgment on himself. That is why many among you are ill and infirm, and a considerable number are dying. If we discerned ourselves, we would not be under judgment; but since we are judged by the Lord, we are being disciplined so that we may not be condemned along with the world.

(1 Cor. 11:27-32)

Let us prepare ourselves to receive Him in a worthy manner! St. Paul says: "And you who once were alienated and hostile in mind because of evil deeds he has now reconciled in his fleshly body through his death, to present you holy, without blemish, and irreproachable before him, provided that you persevere in the faith, grounded, stable, and not shifting from the hope of the gospel that you heard.

(Col. 1:21-23)

The Healing Power of the Holy Spirit

Three Cases

As a family physician, I would like to share three particularly memorable cases of patients that I cared for where the invigorating breath of the Holy Spirit brought about healing of mind, body, and spirit. These cases truly revealed the glorious power of Jesus at work healing the sick and the brokenhearted, allotting to each one the supernatural graces needed to move forward. Believe that Jesus wants to restore you to health and heal your wounds (Jer. 30:17).

Recall the story of the woman who had suffered greatly from hemorrhages for twelve years. She had gone to many doctors, not one of whom was able to cure her. It was a simple act of faith in her encounter with Jesus, merely touching the tassel on his cloak, that healed her instantly of her infirmity (Lk. 8:43-48). Do you have that same faith in Jesus to heal your infirmities?

First Patient: Oscar
Healed Body, Mind and Spirit

I will share with you the story of a patient of mine who was instantaneously healed by the Lord during his last office visit with me. Oscar was a 45-year-old homeless man who had suffered from chronic low back pain, substance abuse, and depression with a history of hospitalizations for suicide attempts in the past. He was under medical treatment and had undergone physical therapy for his back, though this was not enough. During the course of forging a therapeutic relationship with him, he had found lodging at the local YMCA. He had a wife and three children in the Dominican Republic whom he often spoke of wistfully.

I began to wonder how he was able to cope with these overwhelming odds that seemed to be stacked against him. The way he coped with all of this and "stayed sane" he said was by attending church services and praying with others which helped him remain hopeful in spite of his circumstances. I thought, "What faith!"

One morning, Oscar came to see me for a routine follow-up visit. He looked the same on the outside and I didn't suspect anything until he confided in me that he was going crazy. Then ever so gently, I asked him what he meant by this and he proceeded to tell me that he had recently found out that his wife had been cheating on him and would no longer allow him to see the children. He said he had so much anger and rage inside of him that he would kill her if he could. The only thing stopping him was the fact that he didn't have the money to go back to the Dominican Republic which turned out to be a real blessing in disguise.

My heart went out to him as I saw him suffering in pain and anguish and hadn't a clue what to say next. Somehow these words came out of my mouth, "Could I pray for you and lay hands on you?" A small flicker of light appeared on his face and immediately he said, "Yes!" the faith-filled man that he was.

As I laid hands on him, I asked Jesus to pour out the Holy Spirit anew into the wounded heart of this poor man and heal him of his anger, rage, and hardness of heart, and any and all infirmities that were oppressing him and draining life out of him. The verse from John 10:10 came to the light, "A thief comes only to steal and slaughter and destroy; I came so that they might have life and have it more abundantly."

This man began to break down and weep like a child as the "rivers of living water flow(ed) from within him" (Jn. 7:38) to heal and restore what had been stolen from him. His face became radiant (see Ex.34:29-30) and he began to praise God with great joy, the undeniable sign of the Holy Spirit!

Oscar was delivered from the stronghold of the Evil one that day after having encountered the Eternal Father, Jesus, the Divine Physician and the invigorating breath of the Holy Spirit! He had encountered the Holy Trinity in such an intimate and personal way! That day, Oscar received healing of mind, body, and spirit, and left a new man! He had found a peace and joy that he had been searching for his whole life! Praise the Lord!

Pray daily for the infilling of the Holy Spirit, "When you send your Spirit, they are created, and you renew the face of the earth. May the glory of the Lord endure forever; may the Lord rejoice in his works" (Ps. 104:30-31).

There is a balm in the Church that heals crushed souls and wounded hearts and that melts hearts of stone. Come, buy without cost. Take this oil, which comes to you through the Word, the sacraments, and prayer. Take this balm, whether you are sick in heart or sick in mind. Let us all take this balm in massive doses, because the world needs massive doses of the Holy Spirit. With the words of the "Sequence of the Holy Spirit" let us say to the Spirit together: Wounded lives to health restore! Melt the frozen, warm the chill! Guide the wayward home once more!

Fr. Raniero Cantalamessa, O.F.M. Cap., *Sober Intoxication of the Spirit*

Second Patient: Martha
Choosing Life and Not Giving Up Against All Odds

Martha was a 54-year-old morbidly obese woman who had a history of diabetes, high blood pressure, asthma and irritable bowel syndrome. She had been in the hospital for about a month already when I resumed her care. Martha had undergone emergency surgery for a perforated colon from severe diverticulitis and was not expected to survive to this point, let alone the surgery which had been fraught with risks. She was on a ventilator and connected to numerous other tubes, lines and machines that were maintaining her fragile life second after second, minute after minute, hour after hour, day after day and eventually month after month.

We found a way to communicate with each other by using hand signals; squeezing my hand with whatever energy she could muster meant "Yes." Martha was fighting for her life and determined to live in the present moment as best she could. She had a supportive and loving family that came to visit her often, which bolstered her spirits and helped her deal with the painful state that she found herself in. These visits were a healing balm for her depression and loneliness as well.

Martha chose life despite the darkness of infirmity and death that equally fought to consume her. She fought resiliently for her life each waking day hoping for a miraculous recovery. Her family fought with her. The entire medical team fought with her. We were a mighty team chosen by God.

While caring for her, I laid hands on her and prayed for her whenever possible, and encouraged her to persevere and continue to run so as to win the race (1 Cor. 9:24-25, Heb. 12:1-2). And run she did as she made it out of the hospital to a rehabilitation center and eventually back home to be reunited with her family where she belonged! All praise and glory to you Lord! I was left awe-struck, seeing the mighty work of God's hands, the Divine Physician, and was led to meditate on these verses.

O Lord, my God, I cried out to you and you healed me. Lord, you brought me up from Sheol; you kept me from going down to the pit." (Ps. 30:3-4)

For I will restore you to health; of your wounds I will heal you, says the Lord. (Jer. 30:17)

While you wrought awesome deeds we could not hope for, such as they had not heard of from of old. No ear has even heard, no eye ever seen, any God but you doing such deeds for those who wait for him. (Jer. 64:2-3)

For nothing will be impossible for God. (Lk. 1:37)

At the time, all discipline seems a cause not for joy but for pain, yet later it brings the peaceful fruit of righteousness to those who are trained by it. So strengthen your drooping hands and your weak knees. Make straight paths for your feet, that what is lame may not be dislocated but healed. (Heb. 12:11-13)

Third Patient: Victor
To Reconcile with Others before Death

Victor was an elderly man in his seventies, admitted to the hospital for pneumonia and dehydration. He had end-stage chronic obstructive pulmonary disease, a long history of alcohol abuse, and multiple prior admissions. When I first met Victor he was notably weak and had responded very little to the medical treatments.

Jeanie, Victor's wife, who I came to know very quickly, was constantly anxious and worried about her husband, often having to go out to smoke. As Victor's condition worsened, she became hysterical and entreated her doctor to give her a tranquilizer to calm her down. It turns out that Jeanie had suffered years of physical and psychological abuse from her husband which made these turn of events all the more difficult for her to handle. He was a DNR/DNI (do not resuscitate/do not intubate) on admission, and as his respiratory status worsened, was placed on a 100% (oxygen) non-rebreather mask.

Victor was made as comfortable as possible and no other interventions were done. He came in and out of consciousness, and at times was able to nod or shake his head or squeeze my hand ever so slightly to answer questions. As I entered his room the next morning, Jeanie shared with me that Victor was not yet ready to leave this world, which I pondered. That afternoon, I visited Victor who was alone in his room. I held his hand and spoke to him about how frightening it must be to find himself in this situation having no control over the events.

Following the gentle prompting of the spirit, I then proceeded to tell Victor who is Catholic, that the Lord and our Blessed Mother were present with him in a very special way ministering to him, and if there was anything that was preventing him from letting go, to reconcile this in his heart and be at peace.

At that moment, I laid my hands on his withering body and prayed over him for God's mercy and healing. Though I heard only coarse breath sounds and the flow of oxygen, I knew in my heart that he had heard me. When Jeanie came back, I told her what I had told Victor and encouraged her to talk to her husband about everything that was in her heart because he was listening and needed her help to let go.

The following morning, I entered the room and found a totally transformed Jeanie waiting for me! She excitedly began to recall the events of the night before, starting with Victor having received the sacrament of the Anointing of the Sick by the Catholic chaplain! Shortly thereafter, he signaled to her that he wanted to talk to his estranged brother in Canada, and how happy he was to hear his voice over the phone after so many years! And the best part of all she said was how they came to forgive one another that evening! Two days later, Victor died in peace in the company of his beloved family.

Here is what the catechism teaches about The Anointing of the Sick and the sick person before God:

By the sacred anointing of the sick and the prayer of the priests the whole church commends those who are ill to the suffering and glorified Lord, that he may raise them up and save them. And indeed she extorts them to contribute to the good of the People of God by freely uniting themselves to the Passion and death of Christ.

CCC #1499

The man in the Old Testament lives in his sickness in the presence of God. It is before God that he laments his illness, and it is of God, Master of life and death, that he implores healing. Illness becomes a way to conversion; God's forgiveness initiates the healing. It is the experience of Israel that illness is mysteriously linked to sin and evil, and that faithfulness to God according to his law restores life: "For I am the Lord, your healer." The prophet intuits that suffering can also have a redemptive meaning for the sins of others. Finally Isaiah announces that God will usher in a time for Zion when he will pardon every offense and heal every illness.

CCC #1502

The healing power of forgiveness through Jesus in the Anointing of the Sick was revealed so beautifully here and as you can see, was paramount to this man's salvation. The following are verses to meditate on that speak about the necessity of forgiveness and repentance to obtain healing of our whole self, soul and body.

If you forgive others their transgressions, your heavenly Father will forgive you. But if you do not forgive others, neither will your Father forgive your transgressions. (Mt. 6:14)

But do not ignore this one fact, beloved, that will the Lord one day is like a thousand years and a thousand years like one day. The Lord does not delay his promise, as some regard "delay," but he is patient with you, not wishing that any should perish but that all should come to repentance. (2 Pt. 3:8-9)

Be informed before speaking; before sickness prepare the cure. Before you have fallen, humble yourself; when you have sinned, show repentance. Delay not to forsake sins, neglect it not till you are in distress. (Sir. 18:18, 20-21)

Death is swallowed up in victory. "Where, O death is your victory? Where, O death is your sting?" The sting of death is sin, and the power of sin is the law. But thanks be to God who gives us the victory through our Lord Jesus Christ. (1 Cor. 15:55-57)

He delivered us from the power of darkness and transferred us to the kingdom of his beloved Son, in whom we have redemption, the forgiveness of sins. (Col. 1:13)

The Health Benefits of Prayer

What influence does prayer have on the physical body? Dr. Herbert Benson: physician, researcher, and founder of the Harvard's Mind/Body Medical Institute in his book, *Timeless Healing The Power and Biology of Belief,* describes what happens to our bodies during meditative states such as prayer. He describes "the relaxation response" as a state in which metabolic rate, blood pressure, heart rate, breathing rate, and muscle tension are decreased while slow brain waves are increased. He goes on to say that slower brain waves summoned in the relaxation response are often linked to feelings of pleasure which is what we experience in contemplative prayer.

He affirms that giving your body permission to relax yields many long-term benefits in both health and well-being. We experience the opposite of this in the fight-or-flight response which is our body's reaction to stress leading to increased blood pressure, breathing rate, metabolic rate, and muscle tension while brain waves become more frequent and intense. Dr. Benson comments further about the deleterious effects of this, "Higher blood pressure causes enlarged and strained hearts. It also contributes to blockage of arteries-atherosclerosis-and to the bursting of blood vessels, which causes strokes and other forms of internal bleeding. The same adrenaline and noradrenaline can induce cardiac arrhythmias (disturbances in heart rhythms), lower one's threshold for pain, and contribute to higher levels of anxiety, depression, anger, and hostility" (page 128).

Dr. Benson also cited one of the most important summaries done by Dr. Levin who reviewed hundreds of epidemiologic studies to conclude that belief in God lowers death rates and increases health. He goes on further to say that the greater a person's religious commitment, the fewer his or her psychological symptoms, the better his or her general health, the lower the blood pressure, and the longer the survival. These lifetime benefits were seen across the board, in groups of different ages, ethnicities, and religions, and among patients with very different diseases and conditions.

What has the research shown on the benefits of prayer in particular intercessory prayer? Concerning experiments in prayer, Dr. Dossey says in his book *Prayer is Good Medicine*, "We feel that we already have evidence for prayer in our lives, and our lives are the most important laboratories of all." Isn't this the truth? Dr. Dossey mentions that intercessory prayer has been shown to increase the healing rate of surgical wounds, and religious faith is associated with faster recovery from surgery.

Thoresen and Harris in their article, Spirituality and Health: What's the Evidence and What's Needed?, cited two studies that demonstrated the positive effects of intercessory prayer on mortality and morbidity outcomes. The first study was done by cardiologist, Dr. Randolph Byrd who randomly divided heart patients into two groups for a ten-month study. One group (192 patients) received intercessory prayer by Christian prayer groups while the control group (201 patients) had not received prayers. None of the participants in the study knew they were being prayed for. The heart patients who were prayed for had significantly fewer complications than the control group. They were five times less likely to need antibiotics for infections, two and a half times less likely to suffer congestive heart failure, and had lower risk of sudden cardiac arrest (14).

Thoresen and Harris write, "In a replication of the Byrd study, published in *Archives of Internal Medicine* and involving 990 patients, Harris *et al.* found that the prayed-for group in the coronary care unit (CCU) had significantly lower (11%) CCU Overall Course Scores than those with usual care. Course Score is an index of several major in-hospital procedures and outcomes, ranging from need for specific medications to bypass surgery, reinfarction, and death. However, the length and number of hospital stays did not differ significantly." In order to control for response expectancy effects, all participants and healthcare providers were not informed about the study. It was not clear whether baseline differences of the patients were adequately controlled for (10).

Furthermore, they write that not all studies using experimental designs have shown this positive outcome, and point out the need for more studies to demonstrate such effects using a broader range of person, health, and socio-demographic factors. The problem with looking at the possible associations between religious and/or spiritual factors and health outcomes is the limited quality of available studies in terms of research designs and assessments (9). For instance, an assessment of religious involvement has been almost always limited to a person's affiliation with an organized religion or to the frequency of attendance at religious services (9). There is a need to develop better research designs and assessments even more so now as our questions have become more sophisticated and precise (9). Another limitation in studying this association has been a lack of experimental research in this area, except that seen in intercessory prayer and meditation (9).

Prayer Is Our Life

Concerning prayer and science, Dr. Dossey says, "We feel that we already have evidence for prayer in our lives, and our lives are the most important laboratories of all. The scientific understanding of prayer is limited. Science cannot measure the un-measurable. Science deals only with what can be measured by its various detection devices-and scientists do not have a God meter. Some things are beyond science. Everything that counts cannot be counted"(8). Isn't this true? St. Paul tells us "For we walk by faith, not by sight" (2 Cor. 5:7) which speaks precisely of our prayer life. At this point, we need to ask ourselves, "Is prayer our top priority?"

> You are as much a Christian as you are capable of praying.
> Prayer and its particular stages are signs and indications of your closeness or distance from God. Everything depends on God; it is He who decides and only He can give you strength. The tragedy of our Christian activism is that activities really do smother us. The more suppressed you are with activities, the more time you should dedicate to prayer. Otherwise you will be empty; you will have the impression that you are giving something but this will only be an illusion. You cannot give that which you do not have. When a Christian, as a disciple of Christ, stops being a person of prayer, he becomes useless to the world, he becomes like tasteless salt worthy to be: "trampled underfoot" (compare Mt. 5:13).
> Fr. Tadeusz Dajczer, *The Gift of Faith*

In conclusion, when we don't receive what we ask for in prayer, may we find solace in this "Prayer of an Unknown Confederate Soldier" from the *Oxford Book of Prayer* and continue to persevere in faith, hope, and love. God loves us and those we love infinitely more than we could ever fathom:

> I asked God for strength that I might achieve;
> I was made weak that I might learn to obey.
>
> I asked for health that I might do great things;
> I was given infirmity, that I might do better things.
>
> I asked for riches that I might be happy;
> I was given poverty that I might be wise.
>
> I asked for power that I might have the praise of men;
> I was given weakness that I might feel the need of God.
>
> I asked for all things that I might enjoy life;
> I was given life that I might enjoy all things.

I got nothing that I asked for,
But everything I had hoped for.

Almost despite myself my unspoken prayers were answered;
I am, among all men, most richly blessed.

God Given Purpose

God is a God of order as we can see clearly in the story of creation in the book of Genesis. He created each one of us with a purpose and a plan for our lives. For Jeremiah tells us, "For I know well the plans I have in mind for you, says the Lord, plans for your welfare, not for woe! Plans to give you a future full of hope" (Jer. 29:11). He loves each one of us as His own. He says, "I have called you by name: you are mine" (Is. 43:1). We are his beloved creations, his sons and daughters. That is our true identity that we need to make our own.

In the book of Psalms, it says:

> You formed my inmost being; you knit me in my mother's womb. I praise you, so wonderfully you made me; wonderful are your works! My very self you knew; my bones were not hidden from you, When I was being made in secret, fashioned as in the depths of the earth. Your eyes foresaw my actions; in your book all are written down; my days were shaped, before one came to be" (Ps. 139:13-16).

We were not accidents or here simply by chance as we may have first believed. Many of us have been wounded and rejected leaving us unable to receive love that in reality we need so desperately. Deep down inside of us, we may even believe that we are not lovable.

> Even if my father and mother forsake me, the Lord will
> take me in. (Ps. 27:10)
> Let us conquer evil with good. (Rom. 12:21)

Therefore, we reject the lies of the Enemy and counter this evil with good, by claiming our true identity as beloved sons and daughters of the Most High. Psalm 103 tells us who the Lord is: "Merciful and gracious is the Lord, slow to anger, abounding in kindness. As the heavens tower over the earth, so God's love towers over the faithful" (Ps. 103:8, 11). We are the marvelous work of His hands and for this, let us shout for joy! (Ps. 92:5).

May our time spent in prayerful meditation upon these Bible verses cleanse us of any false beliefs or lies about ourselves and of our loving God that have been obstacles to our union with the Holy One. He is always calling His wayward children back to Him, the fount of life. This brings to mind the story of the prodigal son who left home with the share of his inheritance. Living licentiously, he squandered all of his money and ended up not having even anything to eat. Meanwhile, his father waited expectantly for his son to return home. And sure enough, the son came home repentant of all that he had done. The father experienced such joy at his son's homecoming that he immediately embraced him and called forth a celebration because, "his son was dead, and has come to life again; he was lost, and has been found" (Lk. 15:24). Our Abba Father truly waits expectantly for us with open arms. When we come to know our true identity in Him, this is when we begin the journey to live out His God given purpose in our lives to the fullest. We depend on our Abba Father. He then truly becomes our daily bread, our way of life.

A Call to Vigilance: Seeking Health in the Wrong Places

God created the physician to help heal the sick and alleviate pain and suffering from a variety of illnesses. He wants us to utilize the physician, an important instrument of God's healing to restore, maintain, or improve our health and well-being. If you have an infirmity, be it of mind, body, or spirit, first consult a physician who is trained to help you figure out the cause and works alongside you to alleviate your pain. Do not forgo this initial step which is an integral part of God's plan of healing for you. Do not think that you should suffer on your own because of your fears, often times unfounded, ignorance, and/or pre-conceived notions such as "I must have deserved this somehow." The truth is there are good effective medical treatments for many illnesses in which there are known pathophysiologic basis for. Be prudent in choosing the right physician for yourself, one who understands and treats the entire you: mind, body, and spirit. This is what Sirach says about the physician:

> Hold the physician in honor, for he is essential to you, and God it was who established his profession. From God the doctor has his wisdom, and the king provides for his sustenance. His knowledge makes the doctor distinguished, and gives him access to those in authority... He endows men with the knowledge to glory in his mighty works, through which the doctor eases pain and the druggist prepares his medicines; Thus God's creative work continues without cease in its efficacy on the surface of the earth. My son, when you are ill, delay not, but pray to God, who will heal you: Flee wickedness; let your hands be just, cleanse your heart of every sin; Offer your sweet-smelling oblation and petition, a rich offering according to your means. Then give the doctor his place lest he leave; for you need him too. There are times that give him an advantage, and he too beseeches God that his diagnosis may be correct and his treatment, bring about a cure.
>
> (Sir. 38:1-3, 6-14)

There are limitations to what science and medicine can do and explain and there will always be unanswered questions as to why, how and when something happens. Sometimes there are more questions than definite answers. With the complexity of problems presented, affecting the mind, body and spirit and all of its ramifications, it is certainly a greater challenge in this day and age for us physicians and other health care providers to help heal the sick. Furthermore, it is not difficult to see how physicians can be deified in certain ways, for we share in Jesus' healing mission where people come and get relief and/or healing of their ailments. The truth is we are only instruments of God's healing and there is only one Divine Physician who is omnipotent, omniscient, and omnipresent and that is Jesus, the Healer himself! We as physicians can alleviate suffering, but do not control matters pertaining to life or death. This is the exclusive domain of God. This is what the catechism teaches:

> *Human life is sacred* because from its beginning it involves the creative action of God and it remains for ever in a

special relationship with the Creator, who is its sole end. God alone is the Lord of life from its beginning until its end: no one can under any circumstance claim for himself the right directly to destroy an innocent human being.

CCC#2258

As mentioned earlier, the New Age Movement and false idols have influenced every part of society including the field of medicine. They come in the form of alternative medicine such as holistic healing centers that offer the practice of yoga, transcendental meditation, and Reiki to name a few, which all draw from the belief system of Eastern religions, specifically Hinduism and Buddhism. Fr. Daniel Sinisi, T.O.R., says in his preface to the book, The New Age Counterfeit written by Johnnette Benkovic:

We are called to be sons and daughters of God but we are not gods. All that we are, and have, come from God. The fundamental error of the New Age movement distorts this beautiful reality of God's plan for us. It asserts that we can become God by becoming aware of and developing the human potential within us. Tragically, this movement is drawing large number of people into this erroneous and harmful way of life and it is having strong influence in so many areas of human life and society.

Jesus Christ is the Savior of the entire human race. Only in Him are we reconciled to God. He, the Son of God, is the Way, the Truth, and the Life. He is the one and only path to God. He is the revelation of God. He is God's Son and the one and only source of God's Life coming into us. He tells us not to have itching ears listening to false doctrines. He is the Kingdom of God present among us. In Him and through His church we have life, abundant life.

Fr. Daniel Sinisi, T.O.R.

Franciscan University of Steubenville

What does scripture have to tell us about the New Age Movement? There are many bible verses pertaining to this, a few of which I will share.

Do not be carried away by all kinds of strange teaching. It is good to have our hearts strengthened by grace. (Heb. 13:9)

Let there not be found among you anyone who immolates his son or daughter in the fire, nor a fortune-teller, soothsayer, charmer, diviner, or caster of spells, nor one who consults ghosts and spirits or seeks oracles from the dead. Anyone who does such things is an abomination to the Lord. (Deut.18: 10-12)

For the time will come when people will not tolerate sound doctrine but, following their own desires and insatiable curiosity, will accumulate teachers and will stop listening to the truth and will be diverted to myths. But you, be self-possessed in all circumstances; put up with hardship; perform the work of an evangelist; fulfill your ministry. (2 Tim. 4: 3-5)

For if their purpose or activity is of human origin, it will fail. But if it is from God, you will not be able to stop these men; you will only find yourselves fighting against God. (Acts 6:38-39)

They shall be turned back in utter shame who trust in idols. (Is. 42:17)

I will rescue my people from your power. Thus you shall know that I am the Lord. (Ezk.13:23)

I, the Lord, am your God. You shall not have other gods besides me. For I, the Lord, your God, am a jealous God. (Ex. 20: 2-3, 5)

There is no salvation through anyone else, nor is there any other name under Heaven given to the human race by which we are to be saved. (Acts 3:12)

I am bringing up the topic of New Age so that we become aware of the dangers associated with its ideology. Many Catholics are unaware of the spiritual consequences of participating in alternative methods of healing that are based on non-Catholic beliefs. People become frustrated with the limitations of Western medicine in bringing about the relief of their pain. The catechism teaches this about Divination and magic:

All practices of *magic* or *sorcery*, by which one attempts to tame occult powers, so as to place them at one's service and have a supernatural power over others—even if this were for the sake of restoring their health—are gravely contrary to the virtue of religion. These practices are even more to be condemned when accompanied by the intention of harming someone, or when they have recourse to the intervention of demons. Wearing charms is also reprehensible. *Spiritism* often implies divination or magical practices; the Church for her part warns the faithful against it. Recourse to so-called traditional cures does not justify either the invocation of evil powers or the exploitation of another's credulity.

CCC#2117

Johnnette Benkovic informs us further about the New Age movement:

The foundational element in this new perspective is monism, a philosophy teaching that everything is "interrelated, interdependent, and interpenetrating." God is not a personal God, but rather an impersonal energy force that permeates all things. For the New Ager, this "oneness" obliterates even the distinction between good and evil, which is "dualism." Decisions are based on situational ethics instead of moral absolutes.

Certainly on the surface, this can appear to be more attractive and immediately gratifying than living a life of faith where there are no shortcuts or "quick fixes." We need desire, discipline, and patience. Fr. Tadeusz Dajczer describes faith as sharing in the life of God. In faith, we are able to entrust ourselves to Him who is infinitely merciful and loving and desires only good for us. In faith, we are able to die to self and embrace the crosses in our lives with gratitude so that we can grow in holiness and see everything as grace.

People free from attachments are filled with the peace of God. The peace of God builds and strengthens mental health which in turn reflects on physical health. In this way, the soul, the psyche and the body participate in a person's great freedom.

Fr. Tadeusz Dajczer

Mankind's salvation and true peace comes as a result of doing the will of God and living according to His laws.

Johnnette Benkovic

I encourage further study and research into the New Age movement so that we ourselves will not fall prey to counterfeits. St. Paul warns us, "I say this so that no one may deceive you by specious arguments. See to it that no one captivate you with an empty, seductive philosophy according to human tradition, according to the elemental powers of the world and not according to Christ" (Col. 2:4, 8). Johnnette Benkovic says: "As Christians, we must equip ourselves to recognize the 'fable' in our midst and to preach the truth of Jesus Christ when given the opportunity."

In the highly informative article, *Yoga - Health or Stealth*, from *The Cross And The Veil* website, a Catholic Web Resource for Spiritual Discernment (www.crossveil.org), the author poignantly sums up the dangers of energy manipulation.

To most western devotees, these powers are merely the harnessing of energies and physical laws not yet understood in the west. The majority of holistic energy work practices touted as healing science are all built on a science of energy manipulation based on the eastern chakra system. What we in the west do not fully realize, is that any manipulation of energy is tantamount to the practice of magic-using power at the service of the will. Utilizing or even simply channeling these energies sent supposedly by God, angels, extra-terrestrials or the universe opens the yoga practitioner and also the many healers and body workers in the New Age to forces they cannot perceive, understand, or control. Surrender to otherworldly guides, gurus or a yogi adds additional oppressive influences in the dangerous game of kundalini arousal (Johnnette Benkovic explains that: "Hinduism teaches that at the base of the spine is a triangle in which lies the "Kundalini Shakti" or Serpent Power. It is usually dormant but when it is awakened it travels up the spine to the top of the head, passing through six psychic centers called "chakras"). The arousal may not only cause long-term psychological burnout and exacerbation of latent weaknesses but also demonic oppression and possession as a Pandora's Box is literally opened to the spiritual world. Using the Garden of Eden as an analogy, our spines are like the tree of life which holds within them the potential for good or evil. True spiritual development, ecstasies and gifts, however, descend from above and are not the result of conscious control. As Our Lord warned, those who try to enter Heaven without Him are thieves (Jn. 10:7-10).

How do we approach this problem and stem the tide? The author of the above article says:

> In closing, yoga and all New Age practices have filled the void that exists because we have abandoned the greatest source of bliss and comfort, the Eucharist. A return to the Eucharist and a renewed program of instruction on contemplative prayer will bring many Catholics back from these deceptively beautiful practices and philosophies.

I would like to quote Archbishop Norberto Rivera Carrera's Pastoral Instruction on the New Age: A Call to Vigilance.

> Our faith is deep. It has its source in God himself, who reveals himself to all men in Jesus Christ. Over the past 2,000 years, Jesus Christ has guided his Church by means of the Holy Spirit "to the fullness of truth" (Jn. 16:13) as he promised on the night of his passion. A Catholic who experiences his faith, knows it, and lives it in all it greatness, will never feel the need to beg for the New Age's vain promises and half-truths.

> Therefore, we are all obliged to pursue continuous formation to understand New Age, and its attraction for the people of our time. Like the wise man in the Gospel, who draws out his treasure both the old and new (cf. Mt. 13:52), we have to give witness to and preach the inexhaustible richness and penetrating truths of the Catholic faith in an increasingly accessible and attractive way to all those who ask us about the reason for our hope. May the Catholic faithful, with our help, discover that everything that they yearn for (a real spiritual

life, inner healing, forgiveness and reconciliation, an encounter with the unfathomable mystery of the one true God and His saving plan) is already incomparably present in the Catholic faith, into which they were initiated at Baptism.

Healing Power Prayers

Healing Prayer of Isaiah 53

Precious Lord Jesus, I thank you for your loving care. You came into the world to set me free from the consequences of sin. You embraced the violent death of the cross to pay the penalty on my behalf. You suffered the scourging at the pillar, taking the sickness of humanity upon your flesh, so that I could be healed.

I come before you now to place all my sins upon your cross and ask for your precious blood to wash me clean. I place the penalty for my sinfulness, all my sickness, diseases and infirmities upon your cross, and for the sake of your sorrowful passion, I ask to be set free. I accept your sacrifice and receive your gift of reconciliation. I confess your Lordship over every aspect of my life, mind, body, soul, and spirit.

Through the power of your cross Lord Jesus, I now resist all forms of sin, sickness, and disease, that is not your perfect will for my life. I enforce the power of the cross upon you right now.

By the shed blood of the Lord Jesus Christ of Nazareth, I command all forms of sickness and disease to leave my presence immediately. Jesus bore my infirmities. He was wounded for my transgressions. By his stripes I have been healed. No sickness, pain, death, fear or addiction shall ever lord over me again. The penalty has been paid in full. I have been ransomed and redeemed, sanctified and set free. Amen.

Prayer for a Creative Miracle

God of all creation, you who spoke a simple command and brought forth light from the darkness, I call upon you now to send forth your miracle-working power into every aspect of my being. In the same way that you spoke unto the dust of the ground when you created humankind in your own image, I ask you to send forth your healing power into my body. Send forth your word and command every cell, electrical and chemical impulse, tissue, joint, ligament, organ, gland, muscle, bone and every molecule in my body to come under complete and perfect health, strength, alignment, balance, and harmony.

It is through you that I live and move and have my being. With every breath I take, I live under your life-giving grace. I ask you to touch me now with the same miracle-working power that you used when you fashioned me inside my mother's womb. As surely as you have created me in your image and likeness, you can also recreate me now and restore me to health.

Please fill me with your healing power. Cast out all that should not be inside of me. I ask you to mend all that is broken, root out every sickness and disease, open all blocked arteries and veins, restore my internal organs, rebuild my damaged tissues, remove all inflammation and cleanse me of all infections, viruses and destructive forms of bacteria.

Let the warmth of your healing love flood my entire being, so that my body will function the way it was created to be, whole and complete, renewed in your perfect health. I ask this through my Lord, Jesus Christ, your Son, who lives and reigns with you and the Holy Spirit, one God, for ever and ever. Amen.

Prayer to the Divine Physician

Dear Lord Jesus, you went about healing all those who were sick and tormented by unclean spirits. You cleansed the lepers, opened the eyes of the blind and by speaking a simple command, you empowered the crippled to rise up and walk. You sent forth your life-giving power to all those in need, including those you raised from the dead.

O Divine Physician, I come to you now in great need of your intervention. I surrender my life and health into your loving hands. I ask you to send forth your healing power into my heart, mind, body, soul and spirit. Remove from me every lie of the enemy and destroy all the word curses that have been spoken against my health.

If I have accepted medical beliefs that I should not have, I ask for your forgiveness and denounce those beliefs right now. I break every agreement that I have made with my sickness and disease. I denounce every symptom of my illness, and I ask to be set free by the power of your truth.

Please send forth your Holy Spirit to renew my mind and cleanse my thoughts. I refuse to bow down and serve the symptoms of my illness any longer. Please draw my attention away from myself, and help me focus on your enduring love.

O Divine Physician, you are the source and strength of my recovery. Show me how to proceed with your plan for my restoration. I surrender my healthcare into your loving hands. Please help me to discern every aspect of my treatment, medications and recovery process, so that my every thought and action conforms to your good and perfect will for my life. Amen.

Bible Verses for Healing

Trust in the Lord with all your heart. On your intelligence rely not. In all your ways be mindful of him, and he will make straight your paths. Be not wise in your own eyes, fear the Lord and turn away from evil; this will mean health for your flesh and vigor for your bones. (Prov. 3:6-8)

Look to God that you may be radiant with joy and your faces may not blush with shame. In my misfortune I called, the Lord heard and saved me from all distress. The angel of the Lord, who encamps with them, delivers all who fear God. Learn to savor how good the Lord is; happy are those who take refuge in him. Fear the Lord, you holy ones; nothing is lacking to those who fear him. The powerful grow poor and hungry, but those who seek the Lord lack no good thing. (Ps. 34:6-10)

The Lord is close to the brokenhearted, saves those whose spirit is crushed. Many are the troubles of the just, but the Lord delivers from them all. God watches over, over all their bones; not a one shall be broken. (Ps. 34:19-21)

And we have this confidence in him, that if we ask anything according to his will, he hears us. And if we know that he hears us in regard to whatever we ask, we know that what we have asked him for is ours. (1 Jn. 5:14-15)

So strengthen your dropping hands and your weak knees. Make straight paths for your feet, that what is lame may not be dislocated but healed. (Heb. 12:12-1)

Is anyone among you suffering? He should pray. Is anyone in good spirits? He should sing praise. Is anyone among you sick? He should summon the presbyters of the church, and they should pray over him and anoint him with oil in the name of the Lord, and the prayer of faith will save the sick person, and the Lord will raise him up. If he has committed any sins, he will be forgiven. (Jm. 5:13-15)

For this reason they could not believe, because again Isaiah said: He blinded their eyes and hardened their heart, so that they might not see with their eyes and understand with their heart and be converted, and I would heal them. (Jn. 12:40)

He was spurned and avoided by men, a man of suffering, accustomed to infirmity, one of those from whom men hide their faces, spurned, and we held him in no esteem. Yet it was our infirmities that he bore, our sufferings that he endured, while we thought of him as stricken, as one smitten by God and afflicted. But he was pierced for our offenses, crushed for our sins, upon him was the chastisement that makes us whole, by his stripes we were healed...and he shall take away the sins of many, and win pardon for their offenses. (Is. 53:4-5, 12)

He himself bore our sins in his body upon the cross, so that, free from sin, we might live for righteousness. By his wounds you have been healed. You had gone astray like sheep, but, you have now returned to the shepherd, and guardian of your souls. (1 Pt. 2:24-25)

Bless the Lord, my soul; all my being, bless his holy name! Bless the Lord, my soul; do not forget all the gifts of God, Who pardons all your sins, heals all your ills, delivers your life from the pit, surrounds you with love and compassion, fills your days with good things; your youth is renewed like the eagle's. (Ps. 103:1-5)

Better a poor man strong and robust, than a rich man with wasted frame. More precious than gold is health and well-being, contentment of spirit than coral. No treasure greater than a healthy body; no happiness, than a joyful heart! Preferable is death to a bitter life, unending sleep to constant illness.... Do not give in to sadness, torment not yourself with brooding; gladness of heart is the very life of man, cheerfulness prolongs his days. Renew your courage, drive resentment far away from you; for worry has brought death to many, nor is there aught to be gained from resentment. Envy and anger shorten one's life, worry brings on premature old age. One who is cheerful and gay while at table benefits from his food. (Sir. 30:14:25)

For it is easy with the Lord on the day of death to repay man according to his deeds. A moment's affliction brings forgetfulness of past delights; when a man dies, his life is revealed. (Sir. 11:26-27)

The eyes of the Lord are upon those who love him; he is their mighty shield and strong support, a shelter from the heat, a shade from the noonday sun, a guard against stumbling, a help against falling. He buoys up the spirits, brings a sparkle to the eyes, gives health and life and blessing. (Sir. 34:16-17)

While you wrought awesome deeds we could not hope for, such as they had not heard of from of old. No ear has ever heard, no eye ever seen, any God but you doing such deeds for those who wait on for him. Would that you might meet us doing right, that we were mindful of you in our ways! (Is. 64:2-4)

Chapter 7

The Eucharist is Healing and Joy

Allow me, dear brothers and sisters, to share with deep emotion, as a means of accompanying and strengthening your faith, my own testimony of faith in the Most Holy Eucharist. Here is the Church's treasure, the heart of the world, the pledge of the fulfillment for which each man and woman, even unconsciously, yearns. A great and transcendent mystery, indeed, and one that taxes our minds ability to pass beyond appearances! Allow me, like Peter at the end of the Eucharistic discourse in John's Gospel, to say once more to Christ, in the name of the whole Church, and in the name of each one of you: "Lord to whom shall we go? You have the words of eternal life." (Jn. 6:68)

John Paul II, *Ecclesia de Eucharistia*

We feel the emotion of John Paul II throughout the course of his encyclical letter. In fact, we sense that John Paul II can scarcely contain his love of the Eucharist, his gratitude to the Lord, and his hope for the Church for rekindling Eucharistic amazement in the Third Millennium.

Think of the years of infirmity that wrapped around his physical being forming a royal garment of sanctity. Yet, his witness in the world was one of healing. How so? Christ transfigured him into his image so thoroughly that we experienced Christ in our midst. He was an icon of Christ's love! His life poured out like a libation to become a healing salve for the body of Christ. By the example of his life, millions of people could "taste and see the goodness of the Lord!"

I experienced a kind of healing each time I saw him in St. Peter's Square or attended one of his Masses. He was like a physician for the Church, binding up the wounds of the body of Christ. All the while, he was a victim of his own intercession for the Church, dying for the salvation of souls! When I observed his body suffering I still thought to myself, "He is the most healed person I have ever seen!" This is the paradox of discipleship: the cross and the crown of glory intersect!

Holy Communion:
The Particular Healing Grace of the Mass

Christ said, "I came so that they might have life and have it more abundantly" (Jn. 10:10). God created us for fullness of life. The fullness of the abundant life Christ desires for us is primarily conferred through the Eucharist. Health is the condition of being sound in body, mind and spirit. This condition implies the fullness of vitality of life. It also implies freedom from disease and pain. Sickness of body, mind or spirit impairs our vital life organs.

In their respective chapters in this book, Dr. Inga Pak and Dr. Elizabeth Kim, provide a wealth of information on the subject of healing of the body, mind and spirit through Eucharistic transformation. My comments will be brief on this subject. I simply want to make an important distinction between prayers for healing that we pray for one another as part of the Lord's healing ministry and the healing power of the Eucharist. We should be mindful not to put the forms of healing prayer on the same plane.

In the Eucharist, we have direct physical contact with Jesus. This is a most important distinction. In the Gospel accounts of people being healed by Jesus, we discover the fact that everyone who touched Jesus was healed if they did so with expectant faith. "People brought to him all those who were sick and begged him that they might touch only the tassel on his cloak, and as many as touched it were healed" (Mt. 14:35-36). When we receive the Eucharist at Mass, we are touching Jesus and our communion is physical. We are eating of the Body, Blood, Soul and Divinity of Christ

Jesus and this is medicine for our body, mind and spirit. The penetration of the Divine Person of Jesus into our human person is thorough and lasting. In the quote below, Fr. John Hampsch, explains why Holy Communion is healing for our body, mind and spirit.

In Jn. 6:56, Jesus says, "He who eats my flesh and drinks my blood abides in me, and I in him." The Greek word for abide is *meno*. This was one of St. John's favorite words; he uses it in ten places in his Gospel. The word *meno* means to remain intimately present to, to be nestled into, and to be grafted into. It conveys a very deep sense of intimacy, and in no way signifies a temporary encounter. Even though our encounter with Jesus is temporary, the effect is lasting. We are grafted into Christ and we are united with him, like branches united to the vine (Jn. 15:4).

In the liturgy of the Eucharist, several prayers at Communion time refer to the healing power of the Eucharist. For instance, immediately after the Lord's Prayer, the priest says the following prayer (italics added): "Deliver us, Lord, *from every evil*, and *grant us your peace in our day*. In your mercy keep us *free from sin* and protect us *from all anxiety* as we wait in joyful hope for the coming of our Savior, Jesus Christ." Upon closer examination, it becomes apparent that this simple prayer encompasses several distinct forms of healing. First, of all, the priest prays a prayer of deliverance, so that we might all be healed of any extrinsic spiritual disorders that occur from the attacks of demonic forces. This is based on 1 Cor. 10:21 (RSV): "You cannot partake of the (Eucharistic) table of the Lord and of the table of demons." Second, he prays for societal or communitarian healing (i.e., peace that heals interpersonal or intrapersonal conflict). Third, he prays for the healing of our intrinsic spiritual disorders, asking God to free us from our state of sin. Finally, he prays for our emotional healing, freedom from anxiety and guilt feelings so we can experience inner peace and joyful hope.

Later on, the priest has the option of reciting another

prayer that speaks about physical healing (body) and emotional healing (mind) as he prepares to receive Holy Communion himself (italics added): Lord Jesus Christ, with faith in your love and mercy I eat your body and drink your blood. Let it not bring me condemnation, *but health in mind and body.*"

Finally, there is a prayer that the congregation recites before approaching the altar to receive Holy Communion: "Lord, I am not worthy to receive you, but only say the word and I shall be *healed.* This prayer has its origins in the story about the healing of a centurion's servant in Matthew 8:5-13. In faith, he knew that Jesus needed only to say the word for his servant to be healed. "And Jesus said to the centurion, "You may go, as you have believed, let it be done for you" (Mt. 8:13).

In Acts 2:42, we read that the early Christians "devoted themselves to the teaching of the apostles and to the communal life, to the breaking of the bread and to the prayers." It is noteworthy that they did not simply participate in these activities, including the Eucharist (the "breaking of the bread"), but *devoted* themselves to them. The word devoted has several connotations and says much about the expectant faith of those early Christians, especially as they approached Jesus in the sacrament of the Eucharist. It is noteworthy that their devotion had a corporate dimension and was a truly communitarian experience: the whole community had this surging expectancy of faith because they all believed that they were to experience a real encounter with Jesus himself. The fullness of life which Jesus confers on us through the Eucharist is not due to following the ritual but because of him: "The one who feeds on me will have life *because of me*" (Jn. 6:57, emphasis added).

Fr. John Hampsch, *The Healing Power of the Eucharist*

Fr. Hampsch illumines the reasons why we are healed by the Eucharist, he also brings up an important point that has not been mentioned in this book, that of communal faith and prayer at the Mass. This environment is most conducive to healing. Let us pray for the Church to increase in fervor for the Mass and expectant faith in the healing power of the Eucharist.

Suffering: Why Some are Not Healed on Earth

The Holy Spirit gives some a special charism of healing (cf.1 Cor. 12:9) so as to make manifest the power of the grace of the risen Lord. But even the most intense prayers do not obtain the healing of all illnesses. Thus St. Paul learns from the Lord that "my grace is sufficient for you, for my power is made perfect in weakness" and that the sufferings to be endured can mean that "in my flesh I complete what is lacking in Christ's afflictions for the sake of his Body, the Church" (2 Cor. 12:9, Col. 1:24).

CCC # 1508

Moved by such suffering Christ not only allows himself to be touched by the sick, but he makes their miseries his own; "He took our infirmities and bore our diseases" (Mt. 8:17; cf. Isa. 53:4). But he did not heal all the sick. His healings were signs of the coming of the Kingdom of God. They announced a more radical healing: the victory over sin and death through his Passover. On the cross Christ took upon himself the whole weight of evil and took away the "sin of the world," of which illness is only a consequence. By his passion and death on the cross Christ has given a new meaning to suffering: it can henceforth configure us to him and unite us with his redemptive Passion.

CCC #1505

The Catechism reminds us that sometimes even the most intense prayers do not obtain the healing of all illnesses. Quoting St. Paul, we are reminded of the biblical principle of co-redemptive suffering: "In my flesh I complete what is lacking in Christ's afflictions for the sake of his Body, the Church." All men suffer on earth in a variety of ways. This is due to the "original wound," as Fr. Benedict Groeschel aptly calls original sin. We are wounded, sin-sick people. Communion with God heals us always at some level.

Sometimes God chooses people to be victim souls. These people are victims of Divine Love and have a vocation to co-redemptive suffering.

These are usually the hidden saints whose lives are burnt up as a sacrificial offering. Faith in Christ is healing in its many different facets. Healing can take on many appearances. It is proper to our faith to ask, seek and knock for healing in all situations. But if the Lord does not grant the healing we thank the Lord anyway and surrender our will to him, trusting in his providential love. Prayerful discernment sheds light as to the nature of our suffering. We know that our suffering united to the Passion of Christ is truly valuable and saves souls. This is a high calling.

In some manner of speaking, all of us are victim souls for Christ. In scripture, the book of Job beautifully illustrates the role of suffering in the lives of God's chosen ones. The Book of Job is a pearl of wisdom literature that gives an intimate account of one man's struggle with extraordinary trials and sufferings that many of the chosen ones of God endure for love of their faith. All of God's chosen ones are sooner or later put to the test, whether it comes from the evil spirit, or directly from God himself, who wished to try a person's faith amidst great suffering. For all who travel the road toward perfection of love, this is true. Eventually, we are all put to the test. Our reward will come one day if we are faithful. "Blessed is the man who endures trials, for when he has stood the test he will receive the crown of life which God has promised to those love him" (Jm. 1:12).

By holding onto the faith, Job received twice as much as he once had through God's goodness and mercy (Job 42:10). It is beautiful, too, that God blessed Job in his later years even more than in his early years. It seems life is a series of trials and those who hold out to the end receive their eternal reward. "I have fought the good fight, I have finished the race. Therefore, I have kept the faith. Henceforth there is laid up for me, the crown (2 Tim. 4:7-8). We are called to remain firm in God until the end. That firmness is dictated by the crosses we bear, the sufferings we endure, all for love of God (Mt. 7:14).

In my particular family, I have witnessed the good fruit of suffering for the salvation of souls. The cross of Christ is a school of love. When we embrace our crosses for the sake of the glory of God, we further the kingdom of light. The enemy would have us reject the cross and rebel against all suffering. But the enemy is a liar from the beginning and a thief of souls. We boast in Christ Crucified, and imitate him in all things.

Sometimes the Lord may allow us to suffer for long periods of time and then heal us. I prayed for twenty years to be healed of hypertension since the medication to control it caused a chronic dry cough along with other side effects. Just this month, a complete physical revealed that my blood pressure was low-normal and I no longer need to take the medicine. Thank the Lord! We may ask for a healing in one area of our lives and receive the healing in another area. God knows the best manner of healing. It is right to always acknowledge our desperate need of Christ's healing love.

I observed my maternal grandmother remain in the fetal position in a nursing home for six years of long suffering before passing to the Lord. She had Alzheimer's disease. When I visited, I praised God for her life that had meaning and value to the last minute. Her body kept a continuous vigil of intercessory prayer. Whether she suffered this disease as her purgative preparation for Heaven, or as intercessory prayer for her family, I know she willed it. It would be unthinkable to deny her the destiny God ordained from the beginning. It was to be her cross and glory. I prayed for healing all the way. But God chose a different manner of healing: the ultimate healing of passing to her eternal reward. Praise God!

Testimony:
The Ultimate Healing: Passing Into Eternal Life

Providence arranged that my path would cross with an anointed priest of God, Fr. Richard Foley, S.J., from Farm Street Church, London, England. From the moment we first met at a Marian Conference in Orange County, CA, we enjoyed sharing about the spiritual life, what the Lord was doing in our respective prayer lives. It turned out that my priest spiritual advisor desired that I show my prayer journal to Fr. Foley for discernment. Father reviewed all of my writings (published anonymously) and undertook the arduous task of writing a commentary on them.

Over a two-year period of time when he wrote his book, *Mary's Call to Holiness*, which is a commentary on my writings; he suffered much with severe cardiac and pulmonary problems. When we prayed together, however, we kept sensing the Lord was going to heal him. This is what we heard from the Lord in prayer, "You will be healed." We both waited on the Lord in anticipation of the day of his healing. Our intercessory prayer group also interceded for his healing and received the same prophecy of promised healing. I recall a priest in the cenacle said, "The ultimate healing is to go home to the Lord." This is not what I wanted to hear. His health continued to challenge him each day. Yet when we spoke, he was so joyful in fulfilling his task to write a commentary on my writings. Approximately two years later, the book was finished and the manuscript arrived from London for me and the publisher. Father Foley and I rejoiced in his labor of love. Shortly thereafter, he called me from the hospital in London around Christmastime and was very ill; his back had gone out also. We prayed together over the phone and the Lord continued to promise healing. A few days passed and I received a call from one of Fr. Foley's friends advising me that he had passed to his eternal reward. I was so sad, thinking that we certainly were not hearing from the Lord after all.

Following the news of his death, in prayer before the Blessed Sacrament, the Lord reminded me of my first conversation with Fr. Foley at Loyola Marymount School in Los Angeles. At that time, Father confided to me that he had such a longing to see Heaven; that he very much enjoyed reading books on the subject. Often Heaven was the object of his meditations in prayer and he was quite animated about the subject. That week a call came from London from a friend of Father's saying that Father had a message for me before he died. His friend told me, "Father Foley said to tell you that he is going to be healed completely; that he is happy and you should not doubt!" Truly, the ultimate healing is to pass from this earthly exile to paradise. Praise the Lord!

The Catholic Catechism on Jesus, the Healer

1504 Often Jesus asks the sick to believe. (cf. Mk. 5:34, 36, 9:23) He makes use of signs to heal, spittle and the laying on of hands, mud and washing. The sick try to touch him, "for power came forth from him and healed them all (Lk. 6:19, cf. Mk. 1:41, 3:10, 6:56). So in the sacraments Christ continues to touch us in order to heal us.

1506 Christ invited his disciples to follow him by taking up their cross in their turn. By following him they acquire a new outlook on illness and the sick. Jesus associates them with this own life of poverty and service. He makes them share in his ministry of compassion and healing: "So they went out and preached that men should repent. And they cast out many demons and anointed with oil many that were sick and healed them" (Mk. 6:12).

1507 The risen Lord renews this mission: ("In my name... they will lay their hands on the sick, and they will recover") and confirms it through the signs that the Church performs by invoking his name. These signs demonstrate in a special way that Jesus is truly "God who saves."

1509 Heal the sick! (Mt. 10:8). The Church has received this charge from the Lord and strives to carry it out by taking care of the sick as well as by accompanying them with her prayer of intercession. She believes in the life giving presence of Christ, the physician of souls and bodies. This presence is particularly active through the sacraments, and in an altogether special way through the Eucharist, the bread that gives eternal life and that St. Paul suggests is connected with bodily health (cf. Jn. 6:54, 58; 1 Cor. 11:30).

Testimony: Healing Through the Intercession of Padre Pio, Eucharistic Saint

When our son was diagnosed by a blood test with mononucleosis, he was sent home to recover for two months. This meant that he would be unable to graduate with his high school class, a difficult reality to accept. During daily Mass and holy hour, I prayed for him. Observing how sick he was, on the fourth day, I asked Fr. Raymond to visit so that we could intercede for a healing. In prayer, I sensed the Lord was waiting for me to ask for a healing. Father and I proceeded to pray over him and he returned to sleep. We prayed through the intercession of Padre Pio, a Eucharistic saint!

Fr. Raymond has a rosary received at San Giovanni Rotundo in Italy, town of Padre Pio. On pilgrimage there, we visited the sacristy of the old Church where Padre Pio's body is entombed. Padre Pio's friend, Fr. Allesio was our guide for the tour of the Church. Fr. Allesio took one of Padre Pio's blood soaked gloves and touched our rosaries to Padre Pio's glove, making them a third class relic.

When my son awoke the next day, he was well and able to return to school. He graduated on schedule with his class. My desire for his healing was very great, but my faith in God that he would be healed was not. That I had faith enough to ask the Lord's healing on this child, was sufficient for the Lord to work miraculously. This episode speaks of the practicality of God's healing touch. At healing Masses with priests who have the gift of healing, I have witnessed miracles of physical, spiritual and emotional healing. I expected miracles in that setting. But this incident was simply a mother asking God to heal her son. The Lord honored the prayer. Why was I surprised? I have since asked for every kind of miracle for both of our children. This book does not contain the space to tell of the many miracles God has worked in our family. Praise the Lord!

Saint Padre Pio's letter to his spiritual daughter

Let us humble ourselves profoundly, my dear daughter, and confess that if God were not our breast plate and our shield we should at once be pierced by every kind of sin. This is why we must invariably keep ourselves in God by persevering in our spiritual exercises.

On the other hand we must always have courage and if some spiritual languor comes upon us, let us run to the feet of Jesus in the Blessed Sacrament and let us place ourselves in the midst of the heavenly perfumes and we will undoubtedly regain our strength.

I can say no more to you as regards your apprehension over those trials to which the good God is subjecting you, or even as regards your fear in bearing them. Didn't I tell you the first time I spoke of your soul that you dwelled too much on what happens to you in time of temptations; that it is not necessary to think of them except fleetingly?; that women and also men sometimes reflect too much on their evils, and that this confuses their thoughts?, so that the fears and desires embarrass the soul so much that it cannot free itself?

Whom, should we fear, therefore? Listen to our Lord who says to Abraham and to you also: "Do not fear, I am your protector." Therefore, be steadfast in your resolutions. Stay in the boat in which he has placed you, and let the storm come. Long live Jesus! You will not perish. He may sleep, but at the opportune time he will awaken to restore your calm."

Saint Padre Pio, *Letters, Volume III*

Chapter 8

Eucharistic Life
Protects from Evil

Enemy of the Eucharist: Spiritual Battles

In the last paragraph of the introduction to *Ecclesia de Eucharistia*, John Paul II states, "It is my hope that the present Encyclical Letter will effectively help to banish the dark clouds of unacceptable doctrine and practice, so that the Eucharist will continue to shine forth in all its radiant mystery." In the paragraph before this closing sentence, he alludes to liturgical abuses and *shadows* that try to strip the Eucharistic mystery of its sacrificial meaning. Here we are reminded to be vigilant because the Eucharist has an enemy. The enemy of the Eucharist is also the enemy of all souls. "He was a murderer from the beginning...He is a liar and the father of lies" (Jn. 8:44).

Christ's first Vicar on earth, St. Peter, warns us in 1 Peter 5:8, our enemy "is the devil and he is prowling around like a roaring lion looking for someone to devour." Is there spiritual warfare around the Eucharistic Presence? Yes! As St. Paul tells us, our enemy is not flesh and blood, but spirit: "principalities and powers of darkness in the high places" (Eph. 6:12). It is important to understand that the spiritual warfare over our soul is not an intellectual concept of good versus evil. The spiritual warfare around us is between active personal wills. Satan opposes the will of God who is Love. Satan is pure hatred and his will is always turned against God, and against everything having to do with God. Therefore the Eucharist is hated and opposed by him.

As soon as you enter into an intensely Eucharistic life (daily Mass and Holy Hour), you experience the enemy's opposition. It is Satan's will that Jesus be profaned in the Blessed Sacrament, not worshipped! In our day, unfortunately he is able to find people to do his bidding against the Eucharist. It is his intention to prevent the Church from rekindling Eucharistic amazement since when this happens the Church will reclaim lost territory that Satan has stolen. The random assaults of the enemy should be seen for what they are; Satan has yet to concede that Jesus has already won the final battle. As you live an intensely Eucharistic life, be mindful of Christ's victory and know your baptismal authority over your enemy.

Knowing the Enemy

The Gospel narrates the temptation of Christ in the desert which teaches the idea of a personal devil. Christ not only dealt with the devil in the desert but the New Testament contains many accounts of Jesus coming against demonic spirits. Satan is powerless against his Creator God; he hates him because of his goodness. Since he is powerless against God, he turns his hatred against the children of God. Satan was expelled from Heaven because he decided, "I will not serve!" His pride banished him from Heaven. His will is fixed in hatred against the God he will not serve.

As we draw closer to God through the Mass and Holy Hour, we become a real threat to the kingdom of darkness. The enemy attacks us because he is afraid that we will further the kingdom of light (as does every holy soul) thus, he will lose the opportunity to snatch souls from God. The easiest way for Satan to rob God of his beloved adopted children is by tempting us to sin. While we acknowledge that our evil foe would like to carry us off to eternal torment, we are not to be afraid! How often we heard the words, "Be not afraid." from John Paul II! In the Gospel, Christ often said, "Fear Not!" Christ fights for us. St. Michael and legions of good angels do spiritual battle to help save our soul from the foe. Grace is always sufficient to overcome the attacks of the enemy.

A Eucharistic people should not live in a state of indifference about spiritual warfare. This is not an option for the believer because it is contrary to the Gospel. The Bible is filled with explicit accounts of spiritual warfare. Satan tempted Christ. Christ warned his disciples that servants are not above their Master, what was done to him will be done to his followers. People are experiencing the enemy's exertion upon their lives more than ever in the family, workplace and Church. The Catholic Church possesses a spiritual arsenal of armor and weaponry against the enemy. Denial only exacerbates vulnerability to the tactics of the enemy!

When Good is Presented as Evil and Evil is Presented as Good

We are living at a time when good is presented as evil and evil is presented as good. An intensely Eucharistic life will undo the confusion. Jesus has made a provision for such a time as this in human history. The Truth sets us free from the confusion. Know the personality of Jesus and you will know the Truth. The graces of Eucharist prevail in our hearts to reveal the lie from the truth. We know there is a battle for the soul of the church, country and family. This spiritual battle begs our engagement and requires a constant process of discernment of spirits. To relax in this area of spiritual responsibility is to allow evil to advance and claim more territory by taking prisoner more families, more marriages, and more children!

We are not called to be helpless victims in this spiritual battle. We are called to be soldiers for Christ. A soldier trains for battle and engages in it. We should be able to relate to David and Goliath. Our little stones are faith, hope and love. David won the battle over the giant Goliath because God was with him. David said, "The battle is the Lord's." He knew his limitations against his opponent and trusted in the almighty power of God. Still David had to engage; he had to stand against Goliath, aim and shoot that sling shot! So it is with us.

Christians are people who have crossed over from the kingdom of darkness into the Kingdom of Light (Col. 1:12-14). Jesus has defeated Satan and set us free. We don't have to defeat Satan again because the victory Jesus won was complete (Col. 2:15). Our responsibility is to take hold of the power of Christ's victory. This immediately puts us in conflict with the power of darkness. Paul explains this in Ephesians 6:12, "It is not against human enemies that we have to struggle but against sovereignties and powers who originate the darkness in this world, the spiritual army of evil in the Heavens."

Whenever our activities extend the Kingdom of God, they will be a challenge to the kingdom of darkness. We all need to be supported by prayer—our own and other prayer warriors. Intercessory prayer is absolutely necessary. Exodus 17:8-16 shows us the importance of sustained intercessory prayer to win battles. As Joshua battles with the Amelekites on the plain, Moses prays on the mountain top with Aaron and Hur. "As long as Moses held up his hands the Israelites were winning, but whenever he lowered his hands the Amelekites were winning. As Moses grew tired, Aaron and Hur held up his hands and Joshua overcame the Amalekite army with the sword." Joshua was given the credit for the victory but the real battle was fought by Moses in the spiritual realm. Both battles were necessary.

Discernment of Spirits in Scripture

In the first thirty-five years of my life, I never considered "consulting the Holy Spirit" to discern the different movements of my heart or to make life's decisions. Providentially, the Lord allowed my path to cross with Mother Nadine of the Intercessors of the Lamb in 1992. It was through Mother Nadine's teachings that I first heard of St. Ignatius Exercises and the biblical principles of discernment of spirits. I began to distinguish between the Holy Spirit, human spirit and evil spirit. What a practical difference discernment of spirits has made in my walk with Jesus, in my family and in the spiritual battle against the evil one!

St. Paul: The Charism of Discernment of Spirits

St. Paul's first letter to the Corinthians speaks of the charism of discernment of spirits (1 Cor.12:4-10). There are different kinds of spiritual gifts but the same Spirit. To one is given through the Spirit the expression of wisdom, to another the expression of knowledge, to another faith, the gift of healing, mighty deeds, prophecy, discernment of spirits, and to another, the gift of tongues (prayer language). First Corinthians speaks explicitly of the discernment of spirits, listing it among other charisms. In this context, discernment takes on a special meaning; it is a charism, a gift not given to all but only to some as a special gift of service. It is used in deliverance ministry and exorcisms, to determine the presence of evil spirits.

St. John: The Gift of Discernment of Spirits

(1 John 4:1) The first letter of St. John describes the discernment of spirits as both a gift and a duty for all Christians. "Beloved, do not believe every spirit, but test the spirits to see if they are of God." The First Letter to St. John speaks of the discernment of spirits not as a charism but rather as a gift available to all Christians. All Christians are called to discern according to the light of the Holy Spirit.

We find an analogy between the gift of discernment and faith. All Christians have the gift of faith, but only a few have the charism of faith, the charismatic faith that moves mountains. Charismatic faith is highly expectant, animated with confidence that what we pray for will be granted by God according to His will and timing.

All are called to discern by the Spirit what comes from the Lord and what does not, but only some have this gift in such great force that it takes the form of a charism to be used for others. These two texts (1 Cor. 12:4-10, charism of discernment) and (1 John 4:1, gift of discernment) are the beginning of a long Christian tradition of the practice of discernment.

There is no contradiction between Paul's first letter that he wrote to the Corinthians and St. John's first letter. The charism of the discernment of spirits is a special gift, given only to some, for a special ministry according to Paul in 1 Corinthians. The gift of discernment is offered to all Christians, since all need to judge according to the Spirit, and this is the teaching of 1 John.

By the virtue of baptism, we have the gift of discernment of spirits.

We can also pray to God for the charism of discernment as our mission or situation warrants. I truly believe the Spirit is giving the charism of discernment to more people because of the increased intensity of spiritual warfare.

Discernment in the New Testament

The practice of discernment of spirits can be found all through the New Testament. In the Gospels, discernment is seen in the actions and the words of Jesus. Some lack this discernment and some have it. Biblical examples include the following.

- John 6:66-69 As a result of this (Bread of Life discourse), many of his disciples returned to their former way of life and no longer accompanied him. Jesus said to the Twelve, "Do you also want to leave?" Simon Peter answered Him, "Master, to whom shall we go? You have the words of eternal life we have come to believe and are convinced that you are the Holy One of God." (Good discernment.)

- Matthew 12:24-32 But when the Pharisees heard this, they said, "This man drives out demons only by the power of Beelzebub, the prince of demons." But He knew what they were thinking and said to them, "Every kingdom divided against it self will be laid waste, and no town or house divided against itself will stand. And if Satan drives out Satan, he is divided against himself; how, then, will his kingdom stand? And if I drive out demons by Beelzebub, by whom do your own people drive them out?" (Poor discernment.)

- Matthew 1:18-20 Joseph exercises discernment in deciding according to the dream—not to divorce Mary.

- Luke 1:41 Elizabeth (at the Visitation) and Simeon (in the temple) discern the Holy Spirit in Jesus.

The first Letter to the Corinthians reproaches the Christians at Corinth for many excesses, but especially for their puffed up pride (1 Cor. 4:6, 4:18, 5:2 and 13:5) and their lack of spiritual discernment especially in the scripture below:

1 Cor. 2:14 to 3:1 Now the natural person does not accept what pertains to the Spirit of God, for to him it is foolishness, and he cannot understand it, because it is to be judged spiritually. The spiritual person, however, can judge everything but is not subject to judgment by anyone. For "who has known the mind of the Lord, so as to counsel him?" But we have the mind of Christ.

To discern means to "put on the mind of Christ." Gal. 2:19-20: "I have been crucified with Christ; yet I live, no longer I, but Christ lives in me; in so far as I now live in the flesh. I live by faith in the Son of God who has loved me and given himself up for me." The more we are aware of the Divine Indwelling the more thoroughly we possess the mind of Christ. The very nature of Love is mutual possession; mutual gift of self. Creator and creature become bound together as if living out of one heart and one mind.

The Cross of Jesus is the Standard of Discernment

The Cross of Jesus is the standard by which we discern our lives. I mention this as a caution because any discernment that alters the radical message of the Cross into something more "sensible to human wishes" is contrary to the mind of Christ. To simplify discernment look at the life of Christ and conform every decision, every movement of your heart to Christ crucified and risen! Communal discernment is quite valuable (and necessary) for important matters of discernment. While you may not have a priest spiritual advisor on a regular basis, it is advisable to make an appointment when discernment is an issue. Participating in a small faith sharing community or prayer group is also a protection and aid.

God's Armor

One of the great benefits of receiving the Eucharist frequently is purity of mind, soul and body. Receiving the Eucharistic love of Jesus quenches the lust of this world.

St. Augustine says, "It is a victim that we have received

and it is into a victim that we are transformed. Every time we receive Christ, we become bone of his bone, flesh of his flesh, humility of his humility, purity of his purity, and holiness of his holiness." It is especially at the time of receiving the Eucharist that we can say with St. Paul, "I have been crucified with Christ and the life I live now is not my own. Christ is living in me. I still live in my human life, but it is a life of faith in the Son of God, Who loved me and gave himself for me" (Gal. 2:19-20).

It follows that the more you are alive in Christ, the more you are dead to selfishness and sin. A Eucharistic life means that Christ is increasing and you are decreasing. The more your life is hidden in the Eucharistic life of Christ, the more the devil will become afraid of you! (cf. Col. 3:3).

St. Paul clearly teaches that we must put on the armor of God in Ephesians 6:10-17.

Finally, draw your strength from the Lord and from his mighty power. Put on the armor of God so that so that you may be able to stand firm against the tactics of the devil. For our struggle is not with flesh and blood but with the principalities, with the powers, with the world rulers of this present darkness, with the evil spirits in the heavens. Therefore, put on the armor of God that you may be able to resist on the evil day and having done everything, to hold your ground. So stand fast with your loins girded in truth, clothed with righteousness as a breastplate and your feet shod in readiness for the gospel of peace. In all circumstances, hold faith as a shield, to quench all the flaming arrows of the evil one. And take the helmet of salvation and the sword of the Spirit, which is the word of God.

The armor of God

- Draw strength from the Lord's mighty power: deliverance is the Father's. As a baptized child of the Father, you draw from his power and authority. Claim the words of King David: "The battle is the Lord's". Do not act on your human power.

- Stand firm against the tactics of the devil: wait on the Lord. Stand on the rock, Jesus the Almighty Lord. This is a defensive stance, not offensive. Do not be entrapped by the enemy's tactics of engagement. Do not waver from the Truth.

- Belt of Truth: stand fast with loins girded in truth. Let the Truth securely enfold you as a belt enfolds the body. Do not become fragmented or second guess the Truth. The Truth surrounds you like a fortress. Stay in the Truth.

- Breastplate: righteousness is your breastplate. Your heart, center of your being, is protected by God. Keep your heart pure with the righteousness of God. Humility will dispel the enemy.

- Sandals: keep your feet shod in readiness for the gospel of peace: do everything not to lose your peace of soul! The sandals protect your walk as you proclaim the gospel. Guard your peace of soul as a powerful defense from the tornado of turmoil the enemy whips up.

- Shield: hold faith as a shield to quench the flaming arrows of the evil one: the shield protects the whole body so the arrows are deflected. Two shields are better than one: let another soldier watch your back! Soldiers of Christ who walk two by two are better protected from the enemy.

- Helmet: take the helmet of salvation: the battlefield is the mind. Our mind is where we get bombarded by Satan's lies. Claim Christ's salvation and rebuke the lies. Do not be in agreement with them or the helmet is compromised!

- Sword: take the sword of the Spirit, which is the word of God. The word of God is Jesus and Scripture! It is sharper than a two edged sword to cut down the enemy. This is an offensive weapon (all others are defensive). Use the word of God to combat the lies, deceptions and temptations of the enemy. Speak the word of God out loud! Believe in the word of God!

Know God's Strategy: His Word

I present a teaching from Mother Nadine, Intercessors of the Lamb, on the importance of knowing God's strategy. In the spiritual battle we want to know the strategy of Satan and his cohorts. We also want to be familiar with the scriptures about the Lord's strategy to reclaim souls for Christ.

If we are going to combat Satan himself, then we must know God's strategy. You deal with Satan's cohorts, his lieutenants and captains and the rest of the hierarchy of evil. But often you don't bother with the lesser legions. You deal directly with Satan in spiritual warfare as a rule. Look to Moses for insights. He dealt with Pharaoh, the ruler, and gave the command, "Let my people go!" We are asked to do the same. And when we are led by God, Satan has to obey. Can you imagine? Satan has to obey little, insignificant human beings like us when God gives the command. So pray and study the Moses scriptures. Learn from Moses, because the way God led Moses is the way God often leads us. Our mission is the same. Let my people go so that I can lead them into the Promised Land.

Other scriptures are also very insightful. In Joshua 6:1-10, Joshua is instructed very carefully by God on how to take Jericho. Jericho was only one city that Joshua had to capture in order to take possession of the Holy Land. We also retake souls for the Lord, one soul at a time. It is interesting to read that in each village that Joshua took, the strategy of battle changed. Joshua got the victory every time because he listened to God and did exactly as God said.

I would like to say a few words about a spirit that is especially active today. That spirit is the Jezebel spirit. She is the counter part to Satan, Satan's woman. To come against her we use Mary, Mother of God. Mary is God's woman. Everything about Mary is everything that Jezebel is not. Jezebel controls. She particularly wants to exercise control over the priesthood. Everything about Mary is feminine, surrender. That is the weapon: surrender to God. Pray and study the Scriptures that are given about Jezebel and how she works.

A strategy I especially want you to know about is New Age. It is probably the most deceptive form of spirituality we have and it is everywhere today. You can read about New Age and the strategy of Satan in the Book of Judith. The best way to come against the New Age is to call forth the Holy Spirit, the true Living Waters. Pray the baptism of the Spirit again within souls so that people will not drink of the polluted waters anymore. Give people access to the New Wine of Jesus instead.

Whether you are being attacked personally or praying for others who are under attack, an experience of God's love delivers from evil. This is why an intensely Eucharistic life is the most powerful armor. Through daily Mass and Holy Hour, we enter into an intimate personal relationship with the Lord. His love is a healing salve and a spiritual armament. When I experience the attacks of the enemy, I pray a prayer of authority against the evil spirits. In the name of Jesus I bind the evil spirits and cast them out to the foot of the Cross. Sometimes the prayer may be as simple as, "Get thee behind me Satan." Other times, I mention the name of evil spirits (such as spirits of anger, fear, anxiety, etc.), taking authority over them. Then I implore the Holy Spirit to enkindle the fire of Divine Love in my heart. Love casts out all fear, and dispels all darkness. Saint Paul tells us, "Love never fails" (1 Cor. 13). An experience of God's love leads to praise. The enemy will not persist in the presence of praise of God.

Testimony: Young People Healed by the Power of the Eucharist

To bear witness to the Eucharistic power to deliver from evil, I relate an incident that happened at a local Catholic Charismatic Conference. As a volunteer for the Youth Track, I was assigned a group of teenagers to help facilitate their experience on the weekend. I was surprised when I met my group of gang members complete with tattoos! Most of them were brought by their parents or youth ministers and did not want to be there. They were apathetic and rebellious during the teachings and testimonies which were quite good. Throughout the weekend they continued to disobey. Try as I did to facilitate conversations and share the faith with them, they were not interested.

At the end of the day, we were asked to be silent and to kneel because a priest was bringing the Blessed Sacrament into the room to bless the youth. The lights were dimmed, the music was beautiful, and everyone knelt except my group who refused to kneel and just stood there.

When the Blessed Sacrament entered the room I was amazed at what happened. Instantly they all fell to their knees and began to weep! The power of the Blessed Sacrament brought them to their knees and broke open their hearts; all the walls came down and they wept like babies! All the pain locked within them came gushing forth! These teens had many challenges in their respective families and were trying to cope with difficult things: divorced parents, drugs, gangs, peer pressure, lust. They were carrying a lot of anger, even rage. Yet they were afraid.

They were healed by the power of the Blessed Sacrament! They were delivered from many demonic influences that held them in bondage. Only an experience of God's love could heal them! I knelt in Eucharistic amazement, humbled and grateful. It was a scene I will never forget. There is power before the Blessed Sacrament! Human defense mechanisms fall down! We are transparent in His Gaze. He sees us as we are and loves us in spite of our resistance. The young people in my group became full of His love. Their goodness poured forth in a poster signed by all of them thanking me and praising God! They were completely different in the end. The Blessed Sacrament brought them to their knees; a posture of repentance.

Many priests and youth ministers have witnessed young people at conferences like Steubenville West where 5000 youth gather together. There are powerful testimonies and inspiring music but the most amazing thing happens when the Blessed Sacrament is brought into the arena: demons are expelled! There is deliverance from evil spirits by the power and presence of the Blessed Sacrament. Jesus' deliverance ministry, which is part of His healing ministry, continues in and through the infinite graces of the Blessed Sacrament.

The Reality of the Devil, Article

On October 27, 2006, the *National Catholic Register* published an article by Fr. Andrew McNair, LC, entitled, "The Reality of the Devil." Father states:

> "The new millennium marks for many teens and young adults a renewed interest in spirituality. What type of spirituality? Christian? No. Islamic? No. How about an Eastern spirituality like Taoism? Wrong again. Try Satanism. That's right. The occult movement of Satanism ranks number one among teens and young adults as their preferred spirituality. We could dismiss the ascendancy of Satanism in the United States as a fad of the young; something they will grow out of with time. In others words, it's nothing to worry about.

> In my judgment, that's the wrong approach to the spiritual and cultural phenomenon of Satanism. People need to understand that Satanic spirituality leaves deep spiritual and psychological scars on its victims. Christians should know how to recognize and combat satanic spirituality. Where do we begin?

> Let's begin by reaffirming a basic truth: Satan exists. His demonic minions exist. Scripture and Tradition depict Satan as the supreme evil leader of the fallen angels who seek to disrupt God's plan of salvation for humanity.

> The Catechism of the Catholic Church points out: "Behind the disobedient choice of our first parents lurks a seductive voice, opposed to God, which makes them fall into death out of envy. Scripture and the Church's Tradition see in this being a fallen angel, called 'Satan' or the 'devil.'" The Church teaches that Satan was at first a good angel, made by God: "The devil and the other demons were indeed created naturally good by God, but they became evil by their own doing" (No. 391).

> St. Peter the Apostle warns us, "Keep sober and alert, because your enemy the devil is on the prowl like a roaring lion,

looking for someone to devour." Yet despite warnings from Scripture and Tradition about the lure of Satanism, teens and young adults see involvement in satanic occultism as an acceptable cultural and social option. Why? Satanic occultism wears the deceptive guise of white magic. White magic employs the use of occult powers to do good. Black magic, on the other hand, uses occult powers to do evil. The entertainment industry cleverly hammers the notion of white magic in inattentive minds.

On the literary front, we find an entire plethora of books, magazines and columns that speak highly of the occult. For the last few years, the No. 1 best-selling novel in the United States and abroad narrates a story about a young boy wizard that uses white magic to duel the most powerful and evil wizard ever known. Millions of youth, worldwide, look up to this courageous wizard as a perfect role model. Can a sorcerer or warlock be a role model?

Message of the white magic argument is clear: Magic is not bad in itself. It depends, like many things, on how you use it. In view of this assertion, white magic wins approval and respectability in the minds of many. Here, we need to make an important moral clarification.

The difference often made between white magic and black magic is woefully erroneous. The goodness or badness of an act of witchcraft or magic is not determined by the purpose of its use. Its moral quality comes from its origin. The origin of all occult powers is the demonic realm. Consequently, all magic involving the use of occult powers is intrinsically evil. The Catechism of the Catholic Church makes this point abundantly clear: "All practices of magic or sorcery, by which one attempts to tame occult powers, so as to place them at one's service and have a supernatural power over others — even if this were for the sake of restoring their health — are gravely contrary to the virtue of religion. These practices are even more to be condemned when accompanied by the intention of harming someone, or when they have recourse to the intervention of demons." (No. 2116)

The best defense against the lure of satanic influence is an intense life of grace. In the words of St. Paul, the Church invites us to "Put on the full armor of God so as to be able to resist the devil's tactics." This will permit us to utter effectively the powerful words of Christ in the hour of temptation, "Get thee behind me, Satan!"

Legionary Father Andrew McNair

Spiritual vigilance is part of the Church's pillar of prayer. As a good priest pointed out recently that it has been the tradition of the Church to speak more about Christ than to focus too much on his Adversary. For anyone living a sacramental life of prayer, there is nothing to fear. Fear is not of God since as the Bible tells us, "Perfect love casts out fear." Jesus is our armor! The sacramental life of the Church is our protection. Our families are so assailed by the message of the world which is now imbued with fascination with evil spirits. It is consoling to know that the Catholic Church has a treasury of protection and an arsenal of weapons to "set the captives free."

I have the privilege of working on a deliverance team under the leadership of a priest with vast experience in deliverance ministry. I have observed the devastating effects upon people who dabble in the occult. It brings torment into the life of the person and their household. The cases we see are classified as obsession not possession. During the sessions of praying over the troubled person, the presence of the Blessed Sacrament is felt by the evil spirits and does great harm to them. Evil spirits obey the commands of the Catholic priest since he has the authority of the whole Church with him.

In deliverance ministry (which is, again, part of Christ's healing ministry) it is edifying to observe evil spirits vacate the person with cries of protestation as a result of being sprayed with holy water, sprinkled with blessed salt, anointed with holy oil, touched by the priest's stole, hearing the proclamation of the Word of God and the rosary being prayed. Ah! The arsenal of protection is in the fullness of the Church! Christ himself, who works in and through his Church, has "come to destroy the works of the devil" (1 Jn. 3:8).

The Pope also beatified Dina Belanger because of her devotion to Jesus in the Blessed Sacrament. Jesus revealed to Dina the power of the holy hour in making reparation. One form of reparation is the ability to make up for what is lacking in the life of another. One day before her holy hour, Jesus showed Dina a multitude of souls on the precipice of hell. After her holy hours of prayer a multitude of souls go to Heaven that otherwise would have gone to hell as one person can make up for what is lacking in the lives of others by winning precious efficacious graces for their salvation. In other words, Eucharistic Adoration is the outpouring of God's Divine Mercy on the world!

How One Soul Coming Before the Blessed Sacrament Can Change the World

The Sacrament of the Body of the Lord puts the demons to flight, defends us against the incentives to vice and to concupiscence, cleanses the soul from sin, quiets the anger of God, enlightens the understanding to know God, inflames the will and the affections with the love of God, fills the memory with spiritual sweetness, confirms the entire man in good, frees us from eternal death, multiples the merits of a good life, leads us to our everlasting home, and re-animate the body to eternal life.

St. Thomas Aquinas

These devils keep us in terror, because we lay ourselves open to being terrorized. We become attached to honors, possessions, and pleasures. Then they join forces with us, since by loving and desiring what we should loathe we become our own enemies. Then they will do us great harm. But if we loathe everything for God's sake, embrace the Cross and try to serve Him truly, the devil will fly from such realities as from a plague.

Saint Teresa of Avila

Testimony: A Hospice Nurse's Story of Death Bed Spiritual Battles

The teachings of Christ reveal that as we live, so we die. A friend who is a hospice nurse usually shares beautiful stories of how God provides a very merciful passage from this life to the next. The human person has a way of progressing from life on earth into eternal life that is very natural, peaceful and beautiful in many ways. She has a privileged ministry of praying at the bed of dying patients. She relays in her own words, the unusual experience of a recent patient, whom we will call, Robert.

Robert was a high ranking member of a Cultic Order. He was to be buried in his Cult's cloak hung neatly in his closet. Robert was unconscious lying in his bed when I arrived for my shift. He appeared comfortable except he was experiencing some difficulty breathing. Suddenly, I began to sense the tangible presence of demonic spirits in the room. The hair on the back of my neck stood up and a cloud of oppression overcame me. I have been in the ministry of intercession and spiritual warfare for many years. This was the most intense presence of evil that I had ever experienced. The battle for Robert's soul had begun. I quickly discerned what was happening and began to pray a prayer of authority over the evil spirits in the Name of Jesus. I called on the Eternal Father, Mother Mary, St. Michael and the Saints to come to the rescue of this poor soul. I prayed at his bedside, the rosary, and the Chaplet of Divine Mercy. After completing the prayers, I noted that he was in a state of restlessness, appearing to be interiorly tortured. He facial grimacing was accompanied by moans, not of pain, but fear!

I called for back up intercession from the prayer group. Robert's vital signs indicated that he would die soon and I had an overwhelming sorrow for his soul. While I felt delivered from spirits of fear, anxiety and oppression, Robert still appeared to be very troubled. I picked up the Bible and began to read the scriptures, claiming the word of God. As other nurses and facility staff entered the room, they approached the patient with compassion, but quickly they would step back from the bed, troubled at what they observed in his tormented countenance. They asked me if I was all right in the room alone, sensing again the presence of evil. The room felt cold and devoid of love. The battle continued for two more nights. I stayed in contact with my priest spiritual director and prayer partners to discern how to pray for this soul. On the third night the unthinkable entered my mind that perhaps this soul could be lost. In Robert's final hour his face turned grey-white and there were terrible markings upon his forehead that looked like red and black burns in the shape of flames of fire! Robert died in agony. As the nurses came to look upon the patient, they gasped in horror! We covered Robert's body and face completely to prevent his family from seeing him in such a terrible condition.

In prayer, I begged the Lord for some understanding about why the intercession did not seem to help this patient. The Lord gave me to understand that he sent me to intercede, that he offered Robert Divine Mercy! Christ revealed that he had created Robert for eternal beatitude in Heaven; however, God does not violate human free will. We must choose the Lord! Thank God this story is unique in my experience of hospice care.

Prayer against Every Evil

Spirit of our God, Father, Son and Holy Spirit, Most Holy Trinity, Immaculate Virgin Mary, angels, archangels, and saints of heaven, descend upon me. Please purify me, Lord, mold me, fill me with yourself, use me. Banish all the forces of evil from me, destroy them, vanquish them, so that I can be healthy and do good deeds. Banish from me all spells, witchcraft, black magic, malefice, ties, maledictions, and the evil eye; diabolic infestations, oppressions, possessions; all that is evil and sinful, jealousy, perfidy, envy, physical, psychological, moral, spiritual, diabolical ailments.

Burn all these evils in hell, that they may never again touch me or any other creature in the world. I command and bid all the powers who molest me—by the power of God all powerful, in the name of Jesus Christ our Savior, through the intercession of the Immaculate Virgin Mary—to leave me forever, and to be consigned into the everlasting hell, where they will be bound by Saint Michael the archangel, Saint Gabriel, Saint Raphael, our guardian angels, and where they will be crushed under the heel of the Immaculate Virgin Mary. Amen

Fr. Gabriele Amorth, *An Exorcist Tells His Story*

St. John Bosco wrote, "Do you want the Lord to give you many graces? Visit Him often. Do you want Him to give you few graces? Visit Him rarely. Do you want the devil to attack you? Visit Jesus rarely in the Blessed Sacrament. Do you want him to flee from you? Visit Jesus often. Do you want to conquer the devil? Take refuge often at the feet of Jesus. Do you want to be conquered by the devil? Forget about visiting Jesus. My dear ones, the Visit to the Blessed Sacrament is an extremely necessary way to conquer the devil. Therefore, go often to visit Jesus and the devil will not come out victorious against you."

Chapter 9

Testimony and Prayers of Elizabeth J. Kim, Ph.D.

Since so many good people are looking to non-Catholic methods of well-being, we present this chapter as the experiential witness of Dr. Kim. It could be considered as a support to our faith in Christ. Science is not used to verify theological issues since disciples of Christ walk in faith. This presentation is meant to encourage people to consider the good effects of meditative prayer as part of a Eucharistic lifestyle. In John Paul II's encyclical, he states:

> Truly the Eucharist is a mystery which surpasses our understanding and can only be received in faith, as is often brought out in the catechesis of the Church Fathers regarding this divine sacrament: "Do not see" — Saint Cyril of Jerusalem exhorts — "in the bread and wine merely natural elements, because the Lord has expressly said that they are his body and blood: faith assures you of this, though your senses suggest otherwise."

John Paul II, *Ecclesia de Eucharistia*

Proclaiming the death of the Lord "until he comes" (1 Cor 11:26) entails that all who take part in the Eucharist be committed to changing their lives and make them in a certain way completely "Eucharistic". It is this fruit of a transfigured existence and a commitment to transforming the world in accordance with the Gospel which splendidly illustrates the eschatological tension inherent in the celebration of the

Eucharist and in the Christian life as a whole: Come, Lord Jesus!" (Rev. 22:20)

Meditation's Effects on the Brain toward Wholeness

This chapter explains the good effects of meditation using scientific research and personal testimony to rekindle Eucharistic amazement in our hearts.

Life and Stress

Come to me, all you who are weary and find life burdensome, and I will refresh you. Take my yoke upon your shoulders and learn from me, for I am gentle and humble of heart. Your souls will find rest, for my yoke is easy and my burden light. (Mt.11:28-30)

We have all said or thought the words, "I am stressed out." In this hectic and busy world, who is exempt from stress? A dedicated pastor might feel the stress of time pressures. A devoted Catholic might face financial worries. I have even heard a little kindergartner says she is stressed out from school. In the U.S., most people experience some form of stress in the areas of career, traffic in a big city, marriage and family life, health, and finance. God, in His Divine wisdom, gently invites us all to come to His presence in the Eucharist. He wants to minister to us, commune with us, refresh us, and release us from stress. We, as Catholics, can experience the presence of Jesus in the most profound and intimate way through the Blessed Sacrament. We can receive His life, merciful love, and healing in us. We will be nourished, strengthened, healed, and transformed.

Life is stressful; but it is not possible to eliminate stress. Whether you like it or not, stress will come and go. But what matters are not the problems you face; it is your attitude toward those problems. How you deal and cope with problems is key, and the key is in prayer - that inward journey into the heart. Silent prayer gives us Divine perspectives on life's ups and downs.

There are basically two kinds of stress. Good stress, or *eustress*, refers to life events like marriage, the birth of a newborn baby, a career promotion, moving to a better house, and so forth. On the other hand, bad stress, or *distress*, includes the death of a family member or loved ones, divorce, health problems, and financial difficulties. The science reveals that a moderate amount of any stress helps us to become more motivated and excited. So, how to deal with stress is more important than the stress itself.

In the secular world, Dr. Jon Kabat-Zinn founded a world-renowned stress and anxiety reduction clinic and developed a program called Mindfulness-Based Stress Reduction. He uses an eight-week training course in mindfulness meditation (Kabat-Zinn, *et al.,* 1992). The secular world borrows the Christian concept of meditative and contemplative prayers and uses them quite effectively. What about us? We have the entire spectrum of prayers, which, in addition to countless benefits, heal our stress and anxiety. Do we pray as often as we should?

According to H. Benson, there are symptoms that warn of life-threatening stress. These symptoms fall under four categories: physical, behavioral, emotional, and cognitive. To promote our understanding, let's take a look at them.

- *Physical symptoms* include sleep disturbance, headaches, indigestion, stomach aches, sweaty palms, fatigue, neck and shoulder pain, racing heart, and back pain.

- *Behavioral symptoms* are manifested by overuse or abuse of alcohol, excess smoking, grinding of teeth during sleep, critical attitude of others, over eating, and inability to finish things.

- *Emotional symptoms* include crying spells, anxiety, feeling helplessness or hopelessness, apathy, anger, loneliness, sadness, and getting easily upset and frustrated.

- *Cognitive symptoms* consist of forgetfulness, a lack of creativity, decreased memory, indecisiveness, poor concentration, easily worried, and loss of sense of humor.

What can relieve us from all of these terrible symptoms? The answer is stress management: it constitutes prayer, sleep, a healthy diet, and exercise. Of these factors, prayer is the most powerful. Let me explain.

The Effects of Stress on the Brain

Chronic stress negatively impacts the brain. When certain parts of the brain - the limbic system, amygdala, and hippocampus - become activated often and overworked due to severe, chronic stress and fear, other brain regions dealing with complex thought and immune system response are hindered. The mind and body respond to acute, extreme, and stressful situations (for example, fear) with the "fight-or-flight" response. The person has basically two choices: confront the seemingly fearful and life-threatening event ("fight"), or run away from it ("flight"). When the brain undergoes severe stress for prolonged periods of time, it becomes negatively affected by the neurochemistry and changing concentrations of cortisol, norepinephrine, and adrenaline. (INR, *Emotion, Stress, and Disease*, 2007, p. 10-11).

Research by Herbert *et al.* indicates that brain, stress, and mental illness are closely related. The brain adversely responds to stress by modifying the gene expression, which contributes to the development of many mental illnesses like anxiety disorders and depression. Increasing levels of cortisol damage the brain, particularly the hippocampus. The hippocampus is responsible for learning and memory. Adrenaline is another hormone released at higher speed than normal under severely stressful situations. The elevated levels of adrenaline add physical stress on the body and organs, and increase blood pressure and heart rate. Chronic stress is closely related to heart disease, high blood pressure, stroke, and other illnesses. (INR, *Emotion, Stress, and Disease*, 2007, pp. 10-11).

Brain Structure

The human brain is one of the most amazing masterpieces of God's creation. It weighs only three pounds and contains about 100 billion neurons. Neurons are the brain cells responsible for emotion, thought, perception, memory, movement, and sensation.

The brain has basic four large lobes.

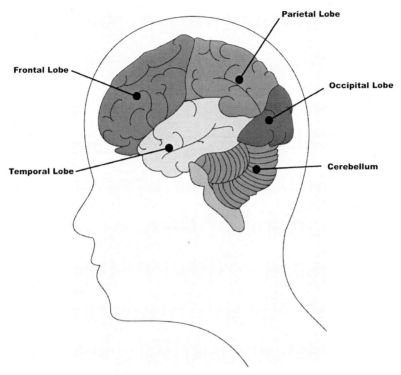

Figure 1: Basic Structure of Brain

The *frontal lobe*, which consists of half the volume of each cerebral hemisphere in humans, deals with sequence of movement, initiation, attention, orientation to sensory input, motivation, speech and emotional expression, critical thinking, and problem solving.

Each *parietal lobe* is concerned with spatial awareness, social-emotional awareness, body relaxation and awareness, and sensory hypersensitivity.

The *temporal lobe* governs auditory processing and emotional regulation. It helps to recognize objects and patterns.

Lastly, the *occipital lobe*, located on the back of the brain, deals with visual processing and visual sensitivity.

Right Brain versus Left Brain

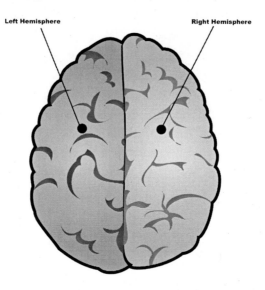

Figure 2: Two Hemispheres

The corpus callosum, meaning "thick-skinned body," divides the cerebral cortex into right and left hemispheres along a line running directly back from the nose.

The right hemisphere perceives input as a whole while the left hemisphere analyzes things. For example, the right hemisphere tends to see the forest while the left hemisphere tends to see the tree. Generally, the left hemisphere processes what was spoken while the right hemisphere processes how it was spoken. The two hemispheres process information from different perspectives, but they work together to create a unified mental experience.

The left hemisphere is involved with right-side motor activity; sequence processing; logical, rational, and analytical thinking; language; text; organization; and conscious awareness.

The right hemisphere excels at controlling the left side of the body, social-emotional awareness, intuition, arts, creativity, abstraction, context, and body and spatial awareness and synthesis.

Can you see toward which hemisphere you are more oriented? No one uses just one side of the brain. We all use and need to develop both hemispheres. During sleep, the left hemisphere rests while the right is active. Thus, during meditative or contemplative prayers, the right hemisphere becomes active.

Brainwave Activity
and Related States of Consciousness

How does the brain work? In short, different brainwave frequency bands produce different behavioral states.

High Beta: 19 Hz and above in frequency

The high beta frequency band encompasses conscious processes and hyper-alertness. Experiences include anxiety, anger, rage, fear, and panic.

Beta: 15 to 18 Hz

The beta frequency band involves conscious processes with an external focus and active alertness. It includes rational-analytical thinking and concentration; here, focus can shift easily.

Sensory Motor Rhythm (SMR): 12 to 15 Hz

The SMR frequency band involves conscious processes with an external focus. It includes calm alertness and calm focus.

Alpha: 8 to 12 Hz

The alpha frequency band encompasses conscious processes with an internal focus. The brain is in a relaxed, non-vigilant state of realistic fantasy or calm and quiet, and creativity exists. This is considered the "no-thought" state.

Theta: 4 to 8 Hz

The theta frequency band includes often unconscious processes with an internal focus. The brain is in an inactive and detached state with receptive drifting, dream-like thoughts and images, and memories of long-past events. This is an intuitive and creative state.

Delta: 1 to 4 Hz

The delta frequency band encompasses deep-sleep processes with an internal focus. Here, the brain loses control over mental processes and awareness; processes slow.

DELTA 1-4 Hz	Sleep	
THETA 4-8 Hz	Drowsy	
ALPHA 8-12 Hz	Relaxed Focus	
SMR 12-15 Hz	Relaxed Thought	
BETA 15-18 Hz	Active Thinking	
HIGH BETA Higher than 18 Hz	Excited	

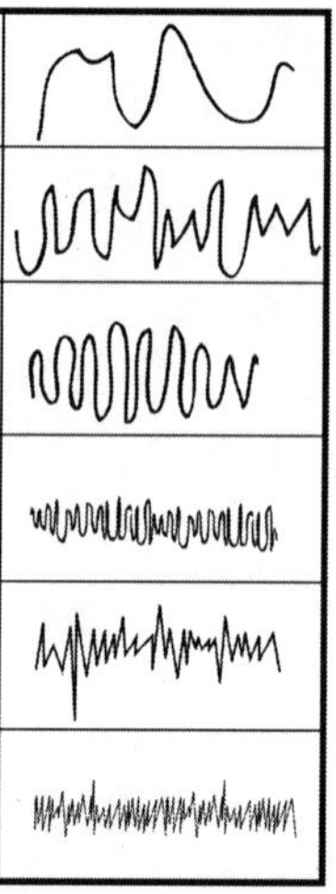

Figure 3: Brainwaves and Related States of Consciousness

How does meditation affect the brain?

Many studies support the idea that meditation reduces the effects of anxiety and stress psychologically and physiologically (R. J. Davidson, 2000). More specifically, the majority of research on the EEG (Electroencephalogram) and meditation generally finds that during meditation, power increases in the alpha and theta bands and overall frequency decreases (Andresen, 2000). In other words, the brain becomes more relaxed and involved in the alpha and theta bands.

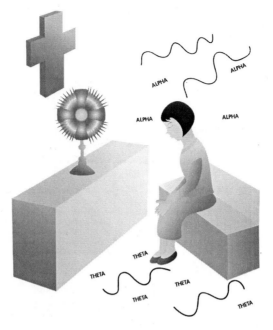

Figure 4: Meditation before the Blessed Sacrament and Brainwaves

As a psychologist and a neurofeedback practitioner, I have observed and treated/trained stressed brains suffering from depression, panic disorder, anxiety disorder, AD/HD (attention deficit/hyperactivity disorder), autistic spectrum disorder, and other disorders for over 15 years.

Neurofeedback, also called EEG Biofeedback, is known as brain exercise in self-regulation. It is a learning process by which you learn to change your brain waves and thus learn to have better control over your brain states. It is done in this fashion: electrodes are attached to the scalp with EEG paste to read brain waves. You are instructed to play a video game only with your brain waves. It is non-invasive and does not apply any voltage or current to the brain.

After improving stability and control of brain state with Beta/SMR (open-eye) training (a term no longer used in the field, but which I use here for context) certain individuals with anxiety, stress, panic disorder, and related conditions receive Alpha/Theta (closed-eye) training. Alpha/Theta training is very relaxing and refreshing for those who are physiologically ready to enter. It allows the reorganization of fears and behaviors formed during early development or traumatic experiences. I witnessed that those who received Alpha/Theta training enjoyed the actual experiences and received healing and relief from trauma, stress and anxiety.

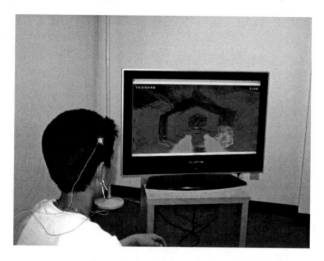

Figure 5: Boy practicing Neurofeedback

A. Newberg, M.D., and his colleague studied brain imaging during meditation, noting unusual activity in the posterior superior parietal lobe. He further experimented to study several Franciscan nuns in prayer. The SPECT (single photon emission computed tomography) scans demonstrated changes during the sisters' most intense spiritual moments.

The sisters tended to describe this moment as a tangible sense of the closeness of God and a mingling with Him. Their accounts echoed those of Christian mysteries of the past, including that of thirteenth-century Franciscan sister Angela of Foligno: "How great is the mercy of the one who realized this union... I possessed God so fully that I was no longer in my previous customary state but was led to find a peace in which I was united with God and was content with everything." Newberg and his colleague further added:

We'd uncovered solid evidence that the mystical experiences of our subjects - the altered states of mind they described as the absorption of the self into something larger - were not the result of emotional mistakes or simple wishful thinking, but were associated instead with a series of observable neuro-logical events, which, while unusual, are not outside the range of normal brain function. In other words, mystical experiences are biologically, observably, and scientifically real (A. Newberg and E. D'Aquili, *Why God Won't Go Away*, p.7).

In their book, *Why We Believe What We Believe*, Newberg and Waldman explain the results of their research on Catholic nuns' meditative prayer. The nuns showed significant increases in the language part of the brain due to the nature of meditation focusing on words. They also showed increased activity in the right hemisphere, which controls meaning, rhythm of speech, and interpretation. They had significant activity in the prefrontal cortex, which is known as the attention area. He formulated "a hypothesis that suggests that spiritual experience, at its very root, is intimately interwoven with human biology. That biology, in some way, compels the spiritual urge." (p. 8).

His hypothesis simply confirms what we already believe, know, and practice in our beautiful Catholic faith. It echoes the words of St. Augustine: "Our hearts are restless until they rest in Thee, O Lord."

The Phenomenon of "Praying in Tongues"

"God wants us to know about the Spiritual Gifts because they are what He uses to keep his Church strong until he comes again" (*Catechism of the Catholic Church*, paragraph 2003). St. Paul instructed us about different kinds of spiritual gifts. "There are different kinds of spiritual gifts but the same Spirit; there are different forms of service but the same Lord .... To each individual the manifestation of the Spirit is given for some benefit. To one is given through the Spirit the expression of wisdom ... knowledge ... faith ... healing ... mighty deeds ... prophecy ... discernment of spirits .... To another, **varieties of tongues** ... interpretation of tongues" (1 Cor. 12: 4-10). In Acts, we learn about Pentecost in the Upper Room: "And they were all filled with the Holy Spirit and began to speak in different tongues, as the Spirit enabled them to proclaim" (Acts 2:4).

During the School of Healing Prayer Conference that I attended in

Florida, May 2007, the International Catholic Charismatic Renewal Services reported that 150 million Catholics around the world have received renewal in the Spirit. This means that many Catholics received the gift of praying in tongues. The gift of praying in tongues is one's personal prayer language. The human language, once divided and confused by Tower of Babel, now the Holy Spirit unifies via gift of praying in tongues. Father Robert Faricy, S.J., often explained praying in tongues as a vocalized, non-conceptual, and contemplative prayer at the SCRC (Southern California Renewal Communities) convention in Anaheim, California. Father Faricy is a Catholic priest and emeritus professor of spiritual theology at the Pontifical Gregorian University in Rome, Italy.

This gift can be exercised at one's will. It does not need to be interpreted and can be used in a group during prayer and singing.

The Spirit too helps us in our weakness, for we do not know how to pray as we ought; but the Spirit himself makes intercession for us with groanings that cannot be expressed in speech. He who searches hearts knows what the Spirit means, for the Spirit intercedes for the saints as God himself wills. (Rom. 8:26-27)

I have personally been using praying in tongues daily since my baptism in the Holy Spirit as a teenager. I often used it in praise with melodies. Sometimes, I use it silently when I intercede for others. Other times, I pray in tongues for discernment and healing or when I do not know how to pray for certain situations. What a wonderful and powerful gift it is! Thank you, Lord, for allowing me to exercise this precious gift in your Spirit.

Not only is praying in tongues a spiritual gift, it can also be classified as a scientific phenomenon supported by recent studies. Newberg's research on this subject showed that, during prayer in tongues, there was a reduction in activity in the frontal lobes. The previously mentioned research on meditation by Franciscan nuns, showed an increase in activity in the frontal lobes and language areas when the brain focused on words or passages. However, in the case of praying in tongues, the language areas had no change. Addressing these unusual results, Newberg suggests that "the language was being generated in a different way, or possibly from some place other than the normal processing centers of speech. For believers, this experience could be taken as proof that another 'entity' had actually spoken through them" (A. Newburg & M. Waldman, *Why We Believe What We Believe*, pp. 200-201). We know it is the Holy Spirit who has spoken through us and prays within us.

Modern scientific research supports the power of prayer and religious/ spiritual/mystical experiences based on a neurobiological basis. As Newberg and Waldman put it in their book *Why God Won't Go Away*, "God is hardwired into the human brain." I might dare to add, that God is also soft wired into the human heart because it is the heart that listens and contemplates. We have a God-shaped vacuum in our hearts. Only God can fill it!

So, how does this all relate to stress management? Prayer, especially contemplation along with exercise, sleep, and a healthy diet, is the best form of stress management. I firmly believe prayer is the number one priority in our lives if we desire to grow in His love and in holiness. It reminds us of Jesus our Lord in the Garden of Gethsemane saying to Peter, "So you could not stay awake with me for even an hour? Be on guard, and pray that you may not undergo the test. The spirit is willing but nature is weak" (Mt. 26:40-41).

Healing Toward Wholeness

May he preserve you whole and entire, spirit, soul, and
body, irreproachable at the coming of our Lord Jesus Christ.
(I Thes. 5:23)

We have studied in this chapter about the effects of stress and meditation on our brain. As opposed to dualism, which views spirit and soul as dignified and the body as ignoble, or as the soul caught in the body, Jesus sees us as a whole. We operate our lives at these three different levels of spirit, soul, and body; God created these parts and cares for them. We know that our emotions and body affect the brain and spirit. Even contemporary psychology recognizes the importance of integrating the different aspects of self in the healing process. Dr. Francis MacNutt states that wholeness is holiness: "Happily, we are now recovering the full proclamation of the good news, that salvation is for the whole person and

that Jesus came to bring us the fullness of life in every possible dimension"
F. MacNutt, *Healing*

Prayer for the Healing of Stress, Anxiety, and Fear

Lord Jesus, you are my light and salvation. Look into my heart and release me from all stress, anxiety, and fear. Help me to move above and beyond the stress that demands of me everyday. Sometimes, I feel I am being stretched too thin. I become a busybody and I often neglect my prayer time with you. In your Holy name, Jesus, break the vicious cycle of "busyness" in my life. I sincerely repent for my lack of prayer while I was too busy and exhausted. Teach me to know what is more important in my life and help me to be constantly led by your Spirit. My daily duties often seem too mundane and unimportant. Help me to do my daily ordinary routines with an extraordinary love for you.

I relinquish all of my concerns and anxieties about the details of tomorrow to you. The more I try to control my life, the more I get out of control. I am helpless and drained. I give you full permission to be in charge of my tomorrows, for you hold my future in your hands and for you are my lord and savior.

O, most compassionate Jesus, I ask you now to heal all of my fear— fear of abandonment, fear of rejection, fear of what other people think of me, fear of illness and death, fear of suffering, fear of failure, fear of intimacy, fear of commitment, and fear of the unknown. Cleanse my fear with your precious blood. In the name of Jesus Christ, I bind any spirits of anxiety and fear. I break a stronghold of fear in your name. I command all these spirits immediately and directly to go to the foot of the Cross. I truly desire to live my life as your little and freed child. I want to walk on the water with you by focusing on you, not focusing on my circumstance. Increase my faith, to be expectant, living, and active. In faith in you, I can conquer the fear and the world. Fill my heart with your peace, joy, and strength that the world cannot give. Thank you for healing me and freeing me from bondage today. In your name, I claim your victory over my life! Amen!

Scriptures for Healing

Indeed, God's word is living and effective, sharper than any two-edged sword. It penetrates and divides soul and spirit, joints and marrow; it judges the reflections and thoughts of the heart (Heb. 4:12).

The Lord is my light and my salvation; whom should I fear? (Ps. 27:1).

O weak in faith! Stop worrying, then, over questions like, "What are we to eat, or what are we to drink, or what are we to wear?" The unbelievers are always running after these things. Your heavenly Father knows all that you need (Mt. 6:30-32).

Martha, Martha, you are anxious and upset about many things; one thing only is required. Mary has chosen the better portion and she shall not be deprived of it (Lk. 10:41-43).

Fear not! Stand your ground, and you will see the victory the Lord will win for you today (Ex. 14:13).

Fear not, for I have redeemed you; I have called you by name: you are mine (Is. 43:1).

Fear is useless. What is needed is trust (Mk. 5:36).

He told them a parable on the necessity of praying always and not losing heart (Lk. 18:1).

In him who is the source of my strength I have strength for everything (Phil. 4:13).

Yes, it was our infirmities that he bore, our sufferings that he endured (Is. 53:4).

It is good to hope in silence for the saving help of the Lord (Lam. 3:26).

I have stilled and quieted my soul like a weaned child. Like a weaned child on its mother's lap, so is my soul within me. O Israel, hope in the Lord, both now and forever (Ps. 131:2-3).

I came that they might have life and have it to the full (Jn. 10:10).

I give you thanks that I am fearfully and wonderfully made; wonderful are your works (Ps. 139:14).

And cure the sick there. Say to them, "The reign of God is at hand" (Lk. 10:9).

At that time he (Jesus) was curing many of their diseases, afflictions, and evil spirits; he also restored sight to many who were blind (Lk. 7:21).

Heal me, Lord, that I may be healed; save me, that I may be saved, for it is you whom I praise (Jer. 17:14).

Hence, declare your sins to one another, and pray for one another, that you may find healing (Jm. 5:16).

Prayer for the Healing of the Brain

My heavenly Father, my Abba, you have created me in your image and likeness, for wellness. I ask you to breathe your life into the areas of my brain that desperately need your healing touch. I ask you to command all parts of my brain to be submissive to your Divine order right now. I ask you to restore and strengthen all neurons, synapses, neurotransmitters, cortical cortex, sub-cortical cortex, basic lobes (pre-frontal, frontal, parietal, temporal, and occipital), each hemisphere, limbic system, cerebellum, brain stem, and brain chemistries. Let your precious blood flow through my brain's pathways and supply your presence and life-giving love. Help my brain to self-regulate the way you have intended.

Come, Holy Spirit, baptize my entire brain in your healing water that flows out of the Father's throne. Heal my brain from depressive disorder, bipolar disorder, anxiety disorder, panic disorder, phobia, obsessive compulsive disorder, sleep disorder, schizophrenia, psychotic disorder, autistic spectrum disorder, AD/HD, learning difficulties, speech problems, head injury, epilepsy, migraine headaches, poor memory, negative thoughts, any form of addiction, and all other neurological dysfunctions known and unknown.

In the name of Jesus, I rebuke the spirit of infirmity and oppression. I command you to go to the foot of the cross right now. Lord Jesus, let all of my brain cells experience the love you create, fully alive in your love. I boldly ask that your miraculous power come through my brain and heal. Any shame, inferiority, inadequacy, self-hatred, anger, resentment, bitterness, and despair I experienced due to my neuropsychological condition, I give to you, Holy Spirit. Heal and transform my brokenness and negativity. I resolve to forgive anyone who hurt me in any way. I make the decision to forgive myself, my parents, and you for having been genetically born with my condition. I ask you to pour out your Divine wisdom, knowledge, understanding, and counsel. I ask you to transform my thoughts to be holy, positive, and constructive. I ask you to grace me to humbly accept my limitation and condition and to continue to take up my cross and follow you. You created my brain and heart to be compelled to your love. I hunger and thirst for your love. I yearn for you. I love you. I surrender my whole life to your most perfect will. Thank you for giving me this life. I praise your name forever. Amen.

My Personal Testimony:
"As I have touched you, touch my people"

Do you believe that miracles still exist? With this story, I hope to remind you that, yes, miracles do still happen. Let me begin with the scripture that sums up my experience of conversion and commission from the Lord:

God chose those whom the world considers absurd to shame the wise; he singled out the weak of this world to shame the strong. He chose the world's lowborn and despised, those who count for nothing, to reduce to nothing those who were something; so that mankind can do no boasting before God.
(I Cor. 1:27-28)

Whoever boasts, should boast in the Lord (I Cor. 3:1). And in that vein, I shall boast of my Abba Father.

Growing up, I was a practicing Catholic like many of you. I did what most practicing Catholics do: attend Sunday Mass weekly, go to confession, and participate in Sunday school. I believed in God and had some faith. Then, during my adolescent years, everything changed. My faith was shaken. I started asking myself, "If God is love, why have I never experienced it? Why do I feel like He doesn't care about me?" I witnessed good people suffering around me. And as I read more books on nihilism and pessimism toward life, I no longer believed in my Catholic teachings. I was able to relate more to Buddha's teachings of "Life is an ocean of suffering." than to "God is love."

I was miserable. It came to a point where I could not buy into the concept of God anymore. Full of confusion and doubt, I concluded that God did not exist. Subsequently, I lost a sense of meaning and purpose in life. Although my Catholic guilt kept me going to church, I no longer knew who I was or what I was. My self-knowledge was filled with lies about the world, and I felt worthless because I could not meet society's standards. I thought everything about me was flawed; I hated myself with a passion. Even a fortune-teller, who happened to stop by our house one day, volunteered to tell my mother that it was my father's fate to have such a daughter with an infirmity. "How did she know about my misery?" I felt shocked and doomed to hear her words.

Then I developed an intense hatred and anger toward my father, who was not a believer at the time. His sins and problems were the cause of my suffering, I thought. It was his fault. It was unfair I said to myself, "Why should I be a victim of my father's problems?" I had reached my last straw: My life was not worth living. This existential crisis of faith led me to utter depression and despair, and I became suicidal. There was no more hope for me in this harsh world. The spirit of death pursued me.

Later, after my conversion, my Abba Father corrected my false judgment against my father and my life with His words: "Rabbi, was it his sin or that of his parents that caused him to be born blind? Neither, answered Jesus. It was no sin, either of this man or of his parents. Rather, it was to let God's works show forth in him" (Jn. 9:1-3). The father of lies, the evil one, perpetually tries to destroy us. However, our Lord always gives us a New Life. I repented for my sin of false judgment against my father. My poor dad! I prayed to be freed from the curse that the fortune-teller uttered against me.

By the time I was sixteen, my mother had become more prayerful and joyful after her completion of a New Life in the Spirit seminar. One day, she invited me and my two brothers to attend a seminar. Little did I know that this was our loving Father's hand, rescuing me while I was a stray, lost sheep. I was skeptical about it in the beginning. But then, I changed my attitude because I sincerely wanted to learn about the Catholic faith and see if there was truth in it. During the eight-week seminar, the daily readings of scripture, personal prayer, teachings, and fellow attendees' intercessory prayers for me gradually opened my heart to His Grace. I learned later that the little prayers I offered in tears and supplications, our blessed Mother took to her Son. She is my powerful intercessor and loving mother. She is a true model of my faith.

So, what was the miracle I experienced? After I was baptized in the Holy Spirit during the seminar, the result was far beyond what I could have ever imagined. The Holy Spirit, the very Spirit that raised Jesus from death, whom I received through the Sacrament of Baptism and Confirmation, was released and alive in me. The baptism in the Holy Spirit helped me to be continually aware of the presence, power, and person of our Risen Christ. I wholeheartedly believe we all need it. As McDonnell and Montague explain in *Fanning the Flame*, "The new living water of the Spirit conforms the believer to Christ, producing holiness, a hunger for God, a search for God." They continue, "Accepting the baptism in the Spirit is not joining a movement, any movement. Rather, it is embracing the fullness of Christian initiation, which belongs to the church" (*Fanning the Flame*, p. 21).

I did not do anything to earn grace. It was given to me, although I did not deserve it. It was total grace, a free gift. It was like the kingdom of Heaven had come down upon me and penetrated this earthen vessel. God's supernatural power touched me and I was no longer the same. For the very first time, I experienced the Father's tremendous love for me. I did not know the Father loved me that much. "The love of God has been poured out in our hearts through the Holy Spirit who has been given to us." (Rom. 5:5) I had truly and personally encountered Jesus as my Lord and Savior, and it turned my life around. This was the miracle.

I was reborn with his new, resurrected Life. This conversion is a process. Because the Spirit of God was released in me, the Lord in his mercy and love healed me miraculously. Through his chosen holy servants, such as Father Xavier Bong Do Choi from Korea and Dr. Francis MacNutt, He healed this poor, broken soul—spiritually, emotionally, and physically. I am convinced that spiritual healing is the most important. Any medical and psychological treatments could not heal and change me as God did. Praise the Lord! God is alive! All the doubt and confusion disappeared. God is truly real! God is profoundly loving and He personally cares for me. I experienced a radical conversion of my soul. I began to establish a new relationship with God as my loving, compassionate Abba. Jesus is the way, truth, and life. This is an awesome truth that I want the whole world to know. The power of baptism in the Holy Spirit must be taught.

> Without the Holy Spirit, God is far away, Christ stays in the past, the Gospel is a dead letter, the church is simply an organization, authority a matter of domination, mission a matter of propaganda, the liturgy no more than an evocation, Christian living a slave morality.

> But in the Holy Spirit: the cosmos is resurrected and groans with the birth-pangs of the kingdom, the risen Christ is there, the Gospel is the power of life, the church shows forth life of the Trinity, authority is a liberating service, mission is a Pentecost, the liturgy is both memorial and anticipation, human action is deified. K. McDonnell and G. Montague, *Fanning the Flame*

Because of the tremendous miracle and healing grace I received, I had a burning desire to serve other people and help them experience the love of the Father, salvation of Jesus, and empowerment of the Holy Spirit. This led me to study psychology and become a psychologist. I felt God's strong calling when I read the Gospel of Isaiah: The Mission to the Afflicted. "The spirit of the Lord God is upon me, because the Lord has anointed me; He has sent me to bring glad tidings to the lowly, to heal the brokenhearted, to proclaim liberty to the captives and release to the prisoners, to announce a year of favor from the Lord" (Is. 61:1-2).

At a Charismatic Renewal Convention, I heard a prophecy given to the group: "As I have touched you, touch my people." I knew, deep in my spirit, that it was the Lord speaking to me. I sobbed and sobbed because His love was so overwhelming. I continued to embrace the words and to live out that calling. As I look back, I cannot adequately express my gratitude and love for what my loving Father had done for me. He delivered me from the power of darkness into His marvelous light, from death to life, from despair to hope, from self-hatred to self-acceptance, from bondage to freedom, healing, and joy.

I have now had the privilege of observing and working with many wounded and beautiful souls for over a decade. Inevitably, I encounter souls caught in spiritual warfare. I consider my degree not only an academic degree, but even more a spiritual one. Mother Nadine Brown from the Intercessors of the Lamb insightfully described the Ph.D. as Prophet, Healer, and Deliverer. I believe it is my calling to be just that. In the name of the Holy Trinity, I will continue to speak the word of God to raise his children with His truth; I will bring His healing love and power to those who are hurting and suffering; and I will deliver those who are in bondage. All is possible with God.

Stories of Healing

I would like to share some of my experiences in the healing prayer ministry. These stories were written in a simple way to highlight their themes, although healing is a continual process which goes through some layers of underlying issues. I use fictional names to protect confidentiality. My hope is for these stories to help readers realize and believe in the same Jesus who healed a multitude in His time. He can do even more for us because "Jesus is same as yesterday, today, and forever." (Heb.13:8) Let us ask God to give us the gift of faith, "even faith the size of a mustard seed which will move a mountain" (Lk. 17:6).

Self-identity: Who am I, Lord?

Judy was in her mid-twenties and came to see me for her depression. She had already been prescribed several antidepressants by her psychiatrist. She had just broken up with her fiancé of two years because she could not bear the severe physical violence anymore. She was obviously suffering from post-traumatic stress disorder. I learned that she was adopted as an infant from Asia, and that she had searched for her biological mother to no avail. During childhood, she had experienced a deep sense of abandonment by her adopted parents, who "never taught her anything." In college, she had given up on her Catholic faith because she believed God had also abandoned her. One day, in her depression, with tears streaming she lamented to me, "No one cares for me. I am nobody. I know who I am supposed to be, but I do not know who I am. Please help!" Right then and there, the Holy Spirit prompted me to show her some scriptures: "But Zion said, 'The Lord has forsaken me; my Lord has forgotten me. Can a mother forget her infant, be without tenderness for the child of her womb? Even should she forget, I will never forget you. See, upon the palms of my hands, I have written your name'" (Is. 49:14-16). These words were like a mirror to her, showing her who she is in the eyes of the Father. The shackle of sense of abandonment was loosened and she was able to see herself as a beautiful daughter of the heavenly Father. Her false-self had to be put to death and her true-self needed to come alive. I said to her, "This is your happiness: God is your loving Father and you are His precious, precious child." Her self-image was corrected and self-identity restored through the healing love of the Father. Now, she has returned to her faith and eagerly participates in Mass.

Prison of Inner Vows

Tall and single, Mike sought a prayer ministry for his ongoing relationship conflict. He had usually been able to form a close relationship with his girlfriends in the past, but his relationships always ended disastrously whenever the issue of marriage came up. He was discouraged and was even afraid of starting a new relationship. He had genuinely loved his girlfriends and could not figure out why he had no luck in relationships. I learned that he came from a violent and abusive family. His father was physically abusive to his mother and to his children, including himself. He remembered many nights when he was terrified and horrified by his father's rage and anger. When we explored his memories and feelings about his early experiences, we, in prayer, discovered that he had made inner vows to himself at the age of six. He said to himself, "If this is what it's like, I will never believe in marriage and family. I hate it." Inner vows are conscious and unconscious self-imposed judgments one makes in order to avoid painful situations. They have very powerful spiritual influences over one's life; they block the flow of life. When Mike was ready, I helped him to renounce his inner vows. I prayed with him: "Lord, in your name I take the sword of the spirit and cut him free from this false judgment of marriage and family. Let your holy will be done in his life." Mike felt incredible freedom and peace when he cast off his inner vows. He learned to appreciate and value marriage and family. He, now, searches for the Miss Right of his life.

The Danger of Unhealthy Soul Ties: Relationships

When a person has co-dependent relationships and connects with someone in unhealthy ways, it is spiritually and psychologically dangerous. Harmful relationships occur when a person over-identifies with someone. I often notice the role of harmful soul ties in 'grief work', unusual difficulty dealing with the death of a loved one, divorce, separation, and so forth. In these cases, the grief process extends unreasonably beyond what is normal. I worked with a ten-year-old girl who began to exhibit strange behavior after her grandfather's death. Her parents were very worried about her newly developed behavior, which included having an imaginary friend whom she talked to at night. The girl deeply loved her grandfather and sorely missed him. While I validated her pain, I prayed for her and helped her to understand about mourning and grief. I also asked her to stop conversing with her imaginary friend, who, she said, was consoling her. I sensed a spiritual tie that needed to be severed through prayer. I prayed, "In the name of Jesus Christ, I break the soul ties between her and her grandfather." (I did this three times to honor the Holy Trinity.) The girl immediately returned to her usual ways and stopped talking to the imaginary figure. She smiled more and was happy. Praise the Lord!

The Beauty of Surrender

"Father, into your hands I commend my spirit." (Lk. 23:46)

About four years ago, I began a large retirement plan. The plan sounded good but was very complicated. I thought about delaying it one more year since I did not thoroughly understand it. In the midst of my busy work schedule, the agents who were involved kept calling me repeatedly and encouraged me to begin the plan soon. In my hurried state, I said okay. That okay got me into more trouble than I had ever anticipated. It turned out that I lost all of my contributions. I consulted lawyers who concluded that I basically had no case and no chance to win. I knew I had made a huge mistake. I could not believe what I did, that I did not pray about this important decision. Normally, I try to listen and to be led by the Holy Spirit. I typically prayed about things, great and little, and asked my spiritual family for guidance. But what happened to me? I asked God to forgive my failure, ignorance and pride. When I had said okay, I was simply operating my life at a purely human level and I miserably failed to consult the Holy Spirit. With prayerful support from the Orange County Magnificat and Intercessors of the Lamb team, I peacefully let this case go. At least I had learned a great life lesson from this mistake. I forgave all who were involved and surrendered the experience to the Lord. I was freed from the situation and completely forgot about it.

Three years had gone by when, one day, I inadvertently found an advertisement from a newspaper sitting on my office table. (Did you know there is no such thing as an accident in a Christian's life?) The advertisement featured a lawyer who specialized in cases like the one of my lost retirement plan. When I contacted him, the lawyer was confident that I had a strong case and wanted to move forward with it. Having learned my lesson, this time I immediately prayed about it. I asked my spiritual family to pray with me. My group and my spiritual director prayerfully discerned the situation and felt a strong sense toward taking legal action. So I did, in obedience, without any attachment to it. It was all in God's hands.

As I write this, my attorney has just informed me that he settled the case in my favor. My settlement would be more than I asked for. When hearing this news, one of my holy and gracious friends said to me, "Our Lord wants to surprise us. So when you are surprised, you know it is the Lord." Praise the Lord for timing this so that I could include my testimony in this book! They say that surrender is the highest wisdom. We learn to surrender in all kinds of situations. We constantly surrender all to God, who indeed knows what He is doing. I surrender so I can be flexible to be led by the Holy Spirit. Thank you, Father, for your wisdom.

Psychology of an Intercessor

The Charism of Intercession describes intercessory prayer as "the prayer of Jesus. It is the 'now' prayer of Jesus. It is what He is doing now because Jesus is at the right hand of the Father, engaged 'in a more excellent ministry now' — that of intercession" (p. 48). It further states that "our power in intercession comes from our union with Jesus. We see, then, that intercession is directly primarily to the Father, in union with Jesus, and in the power of the Holy Spirit" (p. 49).

Intercessory prayers bridge God and a person. These prayers are for others, not for the self. Intercessors offer prayers to God for people, churches, nations, and the world; they pray for others and are invisible. Some people might mistake intercessors as co-dependent people who exist only for other people. Be careful. There are huge differences between the two. Co-dependent people are overly dependent on others. They are generally defined by others and are addicted to people. They *need* to be needed by others. Co-dependent people have a poor self-identity, low self-esteem, and shame about themselves. On the other hand, intercessors have a strong and healthy self-identity and joy about themselves. They have a personal and intimate relationship with God the Father. They know God is their loving Father. They know they are His little beloved children. This relationship is a foundation of who they are. As a follower of the Intercessor, Jesus, who gave His very life for the salvation of humankind, intercessors aspire to imitate Him in every way — even in sacrifice, suffering, and death. With the grace of God, "dying to self" then, becomes a reality because intercessors know to whom they are dying, and why. It is impossible to "die to self" without a healthy self-knowledge.

In psychology, many researchers have studied the stages of human development: cognitive, psycho-social, moral, and spiritual. Most theorists agree that as one becomes more mature, integrated, and authentic, the individual moves from self-centeredness (or ego-centric) to self-transcendent, becoming more inclusive and willing to give of the self for the common good. This parallels the psycho-spiritual development of an intercessor.

In closing, I would like to end with my prayer experiences. In my contemplative Eucharistic Adoration, the Good Shepherd helped me to learn about this truth. When I was infirm as a baby, my loving Father brought me in His Sprit to the foot of the cross of Calvary. He allowed me to participate in the suffering of Jesus for the salvation of souls when I was not even consciously aware of it. He used my suffering to be redemptive for me and for others. I see now that I was invited to be an intercessor from the early part of my life. How I am blessed and privileged! My cross is my victory. I am an intercessor praying for the salvation of souls. Lord Jesus, increase within us our fervent zeal for the souls. Rekindle in us fire of your love. Change us into fire!

"Body of Christ"

O sweet Body of Christ
The bond of human race
Your sacrifice of praise
Our sacrament of grace
O precious Blood of Christ
Holy cup of blessings
Your wine of thanksgiving
Our fountain of healings
O glorious Soul of Christ
Living manna of creation
Your instrument of redemption
Our source of reconciliation
O wondrous Spirit of Christ
Sublime banquet of unity
Exchanging Your divinity
With our fallen humanity
O Eucharistic Heart of Christ
Prepare our hearts for Your callings
Purify our souls for Your comings
Sanctify our spirits for Your dwelling

(Poem-prayer from Intercessors of the Lamb, 2003)

Chapter 10

At the School of Mary, Woman of the Eucharist

Mother Mary in *Ecclesia de Eucharistia*

In *Ecclesia de Eucharistia*, John Paul II, writes:

53. If we wish to rediscover in all its richness the profound relationship between the Church and the Eucharist, we
cannot neglect Mary, Mother and model of the Church. In my
Apostolic Letter *Rosarium Virginis Mariae,* I pointed to the
Blessed Virgin Mary as our teacher in contemplating Christ's
face and among the mysteries of light included the Institution
of the Eucharist. Mary can guide us toward this holy sacrament, because she herself has a profound relationship with it.

At first glance, the Gospel is silent on this subject. The
account of the institution of the Eucharist on the night of Holy
Thursday makes no mention of Mary. Yet we know that she
was present among the apostles who prayed "with one accord"
(cf. Acts 1:14) *in the first community which gathered after the
Ascension in expectation of Pentecost.* Certainly Mary must
have been present at the Eucharistic celebrations of the first
generation of Christians, who were devoted to "the breaking
of the bread" (Acts 2:42).

But in addition to her sharing in the Eucharistic banquet,
an indirect picture of Mary's relationship with the Eucharist
can be had, beginning with her interior disposition. *Mary is*

a *"woman of the Eucharist" in her whole life*. The Church, which looks to Mary as a model, is also called to imitate her in her relationship with this most holy mystery.

May 31, 1996, I attended a Marian Conference at the *Domus Mariae* near the Vatican in Rome. In attendance were many bishops from around the world. Esteemed Marian theologians presented papers on Mary's Maternal Mediation. Mine was a privileged vantage point for a lay woman, very humbling. I listened attentively to Cardinals, bishops, and priests speak affectionately of Mary's role in the life of the Church. In this setting, I began to comprehend the beautiful reality of Mary as Mother of the Church. Here were her priest sons in the heart of the Church and they were imbued with Marian radiance, purity and goodness. They delighted in their Mother of Grace, and I believe Blessed Mother was delighting in her priests also! I thought to myself, they could not exhaust the subject of Mary, there is so much that could and should be said!

The highlight of each day was the celebration of the liturgy in the beautiful Chapel. After listening to lectures on the many faceted roles of Maternal Mediation, we gathered together to partake of the Supper of the Lamb. Mary, Mother of the Eucharist, was tangibly present for her children as the liturgy took place. With Mary as welcomed as she was among her priests, the receptivity to the Eucharist seemed enhanced for the assembly. Her maternal heart united us for the Lord's Banquet. Representatives from many nations came together like one family united in the love of Mary who pointed us to the Eucharist.

While everything was Christ centered, the lovely fragrance of maternal charity inebriated our hearts. Thus the Mother of the Eucharist prepared us to receive her Son with renewed ardor. Mary is present at the Mass to help magnify our "Amen" when we hear the words, The Body of Christ, just prior to consuming the Eucharistic Lord. Mary knows that we cannot love her Son as he deserves, that our hearts are incapable of receiving him with utmost recollection and reciprocal love. Mary helps us to receive Jesus into the depths of our heart and she aids us to receive the maximum benefit of each Holy Communion or Holy Hour.

54. *Mysterium fidei!* If the Eucharist is a mystery of faith which so greatly transcends our understanding as to call for

sheer abandonment to the word of God, then there can be no one like Mary to be our support and guide in acquiring this disposition. In repeating what Christ did at the Last Supper in obedience to his command: "Do this in memory of me!" We also accept Mary's invitation to obey him without hesitation, "Do whatever he tells you" (Jn. 2:5). With the same maternal concern which she showed at the wedding feast of Cana, Mary seems to say to us: "Do not waver; trust in the words of my Son. If he was able to change water into wine, he can also turn bread and wine into his body and blood, and through this mystery bestow on believers the living memorial of his Passover, thus becoming the "bread of life."

55. In a certain sense Mary lives her Eucharistic faith even before the institution of the Eucharist, by the very fact that she offered her virginal womb for the Incarnation of God's Word. The Eucharist, while commemorating the passion and resurrection, is also in continuity with the incarnation. At the Annunciation Mary conceived the Son of God in the physical reality of his body and blood, thus anticipating within herself what to some degree happens sacramentally in every believer, who receives, under the signs of bread and wine, the Lord's body and blood.

As a result, there is a profound analogy between the *Fiat* which Mary said in reply to the angel, and the *Amen* which every believer says when receiving the body of the Lord. Mary was asked to believe that the same Jesus Christ, Son of God and Son of Mary, becomes present in his full humanity and divinity under the signs of bread and wine (Lk. 1:30-35). In continuity with the Virgin's faith, in the Eucharistic mystery we are asked to believe the same Jesus Christ, Son of God and Son of Mary, becomes present in his full humanity and divinity under the signs of bread and wine.

"Blessed is she who believed" (Lk. 1:45). Mary also anticipated, in the mystery of the incarnation, the Church's Eucharistic faith. When, at the Visitation, she bore in her womb the

Word made flesh, she became in some way a "tabernacle"— the first "tabernacle" in history—in which the Son of God, still invisible to our human gaze, allowed himself to be adored by Elizabeth, radiating his light as it were through the eyes and the voice of Mary. And is not the enraptured gaze of Mary as she contemplated the face of the newborn Christ and cradled him in her arms that unparalleled model move love which should inspire us every time we receive Eucharistic communion?

58. In the Eucharist, the Church is completely united to Christ and his sacrifice, and makes her own the spirit of Mary. This truth can be understood more deeply by *re-reading the Magnificat* in a Eucharistic key. The Eucharist, like the Canticle of Mary is first and foremost praise and thanksgiving. When Mary exclaims: "My soul magnifies the Lord and my spirit rejoices in God my Savior," she already bears Jesus in her womb. She praises God "through" Jesus, but she also praised him "in" Jesus and "with" Jesus. This is itself the true "Eucharistic attitude."

At the same time Mary recalls the wonders worked by God in salvation history in fulfillment of the promise once made to the fathers (cf. Lk. 1:55), and proclaims the wonder that surpasses them all, the redemptive incarnation. Last, the *Magnificat* reflects the eschatological tension of the Eucharist. Every time the Son of God comes again to us in the "poverty" of the sacramental signs of bread and wine, the seeds of that new history wherein the mighty are "put down from their thrones" and "those of low degree are exalted" (cf. Lk. 1:52), take root in the world. Mary sings of the "new heavens" and the "new earth" which find in the Eucharist their anticipation and in some sense their program and plan. The *Magnificat* expresses Mary's spirituality, and there is nothing greater than this spirituality for helping us to experience the mystery of the Eucharist. The Eucharist has been given to us so that our life, like that of Mary, may become completely a *Magnificat!*

John Paul II, *Ecclesia de Eucharistia*

Mother Mary's Life is a
Model School of Eucharistic Piety

Immaculately conceived, she possesses the distinct grace to worship the Lord perfectly. Her whole life was a hymn of praise to God! This is the model for your life also. Everything you receive from living an intensely Eucharistic vocation is received through Mary's mediation because she is our Mother of Grace as God, himself, ordains. It is a grace to praise the Lord. We do not know how to pray; it is the Holy Spirit who prays through us. Mary, the pure spouse of the Holy Spirit, is the Mother of praise and worship. You have only to meditate on the sublimity of her *Magnificat* prayer to know that she is our Mother that teaches us how to thank God, and praise his Holy Name. She teaches us how to praise the Lord with exuberance too! Can you image our Jewish Mother praying the words of the *Magnificat* in Luke's Gospel, without tremendous jubilation!

Before each Holy Communion, invoke Mary's name to ready your house for her Son. In every holy hour implore her maternal company that you might assume her posture of humility before God. Be well aware of your poverty of spirit; your inability to worship or thank the Lord as He is worthy to be venerated. Then rely completely on Mary.

How often Mary has said that she holds many graces for God's people; graces that people do not accept so they fall at her feet. In many of her apparitions she tells us that grace is trampled upon every day! Expand your expectations of what the Lord can do for you through Mary! The saints teach that Jesus does not refuse his mother's request on behalf of her children.

The Power of Mother Mary's Intercession: Cana

Mary said, "Do whatever he tells you." She helps you to fulfill this teaching in a manner no other person can. Understand that Mary has singular distinctions before the Throne of God! Think of the biblical scene of the wedding feast at Cana. Mary asked Jesus for a miracle for this family and she knew it would come to pass. Otherwise, why would she tell the servers, "Do whatever he tells you?" (Jn. 2:3). She fully expected Jesus to work the miracle! Would the miracle at Cana, where Jesus changed water into the best wine, have happened without Mary's asking? I do not know. But she did ask. She thought to ask for the miracle that the hosts dared not to ask. Often it is like this with Mary. She thinks to ask God for things on your behalf. She asks for the miracle that you do not yet know that you need!

Cana is an example of Mary's intercession. While she was the mother of Jesus on earth, her life was a hidden life of self denial. Now she is associated with the resurrection power of Jesus and so she is God's mother in power. Maternal mediation is her power for intercession. In Heaven Mary's mediation is broader than when she was on earth. Truth has always taught that Mary obtains grace for the pilgrim people on earth according to the will of God.

The basis of your Eucharistic vocation is found in Mary's mission of obedient love which included the sword piercing her Immaculate Heart. She knew her Son's sacrifice would produce the greater fruit of redemption for his people. She knew that love would be costly. She willed to pay the price in obedient love of God. Mary's life reveals the principles of your Eucharistic vocation. Mary listened and heard God. Mary pondered everything she witnessed so her posture was contemplative receptivity. Mary obeyed the inspirations she heard and believed with surrendered abandonment to God. Mary was always present to the Eucharistic Heart of her Son. She tended to his Sacred Heart with perfect maternal solicitude. She desires to do this for you who are called to be transformed into Christ now.

By virtue of your consecration to the Immaculate Heart of Mary, everything you are, everything you do belongs to her: *Totus Tuus, Maria!* There can be no more perfect way to live an intensely Eucharistic life than to love the Lord Jesus through His mother's pure heart. "Behold your mother," Christ said to the beloved disciple John on Mount Calvary. Jesus does not ask John if he would behold his mother. He tells John to take her as his own mother. Jesus knows how much you need to take Mary into your heart; to enter into the security of maternal solicitude. How can you hope to be a pleasing servant of the Eucharist without consecrating yourself and goods, to the Mother of the Eucharist?

Mother Mary Crushes the Head of the Serpent

Sometimes it happens that when a servant of the Eucharist is participating at Mass or Holy Hour, there is intense spiritual warfare. Mary is there, giving us courage; helping to raise the sword of the spirit against the enemy's tactics. The closer a person draws to the Eucharistic Heart of Jesus, the more he becomes a threat to the kingdom of darkness and can be assailed with various temptations against prayer, against a life of virtue. It is written that the enemy prowls the earth like a lion seeking to devour the disciples of Christ. Mary is the *Woman Clothed in the Sun* and *Crowned with Twelve Stars* who crushes the head of the serpent. The Mother of the Eucharist is profoundly protective of her children and she defends us against the wiles of our enemy who seeks to prevent us from fulfilling our Eucharistic vocation.

5th century Byzantine Hymn on Mary, Invincible Wall of the Kingdom of God

While we sing to your Divine Child, O great Mother of God, we praise you as his living temple. The Lord who upholds the undersea came to dwell in your womb and sanctified and glorified you and taught everyone to cry out to you: Rejoice, tabernacle of the Word of God! Rejoice holiest of all the saints! Rejoice, golden Ark of the Covenant! Rejoice, treasury of Divine life! Rejoice precious diadem of Christian rulers! Rejoice, pride and joy of devout priests! Rejoice, impregnable rampart of the Church! Rejoice, invincible wall of the kingdom of God! Rejoice, giver of victory over evil! Rejoice, destroyer of all who attack us! Rejoice, healing of minds and bodies! Rejoice, salvation of souls! Rejoice, unwedded bride!

Prayer against Malefice from the Greek Ritual
(Invite Mary to pray this with you)

Kyrie Eleison. God, our Lord, King of ages, All-powerful and All-mighty, you who made everything and who transform everything simply by your will. You who in Babylon changed into dew flames of the "seven-times hotter" furnace and protected and saved the three holy children. You are the doctor and the physician of our soul. You are the salvation of those who turn against you. We beseech you to make powerless, banish, and drive out every diabolic power, presence, and machination; every evil influence, malefice, or evil eye and all evil actions aimed against your servant....where there is envy and malice, give us an abundance of goodness, endurance, victory, and charity. O Lord, you who love man, we beg you to reach out your powerful hands and your most high and mighty arms and come to our aid. Help us, who are made in your image; send the angels of peace over us, to protect us body and soul. Mary he keep at bay and vanquish every evil power, every poison or malice invoked against us by corrupt and envious people. Then, under the protection of your authority may we sing, in gratitude, "The Lord is my salvation; whom should I fear? I will not fear evil because you are with me, my God, my strength, my powerful Lord, Lord of peace, Father of all ages."

Fr. Gabriele Amorth, *An Exorcist Tells His Story*

When the evil one disturbs us in any way in prayer, turn to Mary. She will come to the aid of our prayer life. She desires that we pray and is always with us before the Blessed Sacrament. Blessed Mother is pleased to form us into something beautiful for her Son. I often perceive Mary leading me to prostrate myself before the King of Kings and the Lord of Lords! I am speaking here of being able to lay my heart down before the Risen Christ in complete vulnerability; no defenses, no hiding, no fear, no agenda, no desperation, no drama, only the truth! How is this transparency possible without the aid of the Immaculate Conception? I do not know how to imitate her humility before Christ. Therefore, I hide in the Immaculate Heart. Is this not his Living Tabernacle still?

How to Contemplate Jesus as Mary Does

If our life were not under Mary's protection, we might have doubts as to our perseverance and our salvation. Our vocation, which, in a special manner, binds us to the service of the King of kings, makes it a more pressing duty for us to have recourse to Mary. Jesus is the King in the Eucharist and he wishes only trained servitors in his court, only those who have served their apprenticeship. One must learn to serve before presenting oneself to the King! Therefore, Jesus left us his mother to be the mother and model of adorers.

According to general opinion, he left her some twenty years on the earth, that we might learn from her to adore him perfectly. What a beautiful life—those twenty years spent in adoration! When we reflect upon our Lord's love for the Blessed Mother, we are lost in wonder that he consented to separate from her. Was it that the Blessed Virgin was not yet perfect? Was it that she had not suffered enough, she who had endured on Calvary more than all other creatures combined? Ah, yes, she has indeed suffered! But the interests of the Eucharist called for her presence.

Jesus was not willing to remain alone in the Blessed Sacrament, without Mother's Presence. He was not willing that the first hours of Eucharistic adoration should be confided to poor adorers, who knew not how to adore worthily. The Apostles, obliged to labor for the salvation of souls, could not give sufficient time which would have chained them to the Tabernacle, their apostolic duties called them elsewhere. As for the newly made Christians, like unto children still in the cradle, a mother was needed to educate them, a model whom they could copy, and it was his Own Blessed Mother that Jesus left them as such.

All Mary's life, taken as a whole, may be summed up in this one word—adoration; for adoration is the perfect service of God, and it embraces all the duties of the creature toward the Creator.

It was Mary who first adored the Incarnate Word. He was in her womb, and no one on earth knew of it. Oh, how well as our Lord served in Mary's virginal womb! Never has he found a ciborium, a golden vase more precious or purer than was Mary's womb! Mary's adoration was more pleasing to Him than that of all the Angels.

The Lord "has set his tabernacle, in the sun," says the Psalmist. That sun is Mary's heart. At Bethlehem, Mary was the first to adore her Divine Son lying in a manger. She adored him with the perfect love of a Virgin Mother, the love of charity, as says the Holy Spirit. After Mary, St. Joseph, the shepherds, and then the Magi came to adore: but it was Mary who opened up that furrow of fire that was to spread over the world. And what beautiful things, what Divine things, Mary must have said!

Mary continued to adore our Lord: first in his hidden life at Nazareth; afterwards in his apostolic life; and, finally, on Calvary, where her adoration became intense suffering. Notice the nature of Mary's adoration. She adored the Lord according to the different states of His life; Jesus' state determined the character of her adoration.

Her adoration did not stay in a set groove. At one time, she adored God hidden in her womb; at another, as poor and lowly in Bethlehem; again, as laboring at Nazareth; and later on, as evangelizing the country and converting sinners. She adored him in his sufferings on Calvary by suffering with him. Her adoration was always in keeping with the sentiments of her Divine Son, which were clearly revealed to her. Her love brought her into perfect conformity of thought and life with him.

To you, adorers, we say: Always adore Jesus, but vary your adoration as the Blessed Virgin did hers. Recall to your mind all the mysteries of religion in connection with the Eucharist, so as to avoid routine. If your love is not nourished by a new form of devotion, a new thought, you will become stupid in prayer. We should for this reason commemorate all the mysteries of the Eucharist.

It was thus Mary prayed in the Cenacle. When the anniversaries of the great mysteries, wrought under her very eye, came round, it was impossible for us to think that she did not recall their circumstances—the words, the graces. When, for instance, Christmas came, can we imagine Mary's not reminding her son, now hidden under the Eucharistic Veil, of the love that greeted him at his birth, of her smiles, of her adoration and that of St Joseph, the shepherds, the Magi? She wished, thereby to rejoice in the Heart of Jesus by reminding him of her love; and so with all the other mysteries.

How, then, do we act with a friend? Do we always speak to them of the present? Certainly not! We recall past memories, we live them over again together. When we want to pay a compliment to a father and a mother recall their love, their unwearying devotedness, shown to us in our infancy. Similarly, Mary, during her adoration in the Cenacle, reminded Jesus of all that he had done for his Father's glory, in all the great sacrifices he had made, and in this she participated in the Eucharistic grace.

The Eucharist is the memorial of all the mysteries of religion; it renews their love and their grace. And so we must, like Mary, correspond to this grace by contemplating our Lord in all His actions, by adoring and uniting ourselves with Him in all the different states of his life.

The Eucharist had so powerful an attraction for the Blessed Virgin that she could not live away from It. She lived in It and by It. She passed her days and nights at the feet of her Divine Son. She did, indeed gratify the filial devotion of the Apostles and the Faithful who desired to see and converse with her, but her love for her hidden God shone in her countenance and communicated its ardor to all about her.

O Mary! Teach us the life of adoration! Teach us to see, as

thou didst, all the mysteries and all the graces in the Eucharist; to live over again the Gospel story and to read it in the light of the Eucharistic life of Jesus. Remember, O our Lady of the Most Blessed Sacrament that thou are the Mother of all adorers of the Holy Eucharist."

St. Peter Julian Eymard, *Our Lady of the Most Blessed Sacrament*

St. Eymard offers beautiful insight into adopting Mary's art of Eucharistic adoration. Mary's eyes were fixed on Christ always and everywhere. "She kept all these things, pondering them in her heart" (Lk. 2:19). She pondered Jesus in every memory of his life, death and resurrection. Such contemplation never ceased for Mary, even amidst her duties in the early Church. In fact, the prayer of the rosary is a memorial of the life of Jesus. This is why the rosary can be such a contemplative prayer of the heart. Each mystery of the rosary is a mystery of remembrance of what God does for his people. The memorial of the life of Christ should be the basis of Eucharistic adoration. We come into the Presence of the Living God with hearts full of gratitude for what he has done for us and for what he continues to do for us. The Gospels too are an account of his life and they constitute the Living Word, the same yesterday, today and always. This Living Word is always pertinent to our life in the present tense. Like Mary, we ponder different memories of the Lord's life. To ponder the life of Christ is inexhaustible food for thought; source of blessing!

Your Father in Heaven has special graces ordained for you alone. If these graces are not to fall fallow around your feet, draw close to Mary to receive them all. She will help you receive the fullness of grace that God desires to grant you. Though your heart is a small vessel of love, hers is a large vessel of love. Ask her to grant you her Immaculate Heart to capture all the grace God wants to give you! Your Eucharistic vocation is a noble calling that Mary helps you to fulfill. *Ave Maria!*

Why Pray?

We must "always pray and not lose heart." We pray first of all because we are believers. We are, however, Christians, and so we must pray as Christians. The greatest prayer is the Holy Mass because Jesus Himself is fully present. We must continue to pray because we are frail and full of guilt. Prayer gives us the strength for grand ideals, the strength to maintain our faith, charity, purity, generosity; Prayer gives us the courage to emerge from the indifference and sin, if, unfortunately, we have yielded to temptation and weakness. Prayer gives us light by which to see and to consider the events of our own life and of history itself in the salvific perspective of God and eternity. Therefore, do not stop praying! Do not let a day pass without a praying a little! Prayer is a duty, but it is also a great joy because it is a dialogue with God through Jesus Christ.

John Paul II

Our Lady of the Cenacle

Let us follow our Mother to the Cenacle and listen to the lessons that she there teaches us, lessons that she has received from her Divine Son, with whom she conversed day and night. She is the faithful echo of his heart and his love. Let us love Mary tenderly; let us labor under her maternal eye, and pray by her side. Let us be her truly devoted children, for by so doing, we shall honor Jesus who has given her to us for our Mother, that she may teach us how to love him by the example of her own life.

Place yourself, then, under Mary's direction; think her thoughts, speak her words of love, imitate her manners, perform her actions, share her sufferings, and all in her will speak to you of Jesus, of his highest service, of God's greatest glory.

Honor Mary at the foot of the Tabernacle, all the mysteries of her life, for all these were stations, as it were, leading to the Cenacle. In Mary's life there you will find the model and consolation of your own life. In the Cenacle this August Queen kneels as adoratrix and servant of the Most Blessed Sacrament; kneel at your Mother's side and pray with her, and in so doing, you will continue her Eucharistic life on earth.

When you receive Holy Communion, clothe yourself with the virtues and merits of Mary, your mother, and you will thus communicate with her faith and with her devotion. O how happy Jesus will be to find in you the image of his loveable and holy Mother!

St. Peter Eymard, *Our Lady of the Blessed Sacrament*

Chapter 11

The Upper Room:
Place of Eucharist,
Priesthood and Pentecost

The John Paul II, *Ecclesia de Eucharistia*
begins with the following statements:

In a variety of ways, she (Church) joyfully experiences the constant fulfillment of the promise, "Lo, I am with you always, to the close of the age" (Mt. 28:20), but in the Holy Eucharist, through the changing of bread and wine into the body and blood of the Lord, she rejoices in this presence with unique intensity. Ever since Pentecost, when the Church, the People of the New Covenant, began her pilgrim journey toward her heavenly homeland, the Divine Sacrament has continued to mark the passing of her days, filling them with confident hope. (Paragraph 1)

During the Great Jubilee of the Year 2000 I had an opportunity to celebrate the Eucharist in the Cenacle of Jerusalem where, according to tradition, it was first celebrated by Jesus himself, *The Upper Room was where this most holy Sacrament was instituted.* I am grateful to the Lord Jesus for allowing me to repeat in that same place, in obedience to his command: "Do this in memory of me" (Lk. 22:19), the words which he spoke two thousand years ago. (Paragraph 2)

By the gift of the Holy Spirit at Pentecost the Church was born and set out upon the pathways of the world, yet a decisive moment in her taking shape was certainly the institution of the Eucharist in the Upper Room.

Her foundation and wellspring is the whole *Triduum paschale*, but this is as it were gathered up, foreshadowed and "concentrated" forever in the gift of the Eucharist. The thought of this leads us to profound amazement and gratitude. This amazement should always fill the Church assembled for the celebration of the Eucharist. (Paragraph 5)

Through our communion in his body and blood, Christ also grants us his Spirit. Saint Ephrem writes: "He called the bread his living body and he filled it with himself and his Spirit...He who eats it with faith, eats Fire and Spirit...Take and eat this, all of you, and eat with it the Holy Spirit. For it is truly my body and whoever eats it will have eternal life." The Church implores this divine Gift, the source of every other gift, in the Eucharistic epiclesis. In the *Divine Liturgy* if Saint John Chrysostom, for example, we find the prayer: "We beseech, implore and beg you: send your Holy Spirit upon us all and upon these gifts...that those who partake of them may be purified in soul, receive the forgiveness of sins, and share in the Holy Spirit." By the gift of his body and blood Christ increases within us the gift of his Spirit, already poured out in Baptism and bestowed as a "seal" in the sacrament of Confirmation. (Paragraph 17)

John Paul II, *Ecclesia de Eucharistia*

Since the Spirit is our life, let us be led by the Spirit! (Gal. 5:25)

In the Upper Room, on the night before he died, Jesus instituted the sacrament of his body and blood and the sacrament of ministerial priesthood. Fifty days after his resurrection, the birthday of the Church occurs: Pentecost, the descent of the Holy Spirit, takes place as Jesus promised. One Upper Room, three crucial, complimentary initiatives: Eucharist, Priesthood and Pentecost.

When the day of Pentecost came, they were all together in one place. Suddenly a sound like the blowing of a violent wind came from Heaven and filled the whole house where they were sitting. They saw what seemed to be tongues of fire that separated and came to rest on each of them. All of them were filled with the Holy Spirit and began to speak in other languages as the Spirit enabled them. (Acts 2:1-4)

A Eucharistic vocation can only be realized by the dynamism of the Holy Spirit. At baptism you receive the Holy Spirit and come into the state of sanctifying grace. You became gifted with the indwelling Trinity! "Do you not know you are temples of the Holy Spirit and that God dwells in you?" (1 Cor. 3:16). The sacrament of confirmation strengthens you in the Holy Spirit. "It is God who makes us stand firm in Christ. He anointed us, set his seal of ownership on us, and put his Spirit in our hearts as a deposit, guaranteeing what is to come" (2 Cor. 1:21).

Relationship of Rekindling Eucharistic Amazement to Renewal in the Spirit

What is the relationship between rekindling Eucharistic amazement and the grace of renewal in the Spirit? The answer to the question lies in the program John Paul II outlined in *Ecclesia de Eucharistia*, which states, "At the dawn of this third millennium, we, the children of the Church, are called to undertake with renewed enthusiasm the journey of Christian living. ...The program already exists: it is the plan found in the Gospel and in the living Tradition; it is the same as ever. Ultimately, it has its center in Christ himself, who is to be known, loved and imitated, so that in him we may live the life of the Trinity, and with him transform history until its fulfillment in the heavenly Jerusalem. The implementation of this program of a renewed impetus in the Christian passes through the Eucharist."

Look closely at John Paul II's choice of words:

- Renewed enthusiasm about the journey of Christian living
- Renewed impetus in the Christian (personal)
- Rediscovery of the Gospel and living Tradition
- Christ-centered: Proclaiming Jesus is Lord
  (personal and ecclesial)
- Make Christ known, loved and imitated
- Live the life of the Trinity:
  Trinitarian relationship, spirituality
- Transform history until its fulfillment in the heavenly
  Jerusalem.
- Passes through the Eucharist

The phrase "renewed impetus in the Christian" reminds us of what took place in the Upper Room at Pentecost. The Holy Spirit descended with momentum to thrust the Christian community into its mission to transform history.

The phrase, "passes through the Eucharist" also takes us to the Upper Room at the institution of the Sacrament of his Body and Blood. The rekindling of Eucharistic amazement seems to indicate a return to the Upper Room does it not? Everything that was initiated in the Upper Room points the way to:

- Make Christ known (evangelization, testimony)
- Make Christ loved (Eucharistic worship)
- Make Christ imitated (Eucharistic vocation)

He also uses the phrase, "Live the life of the Trinity." How do you intend to do this? At baptism you received the indwelt Trinity. To live the life of the Trinity then has to do with living fully your Sacrament of Baptism. Rediscover your baptismal inheritance! Fan it into flame! We have yet to draw fully from the inexhaustible grace of our Sacramental Baptism. Pray for the grace of the Renewal in the Spirit as a start. This grace will empower your life so you can make Christ known, make Christ loved, and imitate Christ with even greater courage, wisdom and enthusiasm! Let us return to the Upper Room and receive the fullness of the empowerment of the Spirit given the first Apostles gathered in prayer around the Mother of God.

> The gift of the Holy Spirit makes us capable of practicing prayer continually. When the Holy Spirit has established his temple in a person, that person cannot but pray without ceasing. Whether walking or sleeping, prayer does not fade from this soul.
>
> Isaac of Nineveh, *Philokalia*

Renewal in the Spirit for our Eucharistic Vocation

According to Fr. Raniero Cantalamessa, OFM, Cap., Preacher to the Papal Household, what does this term mean for the Church?

The expression *renewal in the Spirit* has two biblical equivalents in the New Testament. To understand the soul of the charismatic movement, its profound inspiration, we must primarily search the Scripture. We need to discover the exact meaning of this phrase that is used to describe the experience of the renewal.

The first text is in Ephesians 4:23-24: "Be renewed in the spirit of your minds and ...clothe yourselves with the new self." Here the word *spirit* is written with a small s, and rightly so, because it indicates *our* spirit, the most intimate part of us (the spirit of our minds), which Scripture generally calls the heart. The word *spirit* here indicates that part of ourselves that needs to be renewed in order for us to resemble Christ, the New Man *par excellence*. "Renewing ourselves" means striving to have the same attitude that Christ Jesus had (see Phil. 2:5), striving for a new heart.

This text clarifies the meaning and the aim of our experience. The renewal should be, above all, an interior one, one of the heart. After the Second Vatican Council, many things were renewed in the Church: liturgy, pastoral care, the *Code of Canon Law* and religious constitutions and attire. Despite their importance, these things are only the antecedents of true renewal. It would be tragic to stop at these things and to think that the whole task has been completed.

What matters to God is people, not structures. It is souls that make the Church beautiful, and there she must adorn herself with souls. God is concerned about the hearts of His people, the love of His people and everything else is meant to function as a support to that priority.

Our first text is not enough, however, to explain the phrase *renewal in the Spirit*. It highlights our obligation to renew ourselves as well as what must be renewed (the heart), but it doesn't tell us the "how" of renewal. What good is it to tell us we must renew ourselves if we are not also told how to renew ourselves? We need to know the true author and protagonist of the renewal.

Our second biblical text, from Titus, addresses that precise issue. It says that God "saved us, not because of any works of righteousness that we had done, but according to his mercy, through the water of rebirth and renewal by the Holy Spirit". (Titus 3:5)

Here *Spirit* has a capital S because it points to the Spirit of God, the Holy Spirit. The preposition "by" points to the instrument, the agent. Then name we give our experience signifies, then something very exact: renewal by the work of the Holy Spirit, a renewal in which God, not man, is the principal author, the protagonist. "I (not you)" says God, "am making all things new" (Rev. 21:5); "My Spirit and only He) can renew the face of the earth" (see Ps. 104:30).

...The Word of God declares, "We need to give the power back to God" (see Ps. 68:35) because the "power belongs to God" (Ps. 62:11). That is a trumpet call! For too long we have usurped God's power, managing it as though it were ours, acting as though it were up to us to govern the power of God.

...The Bible often repeats the command of God, "You shall be holy, for I the Lord your God am holy!" (Lev. 19:2, see Lev. 11:44; Pt. 1:15-16). But in one place in that very same book of Leviticus, we find a statement that explains all the others, "I am the Lord; I sanctify you!" (Lev. 20:8). I am the Lord who wants to renew you with My Spirit! Let yourselves be renewed in My Spirit!

Fr. Raniero Cantalamessa, OFM, Cap., *Sober Intoxication of the Spirit*

The Outpouring or baptism in the Spirit

This outpouring is not a sacrament, but its name implies a connection to a sacrament and even more than one: the sacraments of Christian initiation. The outpouring actualizes or, in other words, renews the Christian initiations. The fundamental connection, however, is with the sacrament of baptism.

The term "baptism in the Spirit" indicates that there is something here that is basic to baptism. We say that the outpouring of the Spirit actualized and revives our baptism. To understand how a sacrament received so many years ago and usually administered in infancy can suddenly come alive and be revived and release such energy as we see on the occasions of outpourings, we must recall some aspects of sacramental theology.

Catholic theology can help us understand how a sacrament can be valid and legal but "unreleased". A sacrament is called "unreleased" if its fruit remains bound, or unused, because of the absence of certain conditions that further its efficacy. One extreme example would be the sacrament of marriage or holy orders received while a person is in the state of mortal sin. In those cases, such sacraments cannot confer any grace on the person. If, however, the obstacle of sin is removed by repentance, the sacrament is said to revive due to the faithfulness and irrevocability of the gift of God. God remains faithful even when we are unfaithful, because He cannot deny Himself (see Tim. 2:13).

In the case of baptism, what is it that causes the fruit of this sacrament to be held back? Here we need to recall the classical doctrine about sacraments. Sacraments are not magic rites that act mechanically, without people's knowledge or collaboration. There efficacy is the result of a synergy, or collaboration, between divine omnipotence (that is, the grace of Christ and of the Holy Spirit) and free will. As St. Augustine said, "He who created you without your consent will not save you without your consent." To put it more precisely, the fruit of the sacrament depends wholly on divine grace: however, this divine grace does not act without the "yes"—the consent and affirmation—of the person. This consent is more of a *conditio sine qua non* than a cause in its own right. God acts like the bridegroom, who does not impose his love by force but awaits the free consent of his bride.

Fr. Raniero Cantalamessa, OFM, Cap., *Sober Intoxication of the Spirit*

Jesus, "the One Who baptizes in the Holy Spirit"

The outpouring of the Holy Spirit is not the only occasion in the Church for this renewal of the sacraments of initiation and, in particular, of the coming of the Holy Spirit at baptism. Other occasions include the renewal of baptismal vows during

Easter vigils; spiritual exercises; the profession of vows, and on a sacramental level, confirmation.

It is not difficult, then, to find the presence of spontaneous outpouring in the lives of the saints, especially on the occasion of their conversion. Although I said the outpouring of the Spirit is not the only time of renewal of baptismal grace, it holds a very special please because it is open to all of God's people, big and small, and not just to certain privileged people who do the Ignatian spiritual exercises or take religious vows. Where does the extraordinary power that we have experienced come from? We are not, in fact, speaking about a theory but about something that we ourselves have experienced. We can also say, with Saint John, "What we have heard, and what we have seen with our...eyes and touched with our own hands... we declare to you...so that you may also fellowship with us. (1 Jn. 1:1-3). The explanation of this power lies in God's will. It has pleased Him to renew the Church of our day by this means, and this is all there is to it!

There are certainly some biblical precedents for this outpouring, like one narrated in Acts 8:14-17. Peter and John, knowing that the Samaritans has heard the Word of God, came to them, prayed for them and laid hands on them to receive the Holy Spirit. But the text we need to begin with to understand something about this baptism in the Spirit is primarily John 1:32-33:

> And John (the Baptist) testified, "I saw the Spirit descending from heaven like a dove, and it remained on him. I myself did not know him, but the one who sent me to baptize with water said to me, "He on whom you see the Spirit descend and remain is the one who baptizes with the Holy Spirit."

What does it mean that Jesus is "the one who baptizes in the Holy Spirit"? The phrase serves not only to distinguish the baptism of Jesus from that of John, who baptized only with water, but to distinguish the whole person and work of Christ from His precursor's. In other words, in all His works, Jesus is the one who baptizes in the Holy Spirit. "To baptize" has a metaphoric significance here: It means "to flood, to bathe completely and to submerge," just as water does with bodies. Jesus "baptizes in the Holy Spirit" in the sense that he "gives the Spirit without measure" (see Jn. 3:34), that He has "poured out" His Spirit (see Acts 2:33) on all the redeemed humanity. The phrase refers to the event of Pentecost more that to the sacrament of baptism, as one can deduce from the passage in Acts: "John baptized with water, but you will be baptized with the Holy Spirit not many days from now" (Acts 1:5).

The expression "to baptize in the Holy Spirit" defines, then, the essential work of Christ, which already in the messianic prophecies of the Old Testament appeared oriented to regenerating humanity by means of a great outpouring of the Holy Spirit (see Joel 2:28-29). Applying all this to the life and history of the Church, we must conclude that the resurrected Jesus baptized in the Holy Spirit not only in the sacrament of baptism but in different ways and at different times as well: in the Eucharist, in the hearing of the Word of God, in all other "means of grace".

The baptism in the Spirit is one of the ways that the resurrected Jesus continues His essential work of "baptizing in the Spirit". For this reason, even though we can explain this grace in reference to baptism and Christian initiation, we need to avoid becoming rigid about this point of view. It is not only baptism that revives the grace of initiation, but also confirmation, first Communion, the ordination of priests and bishops, religious vows, marriage—all the graces and charisms. This is truly the grace of a new Pentecost.

Fr. Raniero Cantalamessa, OFM, Cap., *Sober Intoxication of the Spirit*

My Personal Experience of the Outpouring of the Spirit

In 1991, a member of the prayer group invited me to attend the SCRC convention. I did not know that SCRC meant Southern California Renewal Communities. I was not familiar with charismatic spirituality. Fr. Faricy was leading the assembly in a prayer for the outpouring of the Spirit and the charism of praying in tongues. My main concern was to determine if this experience was in accord with the Church. The program stated that Fr. Robert Faricy, S.J. is Catholic priest and emeritus professor of Spiritual Theology at the Pontifical Gregorian University in Rome, Italy. I followed Fr. Faricy's instructions and surrendered to the Lord. I did not expect much.

Suddenly I experienced a new prayer language that flowed effortlessly. This charism is simply called praying in tongues. The Spirit was initiating the prayer which filled me with ardor for God. Since that day, I continue to pray in this manner and it enhances my spiritual life, especially for praise and for intercessory prayer. I am very grateful to the Lord for blessing me with this useful prayer language. It is incredibly valuable for praying with people at weekly cenacles. It is also a contemplative prayer. Are you skeptical? It might be helpful to consider what the Saints have said about the charism of praying in tongues as presented in the Magnificat *Life in the Spirit Seminar* Handbook.

St. Paul: I give thanks to God that I speak in tongues more than any of you (1 Cor. 14:18). The Spirit too helps us in our weakness, for we do not know how to pray as we ought; but the Spirit himself makes intercession for us with groanings that cannot be expressed in speech. He who searches hearts knows what the Spirit means, for the Spirit intercedes for the saints of God as He himself wills (Rom. 8:26-27)

St. Augustine: This is the way of singing God gives you; do not search for words. You cannot express in words the sentiments that please God—so praise him with your jubilant singing.

Teresa of Avila: Our Lord gives the soul feelings of jubilation and a strange prayer it doesn't understand. I am writing about this favor here so that if he grants it to you, you may give him such praise and know what is taking place. It is my opinion, a deep union of the faculties, but our Lord nonetheless leaves them free that they might enjoy this joy—and the same goes for the senses—without understanding what it is they are enjoying. It seems like gibberish, and certainly the experience is like that, for it is a joy so excessive that the soul wouldn't want to enjoy it alone but wants to tell everybody about it so they might help this soul praise our Lord...I know a saint named Friar Peter of Alcantara—for I believe from the way he lived that he was—one who did this very thing; and those who at one time listened to him thought he was crazy.

Oh what blessedness sisters! If only God would give it to us all! And what a favor he has granted you by bringing you to this house, where, when the Lord gives you this favor and you tell others about it, you will receive help rather than the criticism you would receive in the world.

St. Teresa of Avila, *The Sixth Dwelling Place*

Thereafter, I noticed a consistent change in my spiritual life. My faith in Christ became livelier. My heart was shifting to a mode of receptivity in which I felt the dynamism of the Spirit's activity awakening faith, hope and love. I experienced Christ personally and intimately. It was as if a veil lifted so the things of God became clear and attractive. Pentecost became personal. Some of the initial and continuing effects of my experience of the Outpouring of the Spirit include the following:

- The Holy Spirit animated my life to proclaim "Jesus is Lord!"

- I experienced a strong attraction to prayer. It became a priority of life.

- The Word of God became alive in a personal way.

- I had a strong attraction to read the lives of the Saints. The call to sanctity beckoned.

- My former fascination with material things began to fade away.

- I desired the virtues and became sensitive to sin, confessing more often.

- I received the grace of contemplative prayer before the Blessed Sacrament.

- Charisms of prophecy, word of knowledge, intercessory prayer and counsel were deepened.

- Joy! Praise! These two welled up from within.

Empowerment of the Holy Spirit continues to grow in my life. This has been one of the most profound, lasting spiritual graces of my life. How do you receive the grace of renewal in the Holy Spirit? Ask! Seek! Knock!

At the end of this chapter I give an example of a prayer imploring God for the grace of Renewal of Baptism in the Spirit. Ideally you should prepare by taking a "Life in the Spirit" seminar. This will provide good formation on the history and theology behind the experience and teach prudent use of charisms you may receive. Ideally you would take this seminar with community. After my initial experience, I took a Life in the Spirit Seminar. Through Magnificat and Intercessors of the Lamb, we facilitate Life in the Spirit Seminars and many people are receiving the outpouring of the Spirit to renew their discipleship.

Personal Testimony of
Fr. Raniero Cantalamessa, O.F.M., Cap.

I had the privilege of hearing Fr. Cantalamessa give his personal witness to the grace of the outpouring of the Spirit for his priesthood at the local SCRC conference. We were all edified by his story.

The principal instrument by which the renewal in the Spirit "changes people's lives" is the baptism in the Spirit. This is a rite that occurs with gestures of great simplicity, in peace and joy, accompanied by an attitude of humility, repentance and openness to being children to enter the kingdom. It is a kind of *epiclesis* - that is, an invocation of the Spirit upon a member of the body of Christ. It recalls the invocation, in the Mass after the Consecration, for the Spirit to come upon the assembly of the faithful and make them "a living sacrifice of praise." It is a renewal and an actualization of the whole Christian initiative and not only of baptism. This baptism in the Holy Spirit has come forth in a simple and powerful way to renew the lives of millions of believers in almost all of the Christian churches. We should think very carefully, then, before saying that this is not for us or before automatically dismissing it if the Lord offers us an opportunity to receive it.

I was on the verge of doing that myself, so I want to share my personal experience even if it costs me a great deal. It may be that my difficulties are like those of many other priests and theologians and therefore could help someone else not to succumb to the same danger. It would seem to me a lack of gratitude to God if I were silent about the whole experience which has changed the course of my life. I have even thought that Providence might have placed me in my particular role precisely so that I could humbly testify in the heart of the Church about the rumblings of Pentecost, which in various forms are going through the body of Christ and which constitute a great sign of hope in the midst of all the trials that the Church must still go through in our day.

Another objection I had: "But I am a priest, ordained by a bishop; I have received the Holy Spirit. What else should I still receive, and from lay people, no less?" This time the answer came to me from my own theology. I imagined what Jesus would have answered: "And I, then? Wasn't I sanctified by the Father and sent into the world? Wasn't I full of the Spirit from the moment of my conception in Mary, my mother? And yet I went to the Jordan to be baptized by John the Baptist, who was just a layman!" This is what led me to receive the prayer for a "new outpouring of the Spirit." I received it as a conscious renewal of my baptism, as a definitive first-person affirmation of the "Yes!" and "I believe!" that others had said in my stead at the moment of baptism. It was like surrendering the reins of my life to Christ.

Fr. Raniero Cantalamessa, O.F.M., Cap.,
The Sober Intoxication of the Spirit

Pentecost Events in Rome, 1998 and 2006

An intensely Eucharistic life is animated by the outpouring of the Spirit. The Holy Spirit empowers you to praise and thank the Lord in his Eucharistic Presence. He makes the Mass come alive, draws you into the sacred mysteries and causes the grace of Eucharist to become fruitful in you.

I was privileged to visit Rome during the three years leading up to the Jubilee Celebration. In 1998, John Paul II called all the ecclesial movements of the Church from around the globe to come to Rome in the Year of the Holy Spirit to celebrate Pentecost. The memory of this grand celebration in St. Peter's square with over 500,000 people from every continent still impacts my spiritual life. The Pentecost events in Rome were the liveliest expressions of Catholicism I ever witnessed. American praise bands led the assembly. The Holy Father encouraged us to be fully charismatic to compliment the institutional Church.

Consistent with his predecessor, Pope Benedict XVI also called the ecclesial movements back to Rome for Pentecost events in St. Peter's Square in 2006. Marilyn Quirk, Magnificat founder, could not attend and asked me to represent the ministry of Magnificat at the Pentecost Events. Patti Mansfield, another mother of Magnificat, personally addressed the Holy Father, beautifully sharing her testimony about the Outpouring of the Holy Spirit, and offering gratitude and obedience to the Pope.

Following the Pentecost events in Rome, I attended the ICCRS (International Catholic Charismatic Renewal Services) Conference in Fuiggi, Italy. We were blessed to have with us, Archbishop Stanislaw Rylko, Secretary of the Pontifical Council for the Laity, as well as Fr. Raniero Cantalamessa, O.F.M., Cap, Preacher to the Papal Household. There were many bishops present from different countries. Fr. Raniero Cantalamessa gave his personal testimony about his receiving the grace of renewal of baptism in the Holy Spirit. Father preached on the fruitfulness of the Catholic Charismatic Renewal and also of challenges and misconceptions. He exhorted us to desire the charisms to build up the Church, to respond to the call to holiness and the prophetic mission of the Church in the world. For one week in Fuiggi, representatives from many nations came together to proclaim the marvelous deeds that the Lord is doing in the charismatic lung of the Church. I am very grateful for the opportunity to participate in the events in Rome and Fuiggi, for a variety of reasons, especially that the experience washed away any doubt I had about its Catholicity.

The events revolved around the Eucharist. We heard a clarion call to holiness, personal and ecclesial. We heard the call to offer our lives as a "sacrifice of praise" to God. Accountability and obedience to the Church was stressed. Jubilation penetrated the Pentecost events in Rome with John Paul II, and later with Pope Benedict XVI. Thousands of young people were a part of the events. It is true that when the beauty of the Church manifests in all its solemn liveliness, it attracts young people and fills them up with the good things of God.

Cardinal Ratzinger on the
New Outpourings of the Spirit

For the sake of priests and lay people not familiar with the "Renewal of Baptism in the Holy Spirit", I quote Pope Benedict XVI as Joseph Cardinal Ratzinger, in dialogue with Stanislaw Rylko, Secretary of the Pontifical Council for the Laity, who said the following:

I am glad that the meeting with the (ecclesial) movements last year is now being followed up by a meeting of bishops, because, as I wanted to demonstrate among other things in my address last year, the pastors of the Church are the ones who must guarantee the ecclesial character of the movements. The pastors are not just persons who hold a certain office. They themselves are charismatics; they are responsible for keeping the Church open to the action of the Holy Spirit. We bishops are anointed by the Holy Spirit in the sacrament, and hence the sacrament also guarantees us this openness to the gifts of the Holy Spirit.

To reply to your questions: I think that it was around the mid-sixties that I had my first encounters with the movements that sprang up in the Church after the Council. Three in particular, I was able to get to know then. Perhaps my first encounter was the one I had with the Neocatechumenal Way....

I then came into contact also with the reality of the Charismatic Renewal. In those years I had close contacts with a professor in Paderborn, Heribert Muhlen, who was a great enthusiast of this movement, since he himself had rediscovered the joy of priesthood in it. Thus I had the joy and the grace, I would say, of seeing young Christians touched by the power of the Holy Spirit, of seeing that in a troublesome time for the Church, at a moment when people were speaking of a "winter in the Church," the Holy Spirit was creating a new spring - reawakened in young people, the joy of being Catholic, of living in the Church, the living Body of Christ, the people of God on pilgrimage.

For me this was truly encouraging, because I had two very negative experiences to contrast with it. On the one hand, I saw an academic world that was increasingly losing its enthusiasm for the faith. Anxious to conform themselves completely to the other university disciples, theologians no longer dared to profess the faith openly as the motivating force of their theological work. Instead, they wanted to prove that they were scholars through and through, and so theology became permeated with coldness, a detachment, that seemed to me worrisome and whose effects are still visible. The other negative experience was the growing bureaucratization of the Church in my country. The money that the Church in Germany had at its disposal, in abundance I would say, can undoubtedly be of great help, (for example, in the works of charity). It is not only a help however, it may also become a hindrance that makes the Church materialistic and generates bureaucracies that somehow manage nothing but themselves, becoming something of an end in themselves.

Seeing these two dangers of the Church - a theology that was no longer the attainment of reasonableness by faith but rather oppression of faith by a truncated reason, and bureaucratization, which no longer serves to open doors to the faith, but becomes self-enclosed - at a time when these two factors were all too evident, I really welcomed the newness of the movements as a gesture of God's benevolence: I saw that the Council was bearing fruit, the Lord was present in the Church. I saw that, whereas all our efforts, however well intentioned, both in the theological faculties and in the church bureaucracies, were not bearing fruit but, on the contrary, were becoming counterproductive, the Lord was finding the doors and throwing them wide open for his presence in situations where the sole resources were those of faith and grace.

Cardinal Ratzinger, *New Outpourings of the Spirit*

The Catholic Charismatic Renewal is, for the sake of order, placed in the category of ecclesial movements in the Church. However, it is not a movement, as others are, in that it has no founder, and its beginning is at Pentecost. The grace called, Renewal of Baptism in the Spirit, is however, not captive to any particular movement; rather it is meant for all baptized believers.

My vantage point has been that of a Marian charismatic since my service has been in the area of Magnificat, A Ministry to Catholic Women. Recently, our Magnificat Service Team and Intercessors of the Lamb team, together with several priests, led a Diocesan Life in the Spirit Seminar for 120 people. When the time came to pray for everyone to receive a fresh outpouring of the Spirit, Auxiliary Bishop Dominic Luong, prayed over two hundred people in attendance! The Chapel became an Upper Room. And the people of God became empowered with charisms for service in the body of Christ. The nine classical charismatic gifts given to build others up include: word of wisdom, word of knowledge, charismatic faith, gift of healing, working of Miracles, prophecy, the discernment of spirits, tongues and interpretation and love or charity (1 Cor. 12:4-13).

Prayer for the Outpouring of the Spirit

It is advisable that you seek this grace in the context of a Life in the Spirit Seminar and/or a Catholic charismatic conference or prayer meeting. The prayers below are an example of the prayers offered on your behalf at such gatherings. The prayer for the outpouring of the Holy Spirit is filled with scripture and is beautiful for meditation before the Blessed Sacrament. May the Holy Spirit grant the Church the grace of a new Pentecost and empower her children to transform history at the dawn of the Third Millennium!

Renewal of Baptismal Promises

Response: I do.

1. Do you reject sin so as to live in the freedom of God's children? R.

2. Do you reject the glamour of evil and refuse to be mastered by sin? R.

3. Do you reject Satan, father of sin and prince of darkness? R.

Profession of faith

Divine Savior, you tell me in the gospel of John that "God so loved the world that he gave his only Son, so that everyone who believes in him may not perish, but have eternal life" (Jn. 3:16)

1. Do you believe in Jesus Christ, his only Son our Lord, who was born of the Virgin Mary, was crucified, died and was buried, rose from the dead and is now seated at the right hand of the Father? R.

2. Do you believe in the Holy Spirit, the holy Catholic Church, the communion of saints, the forgiveness of sins, the resurrection of the body and life everlasting? R.

3. This, Lord, is the faith that I confess, and believe in my heart. I not only believe in the truths that you have revealed to me, but, in a special way, I believe in and accept you as the person of Jesus Christ, who is the Son of God and one with the Father and the Holy Spirit.

Invoke the Holy Spirit. Invoke Mary, Spouse of the Holy Spirit. Invoke St. Joseph, Patron of the Interior Life.

Prayer for the Renewal of Baptism of the Holy Spirit

Lord Jesus, I am reminded in St. Paul's first letter to the Corinthians that I am a "temple of the Holy Spirit" and that God dwells in me (1 Cor. 3:16), and "anyone united to the Lord becomes one spirit with him" (1 Cor 6:17).

I want to be "born again" not only of water, but "of water and the Spirit." I want to have the fullness of your Spirit even beyond that of the "born again" experience (Jn. 3:5).

Mindful of your word, as did your disciples and our Blessed Mother on that first Pentecost, I have placed myself symbolically in the Upper Room, prayerfully preparing for the promise of the Father who said he would "send the Holy Spirit" (Acts 1:14). I rejoice that the "promise is for everyone…whom the Lord calls to him" (Acts 2:39). Thank you, Lord, for helping me to prepare to become more open and receptive to receive the Father's promise.

You tell me to ask the Father and he will send me the Spirit (Lk. 11:13), and that you, Jesus, are the "baptizer into the Holy Spirit" (Jn. 1:33). In your name, Jesus, I now ask the Father to send me the Spirit so that I can experience a new spiritual "rebirth" and renewal by your Holy Spirit" (Titus 3:4-6).

Through your prophet Joel you said that you would "pour out your Spirit on all mankind" (Joel 2:28). Pour out your Spirit, Lord. Bring me into that higher level of intimacy of your Spirit's presence and power in me. Bring me into the charismatic dimension of Christian spirituality. As you did to your disciples on that first Pentecost, baptize me and immerse me into the love of the Trinity so that I can experience your Divine embrace. Let my Spirit baptism be one that is distinct from and beyond my conversion and "born again" experience.

Lord Jesus, you tell me that "when the Spirit of Truth comes he will guide me into all truth" (Jn. 16:13), that the Spirit will reveal himself to me and remind me "of all that you have said" (Jn. 14:22). Help me, Lord, by this personal Pentecost, to become more spiritually sensitive so that I will not only look for the Spirit, but will more readily recognize the Holy Spirit's presence and the work that he wants to do in me. I am confident that you who "have begun a good work in me will bring it to completion" (Phil. 1:6).

You said in the gospel of John, that you "give the spirit without measure" (Jn. 3:24); Let this Spirit baptism be the beginning of a continuous filling of my intellect, my imagination, my emotions, my will, my memory, my conscious, my spirit and my body, so that being renewed in Spirit, they will always be used according to your will (2 Cor. 5:16-17).

So that I can have a more personal, childlike and intimate relations with God, my heavenly Father (Gal. 4:6), help me to not only know about you, Lord, but to experience you in my heart as that real person that you are.

Give me a deeper hunger, reverence and understanding of Holy Scripture (Heb. 6:4-5). Help me to understand the importance of obeying the commandments (Jn. 14:21), receiving the sacraments worthily and respecting the authority of the Church (Lk. 10:16, Jn. 10:27).

Through personal and community prayer, help me to "grow in the Spirit" (Heb. 10:25), and be fully united with others in the "bonds of peace and love" (Eph. 2:3). Amen.

Fr. John Hampsch, CMF, *Receiving the Holy Spirit*

Chapter 12

Eucharistic Reflections and Meditations for Visits to the Blessed Sacrament

Prayers for Visits to the Blessed Sacrament

Prayer Before Each Visit to the Blessed Sacrament

My Lord Jesus Christ, I believe that you are really here in this sacrament. Night and day you remain here compassionate and loving. You call, you wait for, and you welcome, everyone who comes to visit you.

Unimportant though I am, I adore you. I thank you for all the wonderful graces you have given me. But I thank you especially for having given me yourself in this sacrament, for having asked your own Mother to mother me, for having called me here to talk to you.

I am here before you today to do three things: to thank you for these precious gifts, to make up for all the disrespect that you receive in this sacrament from those who offend you and to adore you everywhere in the world where you are present in this living bread but are left abandoned and unloved.

My Jesus, I love you with all my heart. I know that I have displeased you often in the past—I am sorry. With your help I promise never to do it again. I am only a miserable sinner, but I consecrate myself to you completely. I give you my will, my love, my desires, everything I own. From now on do what you please with me. All I ask is that you love me, that you keep me faithful to the end of my life. I ask for the grace to do your will exactly as you want it done.

I pray for the souls in purgatory — especially for those who were close to you in this sacrament and close to your Mother Mary. I pray for every soul hardened in sin. My Savior, I unite my love to the love of your Divine heart, and I offer them both together to your Father. I beg him to accept this offering in your name. Amen.

Saint Alphonsus Ligouri, *Visits to the Most Blessed Sacrament and the Blessed Virgin Mary*

Prayer for Spiritual Holy Communion

My Jesus, I believe you are really here in the Blessed Sacrament. I love you more than anything in the world, and I hunger to feed on your flesh. But since I cannot receive Communion at this moment, feed my soul at least spiritually. I unite myself to you now as I do when I actually receive you. Never let me drift away from you.

Saint Alphonsus Liguori, *Visits to the Most Blessed Sacrament and the Blessed Virgin Mary*

Prayer of Praise before the Blessed Sacrament

In prayer, a distinction is often made between praise, petition and thanksgiving. In the Bible, praise and gratitude are often coupled in the same movement of the spirit. God is revealed as worthy of praise for His unfathomable mercies toward mankind. Praise evokes joy! It is most efficacious to begin every prayer session, especially Holy Hour with praise.

Praise immediately places us in a vertical posture of prayer, connecting us to the Lord quickly. Often praise rids us of menacing spirits that attempt to sabotage our prayer session because the enemy of our soul cannot remain amidst praise to the Lord because praise makes us forgetful of self and the enemy gets no attention. This is a prescription for healing! Praise is a sacrifice when we enter it without consolation. It is especially efficacious when we feel an aversion to praise to continue in a sacrificial hymn of praise. Above all, praise is the confession of the grandeurs of God.

Turn all of your attention to God Almighty and pray the **Litany of Praise:**

> Praise You, Jesus, You are my Life, my love.
> Praise You, Jesus, You are the Name above all names.
> Praise You, Jesus, You are Emmanuel, God with us.
> Praise You, Jesus, You are the King of kings.
> Praise You, Jesus, You are the King of creation.
> Praise You, Jesus, You are King of the universe.
> Praise You, Jesus, You are the Lord of lords.
> Praise You, Jesus, You are almighty.
> Praise You, Jesus, You are the Christ.
> Praise You, Jesus, You are Christ, the King.
> Praise You, Jesus, You are the Lamb of God.
> Praise You, Jesus, You are the Lion of Judah.
> Praise You, Jesus, You are the Bright Morning Star.
> Praise You, Jesus, You are our Champion and Shield.
> Praise You, Jesus, You are our Strength and our Song.
> Praise You, Jesus, You are the Way of our life.
> Praise You, Jesus, You are the only Truth.
> Praise You, Jesus, You are the Real Life.
> Praise You, Jesus, You are the Wonderful Counselor.
> Praise You, Jesus, You are the Prince of Peace.
> Praise You, Jesus, You are the Light of the World.
> Praise You, Jesus, You are the Living Word.
> Praise You, Jesus, You are our Redeemer.
> Praise You, Jesus, You are the Messiah.
> Praise You, Jesus, You are the Anointed One.
> Praise You, Jesus, You are the Holy One of Israel.

Praise You, Jesus, You are the Good Shepherd.

Praise You, Jesus, You are the Sheepgate.

Praise You, Jesus, You are the Lord of hosts.

Praise You, Jesus, You are the Rock of all ages.

Praise You, Jesus, You are my Hiding Place.

Praise You, Jesus, You are the Savior of the World.

Praise You, Jesus, You are the Strong Tower.

Praise You, Jesus, You are the Mountain Refuge.

Praise You, Jesus, You are the Bread of Life.

Praise You, Jesus, You are the Font of all holiness.

Praise You, Jesus, You are the Living Water.

Praise You, Jesus, You are the True Vine.

Praise You, Jesus, You are my Maker.

Praise You, Jesus, You are our Fortress.

Praise You, Jesus, You are the Deliverer.

Praise You, Jesus, You are our Victory.

Praise You, Jesus, You are our Salvation.

Praise You, Jesus, You are our Righteousness.

Praise You, Jesus, You are our Wisdom.

Praise You, Jesus, You are our Sanctification.

Praise You, Jesus, You are our Justification.

Praise You, Jesus, You are the Door.

Praise You, Jesus, You are the great I AM.

Praise You, Jesus, You the great High Priest.

Praise You, Jesus, You are the Cornerstone.

Praise You, Jesus, You are the Sure Foundation.

Praise You, Jesus, You are our Joy.

Praise You, Jesus, You are our Portion and Cup.

Praise You, Jesus, You are my Healing and Wholeness.

Praise You, Jesus, You are our Covenant.

Praise You, Jesus, You are the Promise of the Father.

Praise You, Jesus, You are the Everlasting One.

Praise You, Jesus, You are the Most High God.

Praise You, Jesus, You are the Lamb that was slain.

Praise You, Jesus, You are the Just Judge.

Praise You, Jesus, You are the Balm of Gilead.
Praise You, Jesus, You are the Might Warrior.
Praise You, Jesus, You are my Defense.
Praise You, Jesus, You are the Bridegroom.
Praise You, Jesus, You are my Patience.
Praise You, Jesus, You are the Solid Reality.
Praise You, Jesus, You are my Provider.
Praise You, Jesus, You are the Resurrection and the Life.
Praise You, Jesus, You are the Alpha and the Omega.
Praise You, Jesus, You are the Beginning and the End.
Praise You, Jesus, You are all that I need.
Praise You, Jesus, You are all that I want.
Praise You, Jesus, You are worthy of all praise!
Linda Schubert, *The Miracle Hour Booklet*
(used with permission)

Prayer of Spiritual Warfare

Begin with one Our Father, one Hail Mary, and one Glory Be. *"Be strong in the Lord and in His mighty power. Put on the full armor of God so that you can take your stand against the devil's schemes..."* (Eph. 6:12). This scripture exhorts us to be aware of negative spiritual forces that attempt to press upon us in an effort to diminish our capacity to be free, loving people. In Mark 16:17 we are taught that we have been given authority to come against the power of the enemy. The Holy Spirit makes us wise, discerning and courageous in the use of that power.

There may be occasions in your life when you inadvertently opened yourself to some negative spiritual influences. Before the Blessed Sacrament, you can now close the doors. In prayer, place yourself under the protection of the Lord's Precious Blood and take authority over any powers of evil that oppress you.

Heavenly Father, I come before you in praise, worship and adoration. Thank You for sending Your Son Jesus to give me life, to give me forgiveness, to give me a place in your family. Thank you for sending the Holy Spirit to guide me and empower me in my daily life. Heavenly Father, open my eyes that I may see your greatness, your majesty, your victory on behalf.

I place myself now under the cross of Jesus Christ and cover myself in the Precious Blood of Jesus. I surround myself with the light of Christ and say in the name of Jesus that nothing shall interfere with the Lord's work being accomplished in my life.

I put on God's armor to resist the devil's tactics. I stand my ground with truth buckled around my waist and integrity for a breastplate. I carry the shield of faith to put out the burning arrows of the evil one. I accept salvation from God to be my helmet and receive the word of God from the Spirit to use as a sword (Eph. 6:10-11, 14, 16-17).

Heavenly Father, please show me any way that Satan has a hold of my life. I let go of all those ways now. And territory that I have handed over to Satan I now reclaim and place under the Lordship of Jesus Christ.

In the name of Jesus Christ, I bind all spirits of the air, fire, water, ground, underground and nether world. I bind all forces of evil and claim the Blood of Jesus on the air, the atmosphere, the water, the ground and their fruits around us, the underground and the nether world. In the name of Jesus Christ, I seal this room and all members of my family, relatives, associates and all sources of supply in the Blood of Jesus Christ. In the name of Jesus Christ I forbid every spirit from any source from harming me in any way.

In the name of Jesus Christ I reject the seductive lure of evil in all its forms and refuse to let sin have domination over me. I reject Satan and all his works and all his empty promises. Heavenly Father, I ask forgiveness for myself, my friends, relatives and ancestors for calling upon powers that set themselves up in opposition to Jesus Christ. I renounce all openness to the occult, all false worship and all benefits from the magical arts. I renounce every power apart from God and every form of worship that does not offer true honor to Jesus Christ. I specifically renounce _____. (For example, astrology, fortune telling, crystals, tarot cards, Ouija boards, or any occult games, etc.) In the name of Jesus, I break any curses that may be coming against me or my family, and stop the transmission of those curses through my ancestry.

In the name of Jesus Christ, I bind you spirit of _____ _____. (Ask the Lord to reveal the name. If you are not sure about the name, identify it by its negative fruit: anger, unforgiveness, fear, insecurity, illness, traumas, etc.) I bind you away from me now in Jesus' name. Lord Jesus, fill me with your love to replace the fear; fill me with strength to replace the weakness, etc. (after each command, ask the Lord to fill you with the "positive opposite" of the negativity you removed (e.g. fear/love, illness/health, weakness/strength, etc.).

Loving Father, let the cleansing, healing waters of my baptism flow back through the generations to purify my family line of contamination. Thank you, Lord, for setting me free. "...In all these things we are more than conquerors through Him who loved us" (Rom. 8:37). Spend a few moments in praise and gratitude.

Linda Schubert, *The Miracle Hour Booklet*
(used with permission)

Prayer for Receiving and Giving Forgiveness

Lord Jesus, your holy word commands us to "put away all anger...to forgive one another as God, in Christ has forgiven you" (Eph. 4:32). Heal the root cause of the hurt in me that sometimes makes it difficult for me to forgive. With all my heart, and with your help, I now let go of any bitterness, anger and unforgiveness that I have toward you, myself or others.

Forgive me Lord, for becoming bitter and angry with you because I regarded the hard times in my life as punishments from you to me and my family. I know now, that in your eternal wisdom, you sent your only Son, with your healing love that "will never leave me or forsake me" (Heb. 13:5). You "discipline me for my good in order that I may share in your holiness." (Heb. 12:10).

Forgiving Others: Your holy gospel reminds me that whenever I stand praying, I should forgive, so that my heavenly Father will forgive me (Mk. 11:25). With your Spirit of love, I now forgive and let go of any anger, bitterness or resentment that I have toward anyone, especially toward my parents, and other members of my family and relatives living and deceased, and those persons who have hurt me and my family the most. With your help Lord, I forgive my ancestors whose transmitted effects of their sins have resulted in my present sufferings and disorders (Lam. 5:7). Forgive the sins of my ancestors, Lord; unbind them from every form of bondage (Jn. 11:44). Replace that bondage with your healing bonds of love (Col. 3:14). Through you, Jesus, I ask them to forgive me for all the times that I have hurt them. Bless them Lord, and heal all our hurts. Help me to correct my human weaknesses and enable me to understand, love and forgive others.

Forgiving Self: Divine Savior, thank you for helping me to accept and to become more aware of my human weaknesses. Thank you for helping me to forgive myself especially for those sins that have hurt you the most and have kept me in spiritual bondage. With your forgiving love, supply what is lacking in my efforts to love and forgive myself and others as you have forgiven.

Lord, I ask you to forgive me also:

1. For the sinful and selfish use of my intellect, my memory, my imagination, my will and my emotions. R. Forgive and heal me, Jesus.

2. For the sinful and selfish use of my eyes, my ears, my nose, my tongue, my hands and my body. R. Forgive and heal me, Jesus.

3. For the sinful and selfish use of my spiritual and natural gifts, talents, money, position, time and possessions. R. Forgive and heal me, Jesus.

4. For the sinful and selfish use of my family, relatives, clergy,

friends, and other associates. R. Forgive and heal me, Jesus.

5. For causing others to offend you by the bad example of my sinful behavior in what I have done or failed to so. R. Forgive and heal me, Jesus.

6. For being resentful toward you or members of my family and relatives, living and deceased, and toward the persons who have hurt me. R. Forgive and heal me, Jesus.

7. For all the times that I was indifferent and did not thank you, or respond to the riches of your graces that you have freely bestowed on me (Eph. 1:6-7). R. Forgive and heal me, Jesus.

8. For the injuries and pain that I have caused my family, relatives and others by my selfish and sinful behavior. R. Forgive and heal me, Jesus.

9. Lord, both I and my ancestors have sinned and did not remember the abundance of your steadfast love (Ps. 106:6-7). R. Forgive and heal me, Jesus.

10. For being bitter and unforgiving toward my ancestors whose transmitted effects of their sins and possible involvement with the powers of darkness have resulted in the present sufferings, disorders or wrong inclinations in me or in my family. R. Forgive and heal me, Jesus.

Thank you, Lord, for your great mercy, healing and forgiving love. Amen.

Fr. John Hampsch, C.M.F. (used with permission)

Prayer for the renewal of baptism of the Spirit

Lord Jesus, I am reminded in St. Paul's first letter to the Corinthians that I am a "temple of the Holy Spirit" and that God dwells in me (1 Cor. 3:16), and "anyone united to the Lord becomes one spirit with him" (1 Cor. 6:17).

I want to be "born again" not only of water, but "of water and the Spirit." I want to have the fullness of your Spirit even beyond that of the "born again" experience (Jn. 3:5).

Mindful of your word, as did your disciples and our Blessed Mother on that first Pentecost, I have placed myself symbolically in the Upper Room, prayerfully preparing for the promise of the Father who said he would "send the Holy Spirit" (Acts 1:14). I rejoice that the "promise is for everyone…whom the Lord calls to him" (Acts 2:39). Thank you, Lord, for helping me to prepare to become more open and receptive to receive the Father's promise.

You tell me to ask the Father and he will send me the Spirit (Lk. 11:13), and that you, Jesus, are the "baptizer into the Holy Spirit" (Jn. 1:33). In your name, Jesus, I now ask the Father to send me the Spirit so that I can experience a new spiritual "rebirth" and renewal by your Holy Spirit" (Titus 3:4-6).

Through your prophet Joel you said that you would "pour out your Spirit on all mankind" (Joel 2:28). Pour out your Spirit, Lord. Bring me into that higher level of intimacy of your Spirit's presence and power in me. Bring me into the charismatic dimension of Christian spirituality. As you did to your disciples on that first Pentecost, baptize me and immerse me into the love of the Trinity so that I can experience your Divine embrace. Let my Spirit baptism be one that is distinct from and beyond my conversion and "born again" experience.

Lord Jesus, you tell me that "when the Spirit of Truth comes he will guide me into all truth" (Jn. 16:13), that the Spirit will reveal himself to me and remind me "of all that you have said" (Jn. 14:22). Help me, Lord, by this personal Pentecost, to become more spiritually sensitive so that I will not only look for the Spirit, but will more readily recognize the Holy Spirit's presence and the work that he wants to do in me. I am confident that you who "have begun a good work in me will bring it to completion" (Phil. 1:6).

You said in the gospel of John, that you "give the spirit without measure" (Jn. 3:24); Let this Spirit baptism be the beginning of a continuous filling of my intellect, my imagination, my emotions, my will, my memory, my conscious, my spirit and my body, so that being renewed in Spirit, they will always be used according to your will (2 Cor. 5:16-17).

So that I can have a more personal, childlike and intimate relations with

God, my heavenly Father (Gal. 4:6), help me to not only know about you, Lord, but to experience you in my heart as that real person that you are.

Give me a deeper hunger, reverence and understanding of Holy Scripture (Heb. 6:4-5). Help me to understand the importance of obeying the commandments (Jn. 14:21), receiving the sacraments worthily and respecting the authority of the Church (Lk. 10:16, Jn. 10:27).

Through personal and community prayer, help me to "grow in the Spirit" (Heb. 10:25), and be fully united with others in the "bonds of peace and love" (Eph. 2:3). Amen.

Fr. John Hampsch, C.M.F. (used with permission)

Prayer for Healing of Stress, Anxiety, and Fear

Lord Jesus, you are my light and salvation. Look into my heart and release me from all stress, anxiety, and fear. Help me to move above and beyond the stress that demands of me everyday. Sometimes, I feel I am being stretched too thin. I become a busybody and I often neglect my prayer time with you. In your Holy name, Jesus, break the vicious cycle of "busyness" in my life. I sincerely repent for my lack of prayer while I was too busy and exhausted. Teach me to know what is more important in my life and help me to be constantly led by your Spirit. My daily duties often seem too mundane and unimportant. Help me to do my daily ordinary routines with an extraordinary love for you.

I relinquish all of my concerns and anxieties about the details of tomorrow to you. The more I try to control my life, the more I get out of control. I am helpless and drained. I give you full permission to be in charge of my tomorrows, for you hold my future in your hands and for you are my lord and savior.

O, most compassionate Jesus, I ask you now to heal all of my fear— fear of abandonment, fear of rejection, fear of what other people think of me, fear of illness and death, fear of suffering, fear of failure, fear of intimacy, fear of commitment, and fear of the unknown. Cleanse my fear with your precious blood. In the name of Jesus Christ, I bind any spirits of anxiety and fear. I break a stronghold of fear in your name. I command all these spirits immediately and directly to go to the foot of the Cross. I truly desire to live my life as your little and freed child. I want to walk on the water with you by focusing on you, not focusing on my circumstance. Increase my faith, to be expectant, living, and active. In faith in you, I can conquer the fear and the world. Fill my heart with your peace, joy, and strength that the world cannot give. Thank you for healing me and freeing me from bondage today. In your name, I claim your victory over my life! Amen!

    Elizabeth Kim, Ph.D.

Prayer for Healing of the Brain

My heavenly Father, my Abba, you have created me in your image and likeness, for wellness. I ask you to breathe your life into the areas that desperately need your healing touch. I ask you to command all parts of my brain to be submissive to your Divine order right now. I ask you to restore and strengthen all neurons, synapses, neurotransmitters, cortical cortex, sub-cortical cortex, basic lobes (pre-frontal, frontal, parietal, temporal, and occipital), each hemisphere, limbic system, cerebellum, brain stem, and brain chemistries. Let your precious blood flow through my brain's pathways and supply your presence and life-giving love. Help my brain to self-regulate all systems the way you have intended.

Come, Holy Spirit! Baptize my entire brain in your healing water that flows out of the Father's throne. Heal my brain from depressive disorder, bipolar disorder, anxiety disorder, panic disorder, phobia, obsessive compulsive disorder, sleep disorder, schizophrenia, psychotic disorder, autistic spectrum disorder, AD/HD, learning difficulties, speech problems, head injury, epilepsy, migraine headaches, poor memory, negative thoughts, any form of addiction, and all other neurological dysfunctions known and unknown.

In the name of Jesus, I rebuke the spirit of infirmity and oppression. I command you to go to the foot of the cross right now. Lord Jesus, let all of my brain cells experience the love you create, fully alive in your love. I boldly ask that your miraculous power come through my brain and heal. Any shame, inferiority, inadequacy, self-hatred, anger, resentment, bitterness, and despair I experienced due to my neuropsychological condition, I give to you, Holy Spirit. Heal and transform my brokenness and negativity. I resolve to forgive anyone who hurt me in any way. I make the decision to forgive myself, my parents, and you for having been genetically born with my condition. I ask you to pour out your Divine wisdom, knowledge, understanding, and counsel. I ask you to transform my thoughts to be holy, positive, and constructive. I ask you to grace me to humbly accept my limitation and condition and to continue to take up my cross and follow you. You created my brain and heart to be compelled to your love. I hunger and thirst for your love. I yearn for you. I love you. I surrender my whole life to your most perfect will. Thank you for giving me this life. I praise your name forever. Amen.

Elizabeth Kim, Ph.D.

Healing Prayer of Isaiah 53

Precious Lord Jesus, I thank you for your loving care. You came into the world to set me free from the consequences of sin. You embraced the violent death of the cross to pay the penalty on my behalf. You suffered the scourging at the pillar, taking the sickness of humanity upon your flesh, so that I could be healed.

I come before you now to place all my sins upon your cross and ask for your precious blood to wash me clean. I place the penalty for my sinfulness, all my sickness, diseases and infirmities upon your cross, and for the sake of your sorrowful passion, I ask to be set free. I accept your sacrifice and receive your gift of reconciliation. I confess your Lordship over every aspect of my life, mind, body, soul, and spirit.

Through the power of your cross Lord Jesus, I now resist all forms of sin, sickness, and disease, that is not your perfect will for my life. I enforce the power of the cross upon you right now.

By the shed blood of the Lord Jesus Christ of Nazareth, I command all forms of sickness and disease to leave my presence immediately. Jesus bore my infirmities. He was wounded for my transgressions. By his stripes I have been healed. No sickness, pain, death, fear or addiction shall ever lord over me again. The penalty has been paid in full. I have been ransomed and redeemed, sanctified and set free. Amen.

Inga Pak, M.D.

Prayer for a Creative Miracle

God of all creation, you who spoke a simple command and brought forth light from the darkness, I call upon you now to send forth your miracle-working power into every aspect of my being. In the same way that you spoke unto the dust of the ground when you created humankind in your own image, I ask you to send forth your healing power into my body. Send forth your word and command every cell, electrical and chemical impulse, tissue, joint, ligament, organ, gland, muscle, bone and every molecule in my body to come under complete and perfect health, strength, alignment, balance, and harmony.

It is through you that I live and move and have my being. With every breath I take, I live under your life-giving grace. I ask you to touch me now with the same miracle-working power that you used when you fashioned me inside my mother's womb. As surely as you have created me in your image and likeness, you can also recreate me now and restore me to health.

Please fill me with your healing power. Cast out all that should not be inside of me. I ask you to mend all that is broken, root out every sickness and disease, open all blocked arteries and veins, restore my internal organs, rebuild my damaged tissues, remove all inflammation and cleanse me of all infections, viruses and destructive forms of bacteria.

Let the warmth of your healing love flood my entire being, so that my body will function the way it was created to be, whole and complete, renewed in your perfect health. I ask this through my Lord, Jesus Christ, your Son, who lives and reigns with you and the Holy Spirit, one God, for ever and ever. Amen.

Inga Pak, M.D.

Prayer to the Divine Physician

Dear Lord Jesus, you went about healing all those who were sick and tormented by unclean spirits. You cleansed the lepers, opened the eyes of the blind and by speaking a simple command, you empowered the crippled to rise up and walk. You sent forth your life-giving power to all those in need, including those you raised from the dead.

O Divine Physician, I come to you now in great need of your intervention. I surrender my life and health into your loving hands. I ask you to send forth your healing power into my heart, mind, body, soul and spirit. Remove from me every lie of the enemy and destroy all the word curses that have been spoken against my health.

If I have accepted medical beliefs that I should not have, I ask for your forgiveness and denounce those beliefs right now. I break every agreement that I have made with my sickness and disease. I denounce every symptom of my illness, and I ask to be set free by the power of your truth.

Please send forth your Holy Spirit to renew my mind and cleanse my thoughts. I refuse to bow down and serve the symptoms of my illness any longer. Please draw my attention away from myself, and help me focus on your enduring love.

O Divine Physician, you are the source and strength of my recovery. Show me how to proceed with your plan for my restoration. I surrender my healthcare into your loving hands. Please help me to discern every aspect of my treatment, medications and recovery process, so that my every thought and action conforms to your good and perfect will for my life. Amen.

Inga Pak, M.D.

Prayer of Total Commitment to Jesus Christ as Lord

Thank you, Lord, for reminding me that "every perfect gift is from above, coming down from the Father" (Jm. 1:17), and that you are "the Beginning and the End of all things" (Rev. 1:17). Thank you, Jesus, for the gift of loving me into being. Thank you for giving to me the life-giving waters of Baptism by which the Holy Spirit came to dwell in me and I became a child of God and a member of your spiritual Body, the Church (Eph. 4:5). By the power of your Holy Spirit (1 Cor. 12:3), I confess that you, Jesus Christ, are Lord (Phil. 2:11). All things have been created through you and for you (Col. 1:16). Lord Jesus, I want to belong entirely to you. Be Lord of my life. I now unconditionally surrender to you all the areas of my life.

1. Exercise your Divine Lordship over my intellect, my imagination, my memory, my emotions, my will, my spirit, my body and all my natural senses and experiences as well as those of my loved ones. R. Lord, hear my prayer.

2. Be Lord of my family, my business, my money, my plans and my vocation or career in life, as well as that of my loved ones. R. Lord, hear my prayer.

3. Take dominion and be Lord of my past, my present and my future as well as that of all the generations of my family. R. Lord, hear my prayer.

4. You are the Lord of the Universe. All things come into being through you (Jn. 1:1). Be Lord over all your gifts and possessions that I have now and will have in the future as well as those of my loved ones. R. Lord, hear my prayer. Amen.

Fr. John Hampsch, C.M.F. (used with permission)

Saint Therese of Lisieux Prayer before the Blessed Sacrament

Frequently, only silence can express my prayer; however, this Divine Guest of the Tabernacle understands all, even the silence of a child's soul filled with gratitude. When I am before the Tabernacle, I can say only one thing to our Lord: "My God, you know that I love you." And I feel my prayer does not tire Jesus; knowing the helplessness of His poor little spouse, He is content with her good will.

Prayer of Protection: St. Patrick's Breastplate

I bind to myself today,
  The strong power of an invocation of the Trinity,
  The faith of the Trinity in Unity, The Creator of the Universe
I bind to myself today,
  The might of the Incarnation of Christ with that of His Baptism,

The might of His Crucifixion with that of His Burial,
The might of His Resurrection with that of His Ascension,
The might of His coming on Judgment Day
I bind to myself today,
    The Power in the Love of the Seraphim,
    In the obedience of the Angles, in the ministration of the
      Archangels,
    In the hope of resurrection unto reward,
    In the prayers of the Divine Patriarchs,
    In the predictions of the Divine Prophets,
    In the preaching of the Divine Apostles,
    In the faith of the Divine Confessors, in the purity of the Holy
      Virgins,
In the deeds of righteous men, women, angels and saints
I bind to myself today,
    The power of Heaven,
    The brightness of the Sun, the whiteness of Snow,
    The splendor of Fire, the speed of Lightning,
    The swiftness of Wind, the depth of the Sea,
    The stability of the Earth, the firmness of Rocks
I bind to myself today,
    God's Power to pilot me, God's Might to uphold me,
    God's Wisdom to teach me, God's Eye to watch over me,
    God's Ear to hear me, God's Word to give me speech,
    God's Hand to guide me, God's Way to lie before me,
    God's Shield to shelter me, God's Host to secure me
    Against the snares of demons,
    Against the seductions of vices, against the lusts of nature,
    Against everyone who meditates injury to me,
    Whether far or near, whether few or many
I invoke today all these virtues
    Against every hostile merciless power which may assail
    My body, my mind, my soul and my Spirit,
    Against the incantations of false prophets,
    Against the black laws of heathenism, ·

Against the false laws of heresy,
Against the deceits of idolatry,
Against the spells of men, women, smiths and druids,
Against every knowledge that blinds the soul of man
Christ protect me today,
Against evil, against oppression, against stupidity,
Against poison, against wounding, against drowning,
Against burning, against disease of every kind
That I may receive abundant reward
Christ within me, Christ before me, Christ behind me,
Christ above me, Christ under me,
Christ at my right, Christ at my left,
Christ in my lying down, Christ in my sitting,
    Christ in my rising up,
Christ in the heart of everyone who thinks of me,
Christ in the mouth of everyone who speaks to me,
Christ in every eye that sees me,
Christ in every ear that hears me.
I bind to myself today
The strong power of an invocation of the Trinity,
The faith of the Trinity in Unity,
The Creator of the Universe
Salvation is of the Lord, Salvation is of the Lord,
Salvation is of Christ;
May your salvation, O Lord, be with us now and forever!

Prayer of St. Teresa of Avila

I cannot doubt at all Your Presence in the Eucharist. You have given me such a lively faith that when I hear others say they wish they had been living when you were on earth, I laugh to myself, for I know that I possess you as truly in the Blessed Sacrament as people did then, and I wonder what more anyone could possibly want.

Prayer of Padre Pio

O my Lord Jesus Christ, who for the love you bear mankind, remain night and day in this Sacrament, all full of tenderness and love, expecting, inviting and receiving all those who come to visit You. I believe that You are present in the Sacrament of the altar; I adore You from the depths of my own nothingness and thank You for all the favors you have bestowed upon me, especially for having given me Yourself in this Sacrament, and for giving Your most holy mother Mary as my advocate, and for having called me to visit You in this church. I pay my homage this day to Your most loving Heart, and this I intend to do for three intentions: first, in thanksgiving for this great gift; second, in reparation for all the insults you have received from your enemies in this Sacrament; third, by this visit I intend to adore You in all places upon the earth, where you are least adored and most neglected in Your Sacrament. My Jesus, I love you with my whole heart. I repent of having in the past so many times displeased your infinite goodness. I propose with the help of your grace never more to offend you in the future; and at this moment, wretched as I am, I consecrate myself wholly to you. I give to you and utterly renounce my entire will, all my affections, all my desires, and all that I possess. From this day forth do with me and with all that is mine whatever is pleasing in your sight. I ask and desire only your holy love, final perseverance, and the fulfillment of Your Will. I recommend to you the souls in Purgatory, especially those who were most devoted to this Blessed Sacrament and to the Blessed Virgin Mary. I commend to you in like manner all poor sinners. Finally my dear Savior, I unite all my affections with those of your most loving Heart, and thus united I offer them to your eternal Father and I pray Him in Your name be gracious to accept and answer them for love of you. Amen.

Prayer of Reparation to the Eternal Father of the Eucharist

Abba, beloved Father of the Eucharist, be glorified in your weak vessel. Help me to make reparation to appease Divine Justice and draw mercy upon all those who offend your perfect charity by receiving the

Eucharist without proper disposition. Father, all men sin and are unworthy to receive your Son in the Eucharist but at each Mass we pray, "Only say the word and I shall be healed." By means of the Eucharistic Heart of Jesus grant the Church and world be sanctified for the sake of the Precious Blood that gushed from His pierced side for the salvation of sinners. As we drink the Cup may we become one with the Redeemer who glorifies you, His most beloved Father in Heaven! Amen.

Meditations for Visits to the Blessed Sacrament

Meditation:
On the Healing Power of Blessed Sacrament

As they left Jericho, a great crowd followed him. Two blind men were sitting by the road side, and when they heard that Jesus was passing them by, they cried out, "Son of David, have pity on us!" The crowd warned them to be silent, but they called out all the more, "Lord, Son of David, have pity on us!" Jesus stopped and called them and said, "What do you want me to do for you?" They answered him, "Lord, let our eyes be opened." Moved with pity, Jesus touched their eyes. Immediately, they received their sight and followed him." While contemplating this biblical scene, consider this meditation from Matthew 21:29-34.

Disciple, the blind are everywhere. I want to give sight to the blind and revelation of Love so you can see again. In the Light of the Monstrance you visit the Divine Physician. I dispense Heaven's medicine that heals and prevents more sickness. There are areas in you that need healing each day. I gaze into the depths of your being. I know where to apply the healing salve of Divine Mercy. Even before you are sick in spirit or body, I know your vulnerability and give grace to heal you.

When you adore me in the Blessed Sacrament, you enter communion with the Heart of Love. This mystical communion is a healing balm effecting spiritual and physical good in you. Your capacity to love as I love is increased until you become a new creation in my image. The new self emerges. Sanctification progresses; mediocrity vanishes. The lukewarm become committed disciples. You become a person whose heart is receptive to Divine Charity. Whatever suffering you undergo becomes an opportunity for grace. You draw ever nearer to Love that turns all things to joy. You will never remain the same if you continue to participate in the Mass with all of your heart; continue to keep a vigil of prayer before the Monstrance.

In prayer you grow in holiness. The garment of virtue will weave into your being until faith, hope and love adorn you thoroughly. You are made beautiful by communing with me. You are made whole in my Loving Presence. The Eucharistic bond builds a strong foundation that withstands all storms of life. The Eucharist will create a house of prayer in you. My thirst will become your thirst. You will love as I love. Peace begins to reign in you. My divinity begins to fascinate you like nothing else in the world. I am able to impart my divinity upon you through the Eucharist. I make you radiant, like a beacon illuminating the dark world with true light.

Intercessor, holiness is attractive. You will find this to be true. People seek what is holy. You are created to be attracted to sanctity. The mystery of the Eucharist will continue to change the world for good one soul at a time. Let me fashion you into holiness each day. Beauty desires to adorn you in the pure light of transparent sanctity.

Disciple, the graces you are receiving would be impossible without daily Eucharistic communion. Give thanks! Spiritual exercises demand discipline. When you persevere to draw close to me, Heaven rejoices. Each day, countless graces are trampled upon. To those who make good use of each day's grace, untold blessing comes. Disciple, rest in my heart of love. Grace is penetrating you.

Meditation: On Merciful Love

Imagine a dialogue between Jesus and a servant of the Eucharist:

O August Sacrament, I adore you with all my heart. How consoling that I may gaze upon you who are seemingly captive in the Tabernacle for me, a sinner.

Beloved, Love makes me captive for your sake. I am the Light of the world whose radiance illumines creation. I remain in the Tabernacles of the world for the life of the Church. For you I am here where you can approach without fear. Draw close that your face may become radiant with the light of love.

Lord, the world grows darker and many do not perceive your light of love.

Disciple, my nature is infinite love. My love holds creation in existence according to the Divine Will. On earth your perception is obscure. With me you are able to perceive the light of love. I am present in the Host to reveal the nature of Divine Love, to perpetuate the Pascal Mystery, and unite you to myself.

Jesus, what transpires when I come to you in the Blessed Sacrament?

Transformation occurs. My Presence penetrates and transfigures you. An exchange occurs. I look with mercy upon your wounded heart and am compelled to give you a better heart: my Sacred Heart. You receive infinite Good poured into you. As you behold Beauty in the Blessed Sacrament; Beauty beholds you; imbuing you with the virtuous spirit of wisdom. That you come to me in the Blessed Sacrament is an exercise in faith that produces fruitfulness. You come to the source of life to receive new life, renewing your strength for daily battle of good versus evil. You bring me every part of you; body and soul; and the intentions of your heart. You carry to me those you love. I receive your intentions and make them my intentions also. People you love receive grace because you are here with them in mind. I bathe you in the balm of Divine Charity as your spirit rises in adoration of the Holy of Holies. The fecundity of our communion brings healing to every part of your being.

My Lord, It seems that I sleep in your Presence. I am lost in my gaze toward you and enter into rest or sleep.

Disciple, you do not sleep. You are caught up in the dynamism of Love, the realm of the Spirit; into the Mystery of My Presence where we engage in a mutual act of self giving. You rest in My Heart while Love's rhythm resounds in you. I surround your heart like a blanket while I operate to perfect my creature. In adoration you gaze upon the Incarnate Word that speaks in silence instructing your heart to know, love and serve the Eternal Father. I speak on your behalf to My Father saying to Him: "Here Abba is one you gave me! I am bringing her to you." She was lost but I found her and corrected her crooked ways. Father, I will carry her to the room prepared from the beginning.

Child, know that you are being carried in my arms. Even when you insist sometimes on doing things your way, I am patient and surround you to carry you back on the straight and narrow road of sanctity. You ask what occurs in adoration of the Blessed Sacrament. I tell you the world is permeated by My Presence more deeply than the sun rays bathing the globe. And if this ceased to be, all Good would vanish from the globe.

Then Lord, why do so few come?

I am little loved. This does not change My Presence. To some I am invisible; to others I am quite visible. You see me through the eyes of faith in the deepest recess of your heart. If a person so desires; if a person listens with purity of intention and seeks with sincerity to experience me, they can. It is my will that makes it occur. It is I who initiate everything good. The Word Incarnate speaks; silence is the means. In your noisy culture I am not heard. Still I am Present. My word goes out and does not return void. In my Presence there is power.

Lord, what do you mean by "power in your Presence?"

In my presence there is power to convert; to put on the new man; become a new creation. I am ever new. Life in me is ever new. Few people desire to change because of self-contentment and self-deception. The restless human heart fills itself with lesser realities and compromises an eternal inheritance.

Yet there are some who are not absorbed by the spirit of the world. These are prophets and disciples who are the light of the world, salt of the earth. They are sprinkled around the nations and many who would perish are spared because of hidden saints. I am in them and they are in me. A great good is realized through one holy soul. I have many victim souls interceding for humanity in this grave hour. They shine like the stars in the night sky. Often, hidden on earth, they are known in Heaven. Their life burns like incense producing the odor of sanctity. Victims of Love never lose sight of the power of the Cross which becomes for them a nuptial bed.

Lord, this is my prayer then, to be a victim of Love. Please grant me peace amidst life's many tribulations.

In My Presence there is peace. You witness the anxiety of societies.

Observe tension among people that frustrates the flow of grace. People are busy about many things while I remain unchanged and present to all. In the Blessed Sacrament there is presence, power and peace. It is I, the Prince of Peace, standing before you imparting peace the world can never give. I am here and the Church is empty except for a few. I can do much through a few who believe and love as I ask. My Church is built on the foundation of Three In One and her saints are indestructible pillars. Here I shall remain the Hidden God, Silent Teacher, and Risen Life for you, beloved. I remain in the tabernacles of the world for the conversion of all souls.

Disciple, I ask only that you live in My Presence in gratitude. Let your life be a prayer, serve others and not yourself. Keep returning here to commune with me so that like the face of Moses, you radiate my light. Let me see you each day that I may delight in the work of my hands. My Spirit lives in you. I am conquering you daily; teaching you to surrender to the Will of the Father. Go in my peace and do not doubt. I am the Sacrament of Love.

Jesus, be adored in all the Tabernacles of the world. Grant that I may love your more perfectly with every beat of my heart. Be glorified in my nothingness. Amen.

Meditation: Child before the Blessed Sacrament

During Adoration man becomes more a little child in his relations with God.

Lord, I adore you without knowing how to adore you.

Lord, I contemplate you without knowing how to contemplate you.

Lord, I praise you without knowing how to praise you.

Lord, I thank you without knowing how to thank you.

Lord, I perceive you without knowing how I perceive you.

Lord, I believe you are present without knowing how you are present.

Lord, I love you without knowing how to love you.

Lord, I draw close to you without knowing how to draw close to you.

Lord, I experience you without knowing how I experience you.

Lord, I feel your gaze without knowing how I feel your gaze.

Lord, I am sure of you without knowing how I am sure of you.

Lord, I know you instruct me without knowing how you instruct.

Lord, I know I am healed in your presence without knowing how I
am healed.

Lord, I know you extend your heart without knowing how you
extend your heart.

Lord, I know you take my intentions to the Father.

Lord, I believe you draw the veil aside to give a glimpse of Heaven.
You are Heaven!

Lord, I know this time with you is the most important time of
my day.

Lord, I am happy to be with you in this way without knowing how
you make me happy.

Lord, I know this is according to your ordinance of love that I stay
near you.

Lord, I keep watch with you for an hour per day.

Lord, it is enough for me to love you in all simplicity.

Lord, it is enough to believe that you love me in simplicity also.

Lord, the whole world is passing away but you will never pass away.

Lord, I hide myself in you since you make fruitful this encounter.

Lord, it is enough for me to know that for eternity you will delight
in me.

Lord, your love is all that I need. Let my soul sink into your silent
glory.

O pierced heart of Jesus, hide me! Refashion me in your image.

Glory to you, My God. Hush my soul. Silence now! Amen.

After some silence, the Lord seems to speak in the depths of the
heart:

*Child, know that your prayer is pleasing to my ear and consoling to
my heart. I come to you in the Blessed Sacrament, hidden in a little Host.
My littleness is a goal for you. You behold Resurrected Life and infinite
fullness of love for you personally. Your prayer echo's the words of Peter,
James and John on Mount Tabor when they said, "Lord, it is good to be
here! Let us remain here!" Child, see me through the eyes of faith. Faith*

is not a deceiver. Continue to tell me what is on your mind, unburden your heart and present your body as a living sacrifice of praise to my glory. Know that each time you come to me in the Blessed Sacrament my glory is unveiled for you. I expand your soul to receive more of my Glorified Being. I do this to draw you to myself, to heal you and make you free. Child, of all the things that you could do with your time, your being here with me is highest good, producing fruit beyond measure. Here you have a foretaste of the heavenly banquet. You give yourself to me as gift and I give myself to you as gift. Look around, child, not many people are interested in receiving the gift of God! To those who come, I extend my Sacred Heart and welcome you into the deep recesses of Divine Love. I am the Hidden God waiting to be found. I come to live in you and do not leave unless you take in other things that cause me to flee. If your heart erects an idol within, you then send me away. But if you keep yourself pure and free of sin, I am present within you. Nothing of your poverty can drive me away! Know that I want to do extraordinary things through ordinary people of prayer! Be still now and know that I am God.

Meditation:
When You Look at Him and He Looks at You

> *Beloved, the rays of Divine Love are piercing your heart as you adore me in the Blessed Sacrament.*

Lord, I am at peace before the Tabernacle; simply happy to be here near you.

> *Do you want to know more about what happens when you come to me in the Blessed Sacrament?*

Lord, I am here to listen as you will.

> *When you come to Me in the Blessed Sacrament:*
> *I am the Christ Child inviting you to be a child;*
> *I am the Son of Mary sharing My Mother;*
> *I am the Obedient Son imparting obedience;*
> *I am the Word Incarnate speaking unutterable mysteries;*
> *I am the Light of the World dispelling your darkness;*
> *I am the Savior ransoming you;*

I am the Divine Physician healing you;
I am Wisdom Incarnate imparting wisdom;
I am the Divine Teacher instructing you;
I am Humility making you humble;
I am the Good Shepherd reaching for His lamb,
I am the Eternal High Priest interceding for you;
I am the Perfect Sacrifice covering you;
I am the Resurrection bringing new life;
I am the Cornerstone upon which I set you;
I am Truth consecrating you;
I am Living Water satisfying your thirst;
I am The Divine Mercy forgiving you;
I am Love imbuing you;
I am the King conferring a kingdom upon you;
I am the Door you enter;
I am the Gate you pass through;
I am the Vine you are attached to;
I am the Tree of Life sheltering you;
I am the Living God communing;
I am the Pierced Heart opening;
I am the Strong Arm enfolding;
I am the Lover searching;
I am Paradise opened for you;
I am who Am.

My Lord, what do you see when you look at me?
Beloved, I see before me a sinner who is forgiven;
A creature chosen from the beginning;
The work of My Hands;
Clay that I am molding;
Vessel that I am purifying;
Child that I carry;
Someone more precious than gold;
The gem I refine;
A temple of the Holy Spirit;
A ship in the river of grace;

The apple of My eye;
Imitator of My mother;
Messenger of the Word;
Prophet of reconciliation;
Servant of the King;
Apostle of Mercy;
Shepherdess of souls;
Intercessor!
I see a maternal heart;
A generous soul;
Daughter of the Father,
A city being constructed;
A garden blooming;
A lover striving;
You did not spare extravagant oil to anoint My Body.
You are like an alabaster jar broken open;
You have anointed my feet; My head with the balm of your love.
You are listener;
A pupil who sees with the eyes of your soul;
You are sick with love;
Vigilant and engaging in battle;
Impatient for consummation;
Lover of Truth;
You are devoted and single-hearted;
Faithful and true;
Weakness and strength;
This is what I behold in you;
Servant of the Blessed Sacrament!

Thank you Good Jesus for drawing me to the Blessed Sacrament and for condescending to remain on earth in the humble species of the Sacred Host. Be adored! My God! Amen.

Meditation:
Cure of Ars before the Blessed Sacrament

The Spirit of the Lord is upon me, wherefore he hath anointed me to preach the gospel to the poor, he hath sent me to heal the contrite of heart, to preach deliverance to the captives, and sight to the blind, to set at liberty them that are bruised, to preach the acceptable year of the Lord, and the day of the reward (Lk. 4:18). These words which were uttered by thee, O Jesus, in the synagogue of Nazareth, ought to make thy tabernacle dear to me, for they speak to me of thy unceasing ministry there. Thou are always my Savior, my light, and my physician.

Alas! how many Christians are pressed for time, and only condescend to come for a few short moments to visit their Savior who burns with the desire to see them near him and to tell them that he loves them, and who wants to load them with blessings. Oh! What shame to us! If some novelty appears, men leave everything to run after it. But we run away from our God; and the time seems long in his holy presence! What a difference between the first Christians and ourselves! They passed whole days and nights in the churches, singing the praises of the Lord or weeping over their sins; but things are not the same today. Jesus is "forsaken, abandoned by us" in the Sacrament of his love.

The Sweetness of Making Visits to the Blessed Sacrament, and Motives for Making Them:

If we really loved the good God, we should make it our joy and happiness to come and spend a few moments before the tabernacle to adore him, and ask him for the grace of forgiveness; and we should regard those moments as the happiest in our lives. Oh! How sweet and consoling are moments spend with the God of goodness! Are you in sorrow? Come and cast yourself at his feet and you will feel quite consoled. Are you despised by the world? Come here and you will find a good friend whose faithfulness will never fail you. Are you tempted? It is here you will find strong and terrible weapons to vanquish your enemies. Do you fear the formidable judgment, which has made the greatest saints tremble? Profit by the time in which your God is the God of mercies, and while it is so easy to win your pardon from him.

Sinners, ask him with tears and sorrow for the pardon of your sins, and you are sure to obtain it. You, who are reconciled with him, beg for the precious gift of perseverance. Oh! Tell him that if you are to offend him again, you would far rather die. Would you begin to taste the joy of the saints? Come here and you will know the happy beginnings of it. Ah! How good it is to enjoy the pure embraces of the Savior! You have never tasted them! If you had had that happiness you could not leave them. Do not be surprised then, that so many holy souls have spent their life, day and night, in his house; they could not tear themselves from his presence.

St. John Vianney, *Eucharistic Meditations*

Meditation:
St. Faustina at the Foot of the Blessed Sacrament

O Jesus, Divine Prisoner of Love, when I consider your love and how you emptied yourself for me, my senses deaden. You hide your inconceivable majesty and lower yourself to miserable me. O King of Glory, though you hide your beauty, yet the eye of my soul rends the veil. I see the angelic choirs giving you honor without cease, and all the heavenly Powers praising you without cease, and without cease they are saying, Holy, Holy, Holy.

Oh, who will comprehend your love and your unfathomable mercy toward us! O Prisoner of Love, I lift up my poor heart in this tabernacle that it may adore you without cease day and night. I know of no obstacle in this adoration: and even though I be physically distant, my heart is always with you. Nothing can put a stop to my love for you. No obstacles exist for me.

O Holy Trinity, One and Indivisible God, may you be blessed for this great gift and testament of mercy. Amen.

I adore You, Lord and Creator, hidden in the Most Blessed Sacrament. I adore you for all the works of your hands that reveal to me so much wisdom, goodness and mercy, O Lord. You have spread so much beauty over the earth and it tells me about your beauty, even though these beautiful things are but a faint reflection of you, incomprehensible beauty. And although you have hidden yourself and concealed your beauty, my eye, enlightened by faith, reaches you and my soul recognizes its Creator, its highest Good, and my heart is completely immersed in prayer of adoration.

My Lord and Creator, your goodness encourages me to converse with you. Your mercy abolishes the chasm which separates the Creator from the creature. To converse with you, O Lord is the delight of my heart. In You I find everything that my heart could desire. Here streams of grace flow down upon my heart. Here my soul draws eternal life. O my Lord and Creator, you alone, beyond all these gifts, give your own self to me and unite yourself intimately with your miserable creature.

O Christ, let my greatest delight be to see you love and your praise and glory proclaimed, especially the honor of your mercy. O Christ let me glorify your goodness and mercy to the last moment of my life, with every drop of my blood and every beat of my heart. Would that I be transformed into a hymn of adoration of you! When I find myself on deathbed, may the last beat of my heart be a loving hymn glorifying your unfathomable mercy. Amen
Saint Faustina Kowalska

Meditation:
Listening to Mary before the Blessed Sacrament

Imagine the Blessed Mother speaking to you, her beloved child:
Dear child, my Son, Jesus is here in the Blessed Sacrament. Carry the love of the Eucharist within your heart. The Eucharist makes you a child of the light, salt of the earth, bread for the hungry, new wine for the thirsty, a herald of truth, a guardian of life, a humble servant, a victim of Divine Love, and a sword of the Spirit. Allow yourself to be transformed by my Son, Jesus. You know that you belong to Him; that you are His precious possession purchased by his Blood! Continue to worship my Son in the Blessed Sacrament. Continue to bring the nations to the Heart of the Redeemer. Continue to gaze with humble amazement! In the Sacred Host, see the reflection of yourself, for you are there, in his loving countenance.

Dear child, if you do as I ask, you will be my cohort in the peace plan entrusted to my mediation. I am sent from Heaven to be with you mystically because these times call for epic grace. The Church exhorts you to be dedicated to the Eucharist. Continue to be strengthened in his Eucharistic Presence because your faith and hope will be tried; you love will be tested in the terrible spiritual battle for your soul, and that of the Church. My little child, I impart spiritual courage to strengthen your faith. Become part of my army to uphold faith in God against all opposing armies. In the spiritual battle over souls, there is no place for fear since love casts out fear. Fear shrivels the heart and diminishes the flow of Divine grace. Dear child, trust more in God. Believe more than ever before in the power of God to save His people. Suffering on earth escalates but Jesus is able to use suffering to bring about greater good. He is your hope!

You possess him on earth by means of Holy Communion: the fruit of his Perfect Sacrifice! Dear child, as the King of Kings, his Majesty, humbles himself unto the consecrated hands of his ministerial Priesthood, follow his example. Humble yourself before him; entrust your soul unto His Priesthood and come forth as a child of the Father. Bask in his Love and you shall be a new creation! I enfold you in my mantle of grace because I love you dear little child. As Mother I am trying to help you. May your life bear witness to my Son's life, death and resurrection! Be a living monstrance!

Meditation: John Paul II before the Blessed Sacrament Prayer for Lay People: Interceding for the Civilization of Love

O Most Blessed Virgin Mary, Mother of Christ and Mother of the Church, with joy and wonder we seek to make our own your *Magnificat*, joining you in your hymn of thankfulness and love.

With you we give thanks to God, "Whose mercy is from generation to generation," for the exalted vocation and the many forms of mission entrusted to the lay faithful.

God has called each of them by name to live his own communion of love and holiness and to be one in the great family of God's children. He has sent them forth to shine with the light of Christ and to communicate the fire of the Spirit in every part of society through their life inspired by the Gospel.

O Virgin of the Magnificat, fill their hearts with gratitude and enthusiasm for this vocation and mission. With humility and magnanimity you were the "handmaid of the Lord;" give us your unreserved willingness for service to God and the salvation of the world. Open our eyes to the great anticipation of the Kingdom of God and of the proclamation of the Gospel to the whole of creation.

Your mother's heart is ever mindful of the many dangers and evil which threaten to overpower men and women in our time. At the same time your heart also takes notice of the many initiatives undertaken for good, the great yearning for values, and the progress achieved in bringing forth the abundant fruits of salvation.

O Virgin full of courage, may your spiritual strength and trust in God inspire us, so that we might know how to overcome all the obstacles that we encounter in accomplishing our mission. Teach us to treat the affairs of the world with a real sense of Christian responsibility and a joyful hope of the coming of God's Kingdom, and of a "new Heaven and a new earth."

You who were together in prayer with the Apostles of the Upper Room, awaiting the coming of the Spirit of Pentecost, implore his renewed outpouring on the faithful, men and women alike, so that they may more fully respond to their vocations and mission, as branches engrafted to the true vine, called to bear much fruit for the life of the world.

O Virgin Mother, guide and sustain us so that we may always live as true sons and daughters of the Church of your Son. Enable us to establish on earth the civilization of truth and love, as God wills it, for his glory. Amen.

Christifidelis Laici, *Apostolic Exhortation, December 30, 1988*

Meditation: Love is Not Loved

When Saint Francis was newly converted and in the first fervor (which really never left him), he used to go through the streets of Assisi dressed in rags and barefoot, crying, "Love is not loved."

I would condemn myself if I did this because love is not loved by me. But I wish I could at this quiet moment go down into the busy aisles and gates of this airport and shout, "Come to the chapel. Love is waiting there for you. Love is a Person, not a thing. He is risen. He is alive. He is waiting for you. Love is not loved." I can't do that, but I can at least try to act like I believe that Love loves those whom I meet—that He calls to them and is there for them, always and everywhere.

This mystery lights up the whole of the earth and sky. It sanctifies places far away from where the sacrament is reserved. Bishop James Walsh learned this when he prayed in his prison cell in China. And this I think is what the whole Eucharistic Presence of Jesus of Nazareth is about. It doesn't need to be defended, or even explained very much. The presence of Jesus the Christ needs only to be experienced.

Fr. Benedict Groeschel and James Monti, *In the Presence of Our Lord*

Meditation: Servant of God Fulton Sheen before the Blessed Sacrament: On the Church and Awaiting His Coming

Many think they would have believed in Him if they had lived in His day. But actually there would have been no great advantage. Those who do not see Him as Divine living in His Mystical Body today would not have seen Him as Divine living in His physical Body. If there are scandals in some cells of His Mystical Body, there were scandals too in His physical Body; both put forward a human appearance to see Divinity. In the Galilean days, it required faith supported by motives of credibility to believe in the Kingdom He came to establish or His Mystical Body through which He would sanctify men through His Spirit, after His Crucifixion. In these days, it requires faith supported by the same motives of credibility to believe in the Head, of the Invisible Christ, governing, teaching, and sanctifying through His visible head and His Body the Church. In each case a "lifting up" was required. To redeem men, Our Lord told Nicodemus that He had to be "lifted up" to Heaven in the Ascension.

Christ, therefore, still walks the earth, now in His Mystical Body, whereas then in His physical Body. The Gospel was the prehistory of the Church, as the Church is the post-history of the Gospel. He still is denied in the inns, as He was in Bethlehem; new Herods with Soviet and Chinese names persecute Him with the sword; other Satans appear to tempt Him to short cuts of popularity away from the Cross and mortification; Palm Sundays of great triumph come to Him, but they are preludes to Good Fridays, new changes (and often from religious people, as of old) are hurled against Him—that He is an enemy of Caesar, is unpatriotic, and would pervert a nation; on the outside He is stoned, on the inside attacked by false brethren; not even "Judases" who were called to be Apostles are wanting to betray Him and deliver Him over to the enemy; some of His disciples who gloried in His name walk with Him no more, because—like their predecessors—they find His teaching, particularly on the Bread of Life, to be "hard."

But since there is never a death without a Resurrection, His Mystical Body will in the course of history have a thousand deaths and a thousand Resurrections. The bells will always be tolling for His execution, but the execution will be everlastingly postponed. Some final day, in His Mystical Body there will come a universal persecution, when He will go to His death as He did before, "suffering under Pontius Pilate," suffering under the omnipotent power of the State. But in the end, all that was foretold of Abraham and Jerusalem will come to pass in its spiritual perfection, when He will be glorified in His Mystical Body as He was glorified in His physical Body. As John the Apostle described it:

Come, and I will show you the bride, the bride of the Lamb. So in the Spirit he carried me away to a great high mountain, and showed me the holy city of Jerusalem, coming down out of Heaven from God. It shone with the glory of God; it had the radiance of some priceless jewel, like a jasper, clear as crystal. It had a great high wall, with twelve gates, as which were twelve angels; and on the gates were inscribed the names of the twelve tribes of Israel. There were three gates to the east, three to the north, three to the south, and three to the west...I saw no temple in the city; for its temple was the sovereign Lord God and the Lamb. And the city had no need of sun or moon to shine upon it; for the glory of God gave it light and its lamps was the Lamb. By its light shall the nations walk, and the kings of the earth shall bring into it all their splendor. The gates of the city shall never be shut by day—and there will be no night... He who gives this testimony speaks: Yes, I am coming soon! Amen. Come, Lord Jesus! The grace of the Lord Jesus be with you all" Apocalypse 21:9-14, 22-26, 22:20-21.

Servant of God Fulton Sheen, *Life of Christ*

Meditation on the Key to His Eucharistic Heart

Imagine the Eternal High Priest speaking directly to your heart: *Beloved servant of the Eucharist, the key to my Eucharistic Heart is three-tiered, consisting of reverence for Abba Father, surrender to the Divine Will and humility of heart. As you grow in these key virtues, you enter more deeply into your Eucharistic vocation. I call you to a deeper relationship of love; an intimate friendship. The Eucharist sanctifies you. The sacramental fountain of grace perpetuates the life of the Church. It is through the Church that you possess me as I possess you. My hidden self, the Sacred Host, is visible through the eyes of faith.*

The gift of the Incarnation, Redemption and Resurrection is perpetual in the Blessed Sacrament. The Eucharist is a sacred irresistible mystery to some. To others it is a bone of contention. It has been this way throughout the ages. Far above human agencies, divine initiatives prevail, attract and subsist to enliven the Church. The Eucharist is Love's perfect elixir. It is the balm that perfumes my Church; Beauty that attracts the searching. My Eucharistic Heart is the gift that makes you a gift also—a gift to me, to the Church, to others.

The foreshadowing of my Eucharistic life imbued creation since its dawn. As a young child, the aroma of freshly baked bread permeated our humble abode in Nazareth. Now I am the aroma and the bread perfuming and feeding the Church. As a child, I observed the grain of wheat ground up, mixed with water and yeast so the bread could rise in the fire. Do you see? All the Eucharistic species are there: I am the wheat ground up; the yeast is my love; the water is my Spirit; the fire is the Divine Will. As bread must rise, so must my people. Will you join me (mystically) at the right hand of the Father to intercede for the salvation of the world? Reverence, surrender, humility: these are keys to my heart. My heart is for you—servant of the Eucharist. My heart is for you—priests! Allow me to possess you so you know the joy of unutterable Love. My power to heal humanity is manifested at the altar of Sacrifice, in the humble Host. Beloved, rise up in faith, hope and love and I will restore you. Shalom.

Bibliography

Kathleen Beckman References

The New American Bible. 1971. Catholic Publishers, Inc. Washington DC

John Paul II, *Ecclesia de Eucharistia*. 2003. Daughters of St. Paul. MA

St. Faustina. Diary. Marians of the Immaculate Conception. MA. 1147

Fr. Raniero Cantalamessa, O.F.M., Cap. Zenit.org. Article. February 15, 2008

Xavier-Leon-Dufour. *Dictionary of Biblical Theology.* 1995. The Word Among Us and St. Paul Book & Media. 313, 447

Fr. Benedict J. Groeschel, C.F.R., and James Monti. *In The Presence of the Lord.* 1997. Our Sunday Visitor Publishing Division. 74-75

Catechism of the Catholic Church. 1994. Paulist Press. New Jersey

C.S. Lewis. *Mere Christianity.*

Fr. Raniero Cantalamessa. O.F.M., Cap. *This Is My Body.* 2005. Pauline Books & Media. Boston. 61-63

St. Peter Eymard, *Eucharistic Handbook.* 1948. Blessed Sacrament Fathers. Emmanuel Publications. OH. 59-61

Pope Benedict XVI, Spe Salvi Encyclical. 2008. *Inside the Vatican Magazine Special Supplement.* 3-22

Servant of God Fulton Sheen. *The Priest is Not His Own.* 2005. Ignatius Press. SF 176, 230-239

Fr. Raniero Cantalmessa & Carlo Martini. 2003. *St. Francis and the Cross.* Servant Publications, MI. 69, 65-67

St. John Vianney, *Eucharistic Meditations.* 1993. Source Books & Anthony Clarke. 131-133

Fr. Evan, *From the Heart of the Eternal High Priest.* 2005. Queenship Publishing. Goleta CA. 38

John Paul II, *Pastores Dabo Vobis*, Apostolic Exhortation. March 25, 1992

Fr. Garrigou-Lagrange, O.P., *The Three Stages of the Interior Life.* 1989. Volume One. Tan Books and Publishers, Inc. Illinois

Fr. John Hampsch, C.M.F., *The Healing Power of the Eucharist.* 1999. Servant Publications. MI 110-112. Used with permission.

N. Brown, *The Charism of Intercession Formation Program.* 1999. NE Intercessors of the Lamb. 86-87

Fr. Andrew McNair, "The Reality of the Devil." *National Catholic Register Article.* 10-17-06. Zenit.org

St. Thomas Aquinas. *The Quotable Saint.* 2002. R. Guilley. Checkmark Books. NY

Fr. Gabriele Amorth, *An Exorcist Tells His Story.* 1999. Ignatius Press. SF. 199

Fr. Peter Eymard. *Our Lady of the Blessed Sacrament.* 1930. Emmanuel Publications, OH. 10-14

John Paul II, *The Private Prayers of John Paul II.* 1993. Atria Books. NY. 67

K. McDonnell, G. Montague. *Fanning the Flame.* 1991. The Liturgical Press. MI. 9-10

Fr. Raniero Cantalamessa, O.F.M., Cap. *The Sober Intoxication of the Spirit.* 2005. Servant Books. 158-60

Cardinal Ratzinger. *New Outpourings of the Spirit.* 2007. Ingatius Press. SF 70-71

Fr. John Hampsch, C.M.F. *Receiving the Gift of the Holy Spirit.* 2003. Queenship Publishing. Goleta CA. 88-89. Used with permission.

International Catholic Charismatic Renewal Services, 2000. *Then Peter Stood Up.* Vatican City, Italy 76.

K. Beckman. *Praying the Passion of Christ.* 2004. Queenship Publishing. Goleta CA. 55

St. Alphonsus Ligouri. *Visits to the Most Blessed Sacrament and the Blessed Virgin Mary.* 1994. Ligouri Publications, MO. 5-7

L. Schubert. *The Miracle Hour Booklet.* 1992. CA www.lindaschubert.com. Used with permission.

Servant of God Fulton Sheen. *Life of Christ.* 1977. Doubleday. NY 446, 447

Dr. Inga Pak References

The Catholic New American Bible, Second Edition, Personal Study Edition. New York: Oxford University Press, 2007.

English translation of the Catechism of the Catholic Church, Second Edition. Libreria Editrice Vaticana, 1997.

Abba Father. By Rev. Carey Landry.

In His Time. By Diane Ball.

Father Tadeusz Dajczer. *The Gift Of Faith.* Newark: In The Arms Of Mary Foundation, 2001.

Father Raniero Cantalamessa, O.F.M. Cap. *Sober Intoxication of the Spirit Filled with the Fullness of God.* Cincinnati, OH: Servant Books, 2005.

Herbert Benson. *Timeless Healing The Power and Biology of Belief.* New York: Simon & Schuster, 1996, pp. 17,128,131,133.

Larry Dossey. *Prayer Is Good Medicine.* San Francisco: Harper San Francisco, 1996, pp. 5,12,21,23,24.

Thoresen CE, Harris AHS. "Spirituality and Health: What's the Evidence and What's Needed?" *Annals of Behavioral Medicine.* 2002, 24(1):3-13, pp. 4, 8.

Astin JA, Harkness E, Ernst E: "The Efficacy of Distant Healing: A Systematic Review of Randomized Trials." *Annals of Internal Medicine.* 2000, 132:903-910, p. 905.

Shahabi L, Powell L, Musick M, Pargament KI, Thoresen, CE, Williams D, et al. "Correlates of Self-Perceptions of Spirituality in American Adults." *Annals of Behavioral Medicine.* 2002, 24(1):59-68.

Larimore WL, Parker M, Crowther M. "Should Clinicians Incorporate Positive Spirituality Into Their Practices? What Does the Evidence Say?" *Annals of Behavioral Medicine.* 2002, 24(1):69-73.

Koenig HG, George LK, Titus P. "Religion, Spirituality, and Health in Medically Ill Hospitalized Older Patients." *Journal of American Geriatric Society.* 2004, 52:554-562.

Harold G. Koenig. *The Healing Power of Faith.* New York: Simon & Schuster, 1999, p. 223.

"Prayer of an Unknown Confederate Soldier," *The Oxford Book of Prayer.* New York: Oxford Univ. Press, 1985, p. 119.

Johnnette S. Benkovic. *The New Age Counterfeit: A Study Guide For Individual Or Group Use.* Queenship Publishing, Goleta, CA. Revised Edition 1995, pp. VII,VIII, 2,4,11.

Yoga - Health or Stealth? The Cross And The Veil website at www. crossveil.org, pp. 3-5.

Archbishop Norberto Rivera Carrera, "A Call To Vigilance (Pastoral Instruction on the New Age)," January 7, 1996. Taken from the August/ September 1996 issue of *Catholic International* published monthly by *The Catholic Review,* Baltimore, MD.

Healing Power Prayers. Denver, CO: Valentine Publishing House.

Elizabeth Kim, Ph.D., References

The New American Bible. Catholic Publishers, Inc. Washington, D.C. 1971.

H. Benson and E. Stuart. *The Wellness Book.* Simon and Schuster: New York. 1992.

Institute for National Resources. *Emotion, Stress, and Disease,* 2nd edition. California. 2007.

J. Kabat-Jin, *et al.* "Effectiveness of a Meditation-Based Stress Reduction Program." *American Journal of Psychiatry* 149:7, 936-943. 1992.

R. Davidson, D. Jackson, and N. Kalin. "Emotions, Plasticity, Context, and Regulation: Perspectives from Affective Neuroscience." *Psychological Bulletin,* 126, 890-909. 2000.

J. Anderson. "Meditation Meets Behavioral Medicine: The Story of Experimental Research on Meditation." *Journal of Consciousness Studies,* 7, 17-73. 2000.

A. Newberg and E. D'Aquili. *Why God Won't Go Away.* New York: Ballantine Books. 2001.

A. Newberg and M. Waldam. *Why We believe What We Believe.* New York: Free Press. 2006.

Catechism of the Catholic Church. Missouri: Liguori Publications 1994.

F. MacNutt, *Healing.* Notre Dame, Indiana: Ave Maria Press. 1999.

K. McDonnell and G. Montague. *Fanning the Flame.* Minnesota: The Liturgical Press. 1991.

N. Brown. *The Charism of Intercession.* Formation Program. Nebraska: Intercessors of the Lamb. 1999.

About the Authors

The authors are daily communicants and daily adorers of the Blessed Sacrament for many years. Fr. Raymond Skonezny, STL, SSL is their spiritual director.

Kathleen Beckman, LHS is a wife of 33 years and the mother of two grown sons. She is a graduate of Long Beach City College Medical Assisting Program with 15 years experience in medical assisting. She is the Western Regional Representative, Advisory Team member to the Central Service Team, Magnificat, A Ministry to Catholic Women. Since 1992, she is the Coordinator of the OC Queen of Peace Chapter of Magnificat and the Intercessors of the Lamb. She is a Lady in The Equestrian Order of the Holy Sepulchre of Jerusalem. Kathleen was nominated for Orange Diocese Catholic Woman of the Year for her work to aid the poor at the Lestonnac Free Medical Clinic. She has spoken at many Catholic Conferences and Catholic Radio on the subject of Mary, the Eucharist, intercessory prayer and spirituality. She has served in youth ministry, and Cursillo. She is the author of seven books available at Queenship Publishing, Goleta, CA.

Elizabeth J. Kim, Ph.D., is the director of Brain Fitness Center in LA and Orange County. She received her doctorate in Counseling Psychology at USC. She is a Licensed Psychologist, Marriage and Family Therapist, a Certified Neurofeedback Practitioner and member of the American Psychological Association, and Association for Applied Psychophysiology and Biofeedback. She has a dynamic and multi-ethnic practice that incorporates her Catholic faith for healing. She is on the Advisory Team of the OC Queen of Peace Magnificat Chapter. She is a Core Team leader of the OC Intercessors of the Lamb cenacle. She has served in various capacities in ministry including youth and music ministry, and teaching ministry. She served on the Board Member of SCRC (Southern California Renewal Communities); has appeared on Catholic television and radio programs. Elizabeth is received into the Equestrian Order of the Holy Sepulchre of Jerusalem.

Inga Pak, M.D. is certified by the American Board of Family Medicine currently in Family Practice. Inga holds a B.S. in Biological Sciences from

UCI, CA., Post Baccalaureate Studies in Biology, Cal State Fullerton, Diploma in Medicine and Surgery, December 2000 Universidad Autonoma de Guadalajara School of Medicine, Guadalajara, MX, Residency at Greater Lawrence Family Health Center, Lawrence, MA, 2005. Doctor Inga is soon to be married to Paul. She is a member of the Service Team of OC Queen of Peace Chapter of Magnificat, A Ministry to Catholic Women. She is a leader in the OC Chapter of the Intercessors of the Lamb cenacle. She has been involved in the Catholic Charismatic Renewal for many years of formation and leadership. Inga is pleased to incorporate her Catholic faith in her medical practice as part of her healing ministry.